Improving
English
Skills

Desmond W Evans

Pitman

Pitman Publishing Limited
128 Long Acre, London WC2E 9AN

A Longman Group Company

First published 1986

British Library Cataloguing in Publication Data
Evans, Desmond W.
    Improving English Skills.
    1. English language——Usage
    I. Title
    428   PE1460

    ISBN 0–273–02417–5

Typeset, printed and bound in Great Britain at
The Bath Press, Avon

Contents

Part Two Style in English 153

Preface

If you are – or were – one of those people whose school or college report tended to say about your English Language or Communication Studies:

'. . . tries hard, but finds the subject difficult . . .'
'. . . spelling and punctuation problems have impeded progress . . .'
'. . . finds difficulty in expressing his ideas clearly and precisely . . .'
'. . . knows what she wants to say, but cannot easily put it into readable English . . .'

then this book is dedicated particularly to you! It has been specifically designed to enable you to work through its various sections on your own, as they progressively build up your skill and confidence in using the English language in a variety of work and social occasions.

Across the world, several hundred million people use one or other form of the English language in their daily working and personal lives. Indeed, one reason for the continued use of English in many contrasting cultures and countries lies in its richness of vocabulary, wide variety of expressions and differing shades of meaning. Its ability to cope with the language demands of a range of scientific, technical, commercial and industrial topics with both accuracy and interest has also ensured that the English language is, today, a universal tool of communication.

Yet, in both the United Kingdom and abroad, there are also many millions whose problems and difficulties in speaking and writing in English hold them back, and sometimes prevent them from embarking upon the career of their choice or from progressing within it up the ladder of promotion.

In my teaching experience such difficulties are not limited to the 14–19 age group in school or college, but also affect the practising manager more at home, say, with a production engineering problem or a sales challenge than with dictating a letter or drafting a report. Even the postgraduate with an arts background is not immune from the snags and pitfalls of using English correctly or appropriately. There are many reasons put forward nowadays to account for such difficulties in expressing ideas in English:

– 'Children don't read as much as they used to.'
– 'Too much television viewing.'
– 'English teachers don't correct written work as they used to.'
– 'I blame it on computers!'

and so on are examples of the sort of comments made. Whatever may be the true reasons, it is my firm belief that the ability to use English competently and confidently matters enormously – not only to desk-driving managers and office personnel – but also to the many and varied craftsmen and technicians, whether motor-mechanics, hairdressers or laboratory assistants. They cannot escape the need to read, write or speak English at work and rely on it in their social lives – in their ability to apply for a passport, buy a car or arrange a holiday, for example.

It was with these convictions in mind and with the knowledge that an individual's skill in using English can be dramatically improved if the will and effort are present, that I set out to produce a textbook aimed at individual self-study use – a text which would aid the teenager preparing for a first job or the mature person in mid career or in the process of changing jobs.

Progressively, this textbook covers essential grammar and usage in a practical and straightforward way, explains principal rules and guidelines of spelling and punctuation, develops skills in sentence and paragraph writing, enlarges vocabulary and examines the effect of tone and style in particular contexts.

By reading this far into the Preface, you have already demonstrated your desire to attain the skills of which I write. Provided you work steadily through each section of the book and carry out the assignments conscientiously (without peeking prematurely at the answers!), and in your daily life take the trouble to pick up and absorb the new words and expressions you encounter, I am confident that your English will improve beyond your expectations.

But always remember: nothing worth achieving is won without hard work and perseverance!

Desmond W. Evans
1986

Acknowledgements

The author and publishers have made every effort to trace ownership of all copyright material and to obtain permission from the owners of copyright.

Grateful thanks and acknowledgement is given to the following for their permission to reproduce quotations, extracts or listings or to make reference to works during the production of this book:

J. M. Dent & Sons Ltd for a quotation from the Everyman edition of Geoffrey Chaucer's *The Canterbury Tales*, the General Prologue.

A. M. Holden Ltd and Professor Meiklejohn, *The English Language* (publ 1891), for a Saxon quotation from the Gospel According to Saint Luke.

Oxford University Press and A. W. Pollard, *English Miracles, Moralities and Interludes*, for a quotation from the York Miracle Play.

Oxford University Press, *The Concise Oxford Dictionary* (7th edition), for various quotations of entries and listings, including a table of vowel sounds.

Oxford University Press for permission to use various quotations from *The Concise Oxford Dictionary of Quotations* (new edition).

Oxford University Press and H. W. and F. G. Fowler for a quotation from *The King's English* (3rd edition).

Penguin Books Ltd for a quotation from *Jane Eyre* by Charlotte Brontë. Also, for permission to use a number of quotations from *The Penguin Dictionary Of Modern Quotations* (2nd edition).

Penguin Reference Books, *Roget's Thesaurus* (1984), for reproduction of entries, listings and index items as well as the Plan of Classification.

The Reader's Digest Association Ltd for permission to quote from *The Reader's Digest Handbook of First Aid*.

Reading University and Professor Fry for free access to the Graph for Estimating Readability.

Pitman Publishing Ltd. The author has included some extracts from his previous books, *People and Communication* and *Communication at Work*, also published by Pitman.

Scott, Foresman & Co. (USA) for permission to refer to various rules, guidelines and helpful approaches in *Spelling Our Language*, Book 8.

Zenith International Limited, Ashford, Kent, for permission to quote from their assembly instructions for the barbecue Party Chef equipment.

Part One
The mechanics of English

Chapter 1
Obtaining the tools
for the job

No good craftsman – whether carpenter, mechanic or journalist – can expect
to progress very far without equipping himself with the proper tools of his
trade. Basic tools come in for extensive daily use and are carried around,
while specialist tools may be hired for the occasional tricky job.

Where using the English language is concerned, exactly the same prin-
ciples apply. And where an active effort is being made to improve writing
and speaking skills, a 'pocket tool kit' is indispensable. For example, in the
very act of writing the previous sentence, I discovered that I could not recall
whether 'indispensable' had an -ible or -able ending, so I quickly checked the
dictionary at my elbow!

Here then is my checklist of 'essential' and 'useful' tools. Virtually all the
books listed may be purchased as paperbacks and those listed for reference
will be available from your local school, college or public reference library.

Essential

- A good English language dictionary
- A pocket English language dictionary
- A pocket notebook

The larger dictionary should be at hand at your work or study desk, and the
pocket dictionary and notebook should always be carried around for instant
reference or to jot down a new word or expression for later checking and
eventual inclusion in your working vocabulary.

Useful

- A thesaurus of English words and phrases

The thesaurus first compiled by Peter Mark Roget and published originally
in 1852 is one which is in popular use. Basically, an English language
thesaurus is a series of related words and expressions which may be used to
suggest an alternative way of expressing an idea. It is frequently used by
professional writers and is a very helpful means of extending and enriching
your vocabulary.

- A spelling dictionary

If you are one of those people who experiences difficulty in spelling, then for you this dictionary is not only useful but essential! It is a dictionary which shows entries in a simple phonetic form followed by their conventional spelling: *sikoloji* . . . *psychology*. As you can see, the value of such a dictionary is that it does away with the frustration of looking up a word like psychology with its silent p in the s entries of the standard dictionary.

For reference

There are a large number of books, guides and encyclopaedias which will prove helpful to you in the reference section of your library. Below are listed some of these just to indicate the sort of support that exists for the writer of English:

- H. W. and F. G. Fowler, *Fowler's Modern English Usage*
- Sir Ernest Gower, *The Complete Plain Words*
- Michael Swan, *Practical English Usage*
- *English Pronouncing Dictionary*
- *Oxford Dictionary of Quotations*
- *Dictionary of Acronyms and Abbreviations*
- *Titles and Forms of Address*
- *Encyclopaedia Britannica*

It is always tempting to take short-cuts in our busy lives, to take a stab at a spelling instead of checking it in the dictionary, to repeat the use of a tired and well-worn word instead of seeking a better alternative in a thesaurus or to stick to words and phrases we know well instead of seeking to learn and use newly encountered ones. Yet these are precisely the bad habits which slow down or halt progress entirely! So make sure that you determine from the outset of your course of study with this book that you will use the tools of the trade you are now learning!

On pages 18–22 the way to use an English language thesaurus is explained in more detail. Meanwhile, carry out the following assignments as soon as you are able.

Assignments

1 Make a checklist of the particular difficulties you have in writing in English. Check your list against the table of contents of this book to see where you can find help.

2 If spelling is one of your difficulties, visit your local bookshop and look through the range of spelling dictionaries to see which one would suit you best and buy it!

3 Set a date within the next 2–3 days to visit the reference section of your library. Find any of the books listed in this section and browse through them to see what sort of information they provide and how it is presented.

4 Scan the other reference shelves in the library and make a note of any particular reference books which are relevant to your studies. You will find, for example, yearbooks in the fields of construction or engineering, business directories, local government guides and a host of other useful sources of information.

5   Look up the entry for Peter Mark Roget in the *Encyclopaedia Britannica* and read the article.

6   Find the larger version of an English language dictionary kept on your library's reference shelves and compare the detail and extent of its entries with those in your own desk and pocket dictionaries.

Chapter 2
Where the English language came from

A source of pleasure and indeed effectiveness in choosing the best word for a particular job lies in having an understanding of the various old languages and historical movements of peoples which, together, helped to form the English we know and use today.

Such a knowledge also helps us to appreciate that the English language never remains static or stagnant. It is always in the process of discarding old words and expressions as they fall out of use, and of absorbing new ones which are coined or taken into English from other languages to describe new technologies or fresh social or cultural developments. Very often such words start off their lives in English as slang or colloquial expressions:

zilch = nothing, nil (from American)
boot up = get the computer started (from American)

The English which we use today began to settle down between the fourteenth and sixteenth centuries in Britain, yet its roots go much further back – well over 2000 years to the time when the British Isles were inhabited by the people known as Celts. Some of their words have come down to us – *whisky, glen, barrow, slogan* – yet their history of repression and isolation in the more inaccessible parts of Britain meant that the Celts did not play a large part in the evolution of the English language.

One of the causes of this repression was the arrival of the Romans in the south of England in 55 B.C. The famous and indeed arrogant remark of Julius Caesar, *'Veni, vidi, vici'* (I came, I saw, I conquered), certainly held true for some 450 years, during which time the Romans successfully pacified England and much of Wales and Scotland, and settled this 'far northern colony', marrying local inhabitants and spreading the use of their Latin language.

Indeed, very many of our modern English words which deal with government, administration, settlement and so on derive from Latin:

viaduct   aqueduct   castle   domicile   governor

Many were also taken on by the church to communicate the religion of Christianity:

crucifix   charity   bible   resurrection   communion

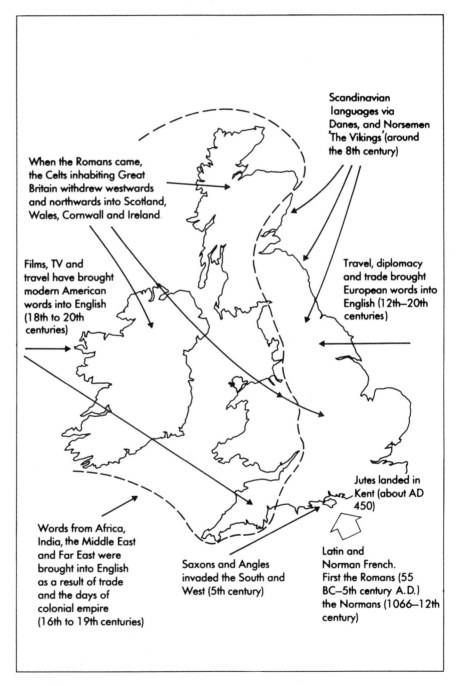

When the Romans came, the Celts inhabiting Great Britain withdrew westwards and northwards into Scotland, Wales, Cornwall and Ireland.

Scandinavian languages via Danes, and Norsemen 'The Vikings' (around the 8th century)

Films, TV and travel have brought modern American words into English (18th to 20th centuries)

Travel, diplomacy and trade brought European words into English (12th–20th centuries)

Words from Africa, India, the Middle East and Far East were brought into English as a result of trade and the days of colonial empire (16th to 19th centuries)

Saxons and Angles invaded the South and West (5th century)

Jutes landed in Kent (about AD 450)

Latin and Norman French. First the Romans (55 BC–5th century A.D.) the Normans (1066–12th century)

Figure 1   Where the English language came from.

Many of the current place names of English towns and villages stem from the period of the Roman occupation

Winchester   Doncaster   Chichester   Chester

and there is much evidence, both in the language of modern English and in the archaeological remains they left behind them, of the deep impact the Romans had upon the history of Britain.

Nevertheless, the threatening tribes of northern Europe called the Romans back to Italy in approximately A.D. 450, and left the British Isles a prey to the aggressive peoples of Scandinavia and North Germany. In successive waves, between A.D. 450 and 800, tribes of Danes, Vikings, Saxons, Jutes and Norsemen invaded different parts of England and Scotland. With them they brought a series of languages and dialects very different from the Latin of the Romans. For example, the Old Saxon word *sterban* 'to die' evolved into the English word to 'starve'. Similarly, the Old Norse word *svin* meaning 'pig' became the English word 'swine'.

Many words stemming from these old European languages have come to form the very heart of English words which describe the countryside, food or parts of the human body:

field   hedge   mere   valley   hill   wood   sea   brook
bread   fat   butter   grain   apple   wine   beer   ale
head   arm   nose   foot   leg   breast   elbow   finger

Indeed, some of the most deeply felt words in English stem from the various dialects of the Germanic and Scandinavian settlers. Poets and authors down the ages have much preferred to use such words in preference to their Latin counterparts:

Germanic/Scandinavian word	Latinate equivalent
fire	conflagration
home	domicile
think	cogitate
farming	agriculture
kill	exterminate
drunken	bibulous

One particularly interesting effect of the invasion and settling of various parts of the British Isles by different northern European tribes was the different dialects of English which could be found in use as late as the fifteenth century in different parts of Britain. The first extract below was written about A.D. 1430 in York as part of a religious play portraying the expulsion of Lucifer from Heaven:

Second Devil
Owte! owte! I go wode for wo, my wytte es all wente nowe
All our food es but filth, we fynd us beforn,
We that ware beelded in blys in bale are we brent nowe,
Owte! on the Lucifer, lurden! oure lyghte has thu lorne.

(Alas and woe! I am going mad from misery, my reason
has all gone now. All our food is but filth, which
we find before us, we who were created in bliss
are now burned in evil. Woe to you Lucifer! You
clown who has lost us our light!)

(Extract from the York Miracle Play, *The Fall Of Lucifer*, *circa* 1430. Courtesy of Oxford University Press.)

A Knyght ther was, and that a worthy man,
That fro the tyme that he first began
To riden out, he loved chivalrie,
Trouthe and honour, fredom and curtesie.
Ful worthy was he in his lordes werre,
And thereto hadde he riden, no man ferre.

(There was a knight, and a worthy man at that,
who from the first time he set out on his knightly
travels loved chivalry, truth and honour, freedom
and kindness. He fought nobly in his lord's wars
and no man had ridden further than he had.)
(Extract from 'The Knight's Tale' of *The Canterbury Tales* by Geoffrey Chaucer, *circa* 1387. Courtesy of J. M. Dent & Sons Ltd.)

As you can see, the English of the Second Devil is rather more unfamiliar to us than that of Geoffrey Chaucer introducing his knight, even though he was writing some forty years earlier than the York Miracle Play was composed. It is said by some English language scholars that the English of that part of England known in Saxon days as Wessex had most influence upon the development of modern English.

However, if we move back some 400 years in time to the England of the Norman invasion and William the Conqueror, the language spoken by the resident Saxons of the time would have been quite unintelligible to us:

Wendon daet he on heora gefere waere, da comon hig anes dages faer, and hine sohton betweox his mages and his cudan.

(They presumed that he was among their company when they came one day's journey and looked for him among his friends and relations.) (Anglo-Saxon version of the Gospel According to Saint Luke, *circa* 995. Courtesy of A. M. Holden, London.)

As a result of the Norman Conquest, the language of Norman French, in its turn, played an important part in the evolution of modern English during the eleventh to fourteenth centuries. Possessing itself many words deriving from the Latin of the Roman occupation of Gaul, Norman French began in England very much as a separate language used by the Norman overlords – much in the way that French was spoken by the Russian nobility in the eighteenth and nineteenth centuries.

Some of the words which came into modern English via Norman French were:

obeisance: obedience   *usage*: usage, custom   *remenant*: rest, remnant
doute: doubt

Indeed, the years which spanned the Norman Conquest of 1066 to the accession of Elizabeth I to the English throne in 1558 saw English blossom and flourish into an extremely rich language, full of alternative words and expressions as a result of its Celtic, Latin, Saxon, Norse, Danish and Norman French roots.

When it came to spelling, however, the Elizabethans followed very much a hit or miss approach. For example, William Shakespeare's name is to be found spelled as

Shagsper   Shakspere   and Shakespeare.

Not until scholars called lexicographers in the sixteenth and seventeenth centuries began to compile dictionaries did the spelling of English words begin to stabilize. Little wonder, then, that we find very often scant similarity between the pronunciation and spelling of certain words:

receipt: 'risseet'   *debt*: 'dett'   *solemn*: 'sollum'

The contacts which grew with foreign peoples during the period from 1600 to the present day resulted in many words being brought back to England and into the language from far-off lands:

al-qaliy: alkali (Arabic)   *jangal*: jungle (Hindu)   *ch'a*: char (slang for tea) (Chinese)   *magrama*: macramé (string-made object from the Turkish word for towel)

In recent times, a wealth of new expressions has been coined in English – many coming from the USA as a result of the screening of American programmes on television and the development of computer or microchip technology:

– It's a rip-off! = I'm being overcharged!
– Having booted up your computer, you will need to format a floppy disc = Having switched on your computer and transferred its operating system into its memory, you will need to prepare a floppy disc to store your information upon.

Other words which have now become part of everyday English are

robotics: machine processes used in factories to perform routine tasks
compact disc: a form of record which stores music that is played back by means of a laser so that it is never scratched by a needle touching its surface
plastic money: a reference to the many plastic credit cards which are used to obtain cash or to demonstrate creditworthiness in shops, petrol stations or banks, etc.

Summary

This section has traced briefly the major milestones and developments which brought about the English language, which is used today by over 700 million people across the world – many of whom have their own words common to that part of India, the Pacific or North America where they live – which have also become part of their particular living English.

In addition, this section will, all being well, have helped you to understand why it is that English is so rich in words and expressions which may be used as alternatives to each other. For example:

How are you feeling?   Great!
Perfectly well.
In the pink!
Fine, thank you.
Enjoying the best of health!
All right, I suppose.
Very well, I'm happy to say.

The above answers represent just some of the many ways that someone feeling in good health might answer the enquiry after his or her health. The following checklists also provide an idea of the many variants which are available to us to describe a particular idea:

fire: blaze conflagration inferno pyre
hot: boiling scalding scorching blistering

Sadly, however, human nature being what it is, all too often people become lazy and settle for the most familiar way of saying something, even though the expression may have become old and tired:

– I came over *sort of funny* really.
– We had a *nice drive*, found a *very nice pub* and had a *really nice lunch*.
– It was *OK*, I suppose, but *nothing out of the ordinary*.
– Last night at the dance? Oh, *I felt really awful*! There was this *awful bloke* with a *really terrible haircut* came over to ask me for a dance – Wasn't funny! Anyway, he had this *queer sort of accent*, and I said to him, *you don't half talk funny*, so he wandered off. *I felt a bit funny myself afterwards* – I mean, his haircut wasn't that bad.

In each of the above extracts taken from everyday conversation, the speaker is really communicating very little, since words like *funny, nice, OK, awful, terrible, queer* and so on have been used so often in so many situations that they have virtually lost their meaning. Such words or expressions are called clichés, and the benefit to you of making the decision to extend your vocabulary and mastery of English so as to avoid them will be that the people you talk to will sit up and take notice of what you have to say because it will be interesting and not a dull repetition of worn-out clichés!

Moreover, if you think about it, it seems a pity not to be able to use more of the 200,000 or so English language words which have been assembled over a period of some 2000 years just for us to have access to and to enjoy using!

Assignments

1 First find the section of your dictionary which lists the abbreviations for the origins of words. For example, in many dictionaries, L stands for Latin, F is for French, OS stands for Old Saxon, etc. Then as a means of getting the feel of the origin and history of words, look up the following words and make a note of their etymology – their origin or source:

kayak carpet-bagger guitar pork friar sword ambidextrous
photograph hermit kindergarten mackintosh

2 Again, using your dictionary, check the plural form (or forms) of the following words:

ox scarf handkerchief aquarium stadium monsieur basis
tobacco louse hero

3 Turn to the examples of cliché-ridden conversation above and write down what you think would be more interesting versions of these clichés:

sort of funny   nice drive   very nice pub   really nice lunch   OK, nothing out of the ordinary   felt really awful   awful bloke   terrible haircut queer sort of accent   you don't half talk funny   I felt a bit funny myself afterwards

4   Consult your dictionary and make a note in your pocket notebook of the following words which are used in this section so that, if they were unfamiliar to you, you can add them to your active vocabulary:

static   colloquial   repression   inaccessible   domicile archaeological   bibulous   unintelligible   evolution   accession lexicographer

While you are looking them up, make sure you check which language each derives from – I think you will be surprised – or yet again probably not if you have taken the message of this section to heart!

When – but only when – you have carried out all your work on the above assignments, consult page 211 for the solutions and further advice on use and meaning.

Chapter 3
How to use your
dictionary effectively

One of the main reasons why many people continue to suffer from the limitations and frustrations of having a restricted vocabulary at their disposal is, quite simply, that they cannot be bothered to look up and digest the meaning and information about a new and unfamiliar word in a good dictionary! If you really *do* wish to improve and extend the range of your active vocabulary, then you must take the trouble to carry out this essential work each time you meet an unknown word and then to make the effort to introduce it into your talking or writing as soon as possible. Your constant companions from now on should be your pocket notebook and your pocket dictionary – supported by your larger dictionary on your study or work desk.

There are a number of helpful and informative dictionaries on the market and, as with most purchases, you will tend to get what you pay for. It is a false economy where a dictionary is concerned to consider price as the only factor – your studies are likely to be amply rewarded by purchasing the best you can afford.

Using the dictionary

The following sections discuss some of the principal features you should take into account before buying your dictionary.

Age

Check when the dictionary was last revised or a new edition published. There have been so many new words added to English recently that a dictionary which has not been revised for ten or so years will be very much out of date when it comes to current usage and popular meaning of words.

Pronunciation

Most dictionaries include an introduction which explains the signs and symbols which it uses to indicate how words are pronounced. Make sure you read through this carefully. For example, the sign ' immediately after a syllable means that it is the stressed one:

con'trast   exhil'arate   psychol'ogy

The sign ˘ is used to signify a short, unstressed syllable:

arĭthmetĭc   cŏntĭněn'tal   ĭllŭ'strĭous

The sign ‾ is used to convey a long vowel sound of a syllable:

lī'lac   refri'gerāte   contribū'tion

A dot over an *è* indicates that it is pronounced 'igh':

nak'ėd   mag'nètize

Such an introduction will also provide help on general pronunciation and the way in which a phonetic (how the word sounds) system is employed in the dictionary entries.

Plurals

The plural form of words is also an essential part of an entry in a good dictionary and is often shown as:

goose n. (pl. geese pr. gēs)

Here the plural spelling of the word is shown and its pronunciation indicated by the symbol for a long *e*.

Abbreviations

A checklist of the various abbreviations used in the dictionary will also be found as a rule in the introduction of a good dictionary. Such a list will include a range of letters to signify the part of speech of the entry – *n* for noun, *v* for verb and so on. Also, the word's origins (etymological roots) will be shown as we have already learned in the section *Where English Came From* – MHG would mean Middle High German, for instance.

Your efforts in learning what the abbreviation symbols mean will be amply repaid in strengthening your word power and confidence in using words.

Many dictionaries also provide an appendix or other form of checklist of commonly used abbreviations or acronyms (words formed from the first letters of a title, for example BBC for British Broadcasting Company). Often to be found in such checklists are entries like:

GP = General Practitioner   RSVP = Répondez S'il Vous Plaît
TUC = Trades Union Congress

Tables of weight, volume, distance, conversion

The good dictionary will often include various tables which set out the principal points of, say, imperial or metric measurement, the metric system of measuring areas and volume or the conversion of inches into centimetres, and so on.

Words of foreign origin

In addition, it is usual to find foreign words listed with a detail of their pronunciation in English, and what anglicised pronunciation is commonly accepted:

Marseilles: Marsales

Otherwise the pronunciation in the foreign language is mirrored:

coiffeur: kwahfer'   pièce-de-résistance: pēās de rāze'stahns

The addenda section

As you can imagine, the compilation of a dictionary takes a long time, and during its course, a number of words may have extended their meaning or new ones may have been coined. Others may have been omitted in error. Thus an addenda or 'additions' section is often to be found at the back of dictionaries which is well worth browsing through – *bug*, for example, is likely to be shown as a concealed microphone as well as the general word for a type of insect, or *pad* as the launching platform for a rocket and not merely as a compress or layered cloth!

Extracting the meaning of a typical entry

The following entry is taken from the seventh edition of the *Concise Oxford Dictionary* and it has been selected to show you how a typical entry is made up, and what may be learned from it.

swīne *n.* (*pl.* same). **1.** (US, formal, or Zool.) = PIG 1, whence **swī'nERY**[3] *n.*; PEARL[1]*s before swine.* **2.** person of greedy or bestial habits; (colloq.) unpleasant thing. **3.** ~-**fever,** infectious intestinal virus disease of pigs; ~-**herd,** one who tends pigs; ~-**plague,** infectious bacterial lung-disease of pigs. **4.** Hence **swī'nISH**[1] *a.* (esp. of persons or their habits). [OE *swīn,* = OS, OHG *swīn,* ON *svín,* Goth. *swein* f. Gmc **swīnam,* neut. (as n.) of a. f. IE **suw-* pig]

From an initial survey of this entry, the reader might be forgiven for thinking that he or she needs a dictionary to decipher the dictionary entry! Phrases like

infectious intestinal virus disease of pigs

takes some sorting out and words like 'bacterial' and 'bestial' do indeed tend to 'hit us between the eyes'! Never mind, the same dictionary can deal with these too.

In looking at the entry for 'swine', it is worth noting that the alphabetical arrangement of the words in the dictionary follows a strict system. Clearly all the words starting with *a* come before all those starting with *b* and so on. Moreover, within each letter section – *a*, *b* or *c*, etc. – the system also is enforced:

aback comes before *acacia*

simply because the second letter of *aback* is *b* and that of *acacia* is *c*. In the same way, the entry *abbreviate* comes before *ABC*, because the third letter of *abbreviate* is a *b* (the other two being identical) and that of *ABC* is a *c*.

The next entry against 'swine' is 'n'. This abbreviation, as we know, means that the word 'swine' is a noun or the naming word of something.

We also learn from '(*pl.* same)' that the word swine does not change in its plural form – for example, 'Many swine browsed in the meadow.'

The entries which follow the numbers 1, 2, 3, 4 illustrate different meanings or uses of the word and show how it may be used in conjunction with another, for example, 'swine-fever', to form a further word of different meaning.

The entry takes the trouble to inform us that the word 'swine' is used formally in the USA and in zoology to mean pig and that in the USA (as opposed to elsewhere) 'swinery' is used for a place where pigs are housed.

A further part of the entry refers to the proverbial expression taken from the Bible of 'casting pearls before swine'.

The smaller numbers 1, 2, 3, 4 invite us to check the entry in the dictionary, for example for -*ish*.

Lastly, the entry concludes by showing us the origin of 'swine' from the Old English swin, or the Old Saxon and Old High German swin, the Old Norse svin and the Gothic swein.

It is remarkable how much information surrounds a simple five-letter word, but then it has been around in English for a long time! Of course, you will not always wish to study a dictionary entry in such detail – you may simply wish to check on the spelling of a word or a particular meaning or use of it. Nevertheless, it is worth knowing precisely what sort of information you may expect to obtain from the entry of a word in a reputable dictionary:

- Its correct spelling (or spellings).
- Its accepted pronunciation (or alternative pronunciations).
- How is it spelled in the plural, including accepted alternative spellings.
- What part of speech it is, and what parts of speech its derivative words are (e.g. swine, n.; swine-fever, n.)
- The ways in which it is used and its meaning (or meanings).
- How is it linked to other words or expressions to form words (especially hyphenated ones of an extended meaning).
- The origins of the word from old (or current) languages.

Bear in mind that 'swine', though it has served to show some of the major factors of a dictionary entry, by no means includes all the signs and symbols which may be employed, so do spend some time browsing through those in your dictionary's introduction. Here are some you may expect to find:

app.: apparently   Bbl.: Biblical   c. circa: about the time of   colloq.: used colloquially or as slang   sl.: slang   sp.: spelling   P: proprietory name, e.g. Hoover   D: disputed usage

Provided that you are prepared to devote some time to familiarizing yourself with your dictionary's system of codes and symbols, you will find it a lifelong friend as well as a most helpful and informative tool. Correspondingly, your word power will increase, and with it your self-confidence and ability to capture and hold other people's attention.

Those words we love to use which do not exist!

Just as we have had to consign 'alright' to our language dustbin, there are, alas, other old favourites which do not exist in correct English. Here are some of those popular – but wrong – favourites:

I liked your book *alot*.

Wrong! 'alot' must *always* be written as two words, and is usually better replaced by 'very much' or 'a great deal'.

Thankyou for sending me a very smart tie for my birthday.

Wrong! 'Thankyou' is also always to be written as two separate words: Thank you ...

I look *foreward* to seeing you.

Wrong! There is no such word. The spelling should be 'forward', which means 'in the future'.

Remember: whenever you are not absolutely sure of a word's spelling or meaning – check it in your dictionary!

Writing it right!

Assignments

1 Find out how the following words are pronounced in English:

raison d'être charabanc lingerie vol-au-vent

2 Find out what the following abbreviations stand for:

AAA cl. do. exc. HRH Mme NALGO prop. WHO UNESCO E&OE prov. pp.

3 How many meanings can you find out for the following:

peer rig grave fair catch bind

4 Find out what the following prefixes and suffixes mean: (note: prefix is that part of a word which comes first, and suffix that part which comes last.)

Prefixes	Suffixes
pre-	*-ist*
bi-	*-ism*
hyper-	*-ious*
contra-	*-graph*

While you are investigating, check out the origins of these prefixes and suffixes.

5 Use your dictionary to find out and list the proverbial expressions associated with the following words:

pride blue die fine fool

6 By using your dictionary, find out whether the following words are (a) all one word, (b) joined by a hyphen, (c) two separate words:

race/track race/horse post/card sea/breeze ladies'/tailor stomach/ache under/ground all/right

Chapter 4
How to use an English language thesaurus profitably

An English language thesaurus of words and phrases may best be described as a giant key which can unlock a vast treasure-house of English vocabulary and expressions. Learn how to use this straightforward key and you will gain access to a fascinating way of extending your vocabulary quickly and painlessly!

Peter Mark Roget, the most famous of the thesaurus compilers, was born in 1778, and was a doctor by profession. He developed a lifelong passion for words and for classifying them into helpful categories as an aid for writers, public speakers and, in fact, anyone with an interest in developing a wider vocabulary.

Roget's Thesaurus has become a faithful friend and companion for all whose stock-in-trade is words. Even the most fluent journalist or politician sometimes becomes stuck for an alternative to a particular word or expression he would like to use again, but does not wish to repeat exactly for fear of becoming repetitive or boring. Similarly, inexperienced writers suddenly notice that they have used the same tired old phrase three times within eight lines of text. In either case, the thesaurus can resolve the problem by offering a series of lists of words and phrases collected in groups sharing a similar or identical root meaning and branching out in a logical progression to words more distant from the root word. Consider the following example taken from *Roget's Thesaurus*, updated to meet current language needs:

556. Artist – N. *artist*, craftsman *or* -woman 686 *artisan*; architect 164 *producer*; art master *or* mistress, designer, draughtsman *or* -woman; fashion artist, dress-designer, couturier, couturière; drawer, sketcher, delineator, limner; copyist; caricaturist, cartoonist; illustrator, commercial artist; painter, colourist, luminist; dauber, amateur, pavement artist; scene-painter, sign-p.; oil-painter, watercolourist, pastellist; illuminator, miniaturist; Academician, RA; old master; art historian, iconographer; aesthetician.

sculptor, sculptress, carver, statuary, monumental mason, modeller, moulder.

engraver, etcher, aquatinter, lapidary, chaser, gem-engraver; typographer 587 *printer*.

Here we find set out in an organized form some sixty alternative words or phrases which derive from the root idea of *artist*, and almost certainly we should find an alternative word here for *artist*, whether in the field of painting, sculpture or printing.

Similar groups of words set down as nouns, verbs, adjectives or other parts of speech (these are dealt with in detail in the grammar and syntax sections which follow) are displayed throughout the thesaurus according to the following classification:

Class	Section	Heads
1 Abstract Relations	*1 Existence*	1–8
	2 Relation	9–25
	3 Quantity	26–59
	4 Order	60–84
	5 Number	85–107
	6 Time	108–142
	7 Change	143–155
	8 Causation	156–182
2 Space	*1 Space in general*	183–194
	2 Dimensions	195–242
	3 Form	243–264
	4 Motion	265–318
3 Matter	*1 Matter in general*	319–323
	2 Inorganic matter	324–357
	3 Organic matter	358–446
4 Intellect the exercise of the mind		
Division one:	*1 General*	447–452
Formation of ideas	*2 Precursory conditions and operations*	453–465
	3 Materials for reasoning	466–474
	4 Reasoning processes	475–479
	5 Results of reasoning	480–504
	6 Extension of thought	505–511
	7 Creative thought	512–513
Division two:	*1 Nature of ideas communicated*	514–521
Communication of ideas	*2 Modes of communication*	522–546
	3 Means of communicating ideas	547–594
5 Volition: the exercise of the will		
Division one:	*1 Volition in general*	595–616
Individual volition	*2 Prospective volition*	617–675
	3 Voluntary action	676–699
	4 Antagonism	700–724
	5 Results of action	725–732
Division two:	*1 General social volition*	733–755
Social volition	*2 Special social volition*	756–763
	3 Conditional social volition	764–770
	4 Possessive relations	771–816
6 Emotion, religion and morality	*1 General*	817–823
	2 Personal emotion	824–879
	3 Interpersonal emotion	880–912
	4 Morality	913–964
	5 Religion	965–990

As you can see from the above table, Roget broke down his thesaurus into six classes:

1   A class given over to such abstract ideas as, relationships, time, change, etc.
2   A class for the words associated with space, form and motion.
3   A class for words to do with all forms of matter.
4   A class about the intellect, or the exercise of the mind, thought processes and the communication of ideas.
5   A class on the exercise of the will or freedom of choice.
6   And lastly, a class on emotion, religion and morality.

As you will have noticed, some classes are split into divisions. Also, each class has a further subdivision entitled 'Sections' and each section is made up of a series of numbered heads. Thus, class 4 has two divisions, the second called *Communication of ideas*. This division is further subdivided into three sections, the second of which is termed *Modes of communication*, and contains twenty-four different heads. The first, numbered 522 starts with a list on *manifestation* – as of spirits appearing – and goes on to include words to do with exhibits, displays and so on. The third heading, 524, deals with the idea of *information*, and provides words and ideas such as: 'viewdata', 'computer', 'hearsay', 'broadcasting', and so on.

However, the user of the thesaurus is most unlikely to approach the use of the thesaurus in this way. He or she is much more likely to turn straight to the back of the thesaurus, to the index. Here, the root words of the 990 heads which make up the thesaurus are listed alphabetically. Suppose, for example, we wanted to find an alternative to the word 'information'. We would look it up in the alphabetical list, and, lo and behold, find against it the reference 524 n. This means that we should turn to head number 524 in the book and find that alternative nouns or naming words for information are set down there. The further use of this index is that it supplies under the root word different meanings or versions of the idea:

inform	—against
inform 524 vb.	*inform* 524 vb.
educate 534 vb.	*accuse* 928 vb.

Thus in the area of the idea *inform* we are given two places to look, either under 524 vb, where the idea is basically *to tell*, or under 534 vb, where the idea is *inform meaning to educate*. Alternatively we might be seeking the list of words where the idea is to *inform against someone*. In this instance, we are referred to head 928.

Should we turn to head 928, we would find it starts with: *Accusation*, and goes on with 'complaint', 'charge', 'home truth' and so on. Having exhausted the nouns or naming words for 'to inform against', it proceeds to list adjectives like 'accusing', 'incriminating', 'suspicious', etc. and then provides verbs like 'to accuse', 'challenge', or 'defy'.

In this way, the thesaurus can supply help, whether you are looking for another word for 'accusation' as a noun, or for the verb 'to accuse'.

And, as if this were not enough, the head 928 provides for certain words a cross-reference to another head in the thesaurus. For example, if the sense of the word we seek in Head 928 for 'accusation' is to reproach someone, or cause them to think again about an action, then we are referred to head 924. A section under 924 begins with the word 'reproach' and includes 'hard words' and 'reprimand'. In this way, the reader is able to travel backwards

Boost your spelling power

Learn these key words by heart

Over recent years, the Pitman Examinations Institute has amassed a checklist of about 200 key words – and those words formed from them – which students of English commonly misspell.

In each unit, ten of these words will be given for you to study carefully. Try to 'photograph' each of them in your mind's eye, then write down each word in your vocabulary notebook. Notice particularly where the vowels – a, e, i, o, u, – come and whether the common consonants – c, d, f, g, l, m, n, p, r, t, are present singly or in pairs – cc, dd, ff, gg, mm, etc. An asterisk after a word indicates that it is *very commonly misspelled*. Words formed from the base word are shown in brackets and an abbreviation shows each word's part of speech. Finally, the parts of each word which tend to be mispelled are underlined:

absence*, n.   familiar*, adj.
beginning*, n.   gauge, v., n.
ceiling, n.   harassed, v.
deceive, v. (deception, n.)   immediately, adv.
efficient, adj.   knowledge, n. (knowledgeable, adj.)

and forwards through the thousands of words of the thesaurus until just the right alternative word or phrase is found – and this can be a godsend to a tired brain!

Summary

To summarize, then, all you need to be able to use an English language thesaurus successfully are:

- the price of an average paperback or a library ticket;
- the ability to spell reasonably, so as to use the alphabetically set out index;
- the ability to leaf through a numerical sequence between 1 and 990;
- the ability – gained from this book – to identify a word as a noun, verb, adjective, etc.;
- and, most important, a sufficiently open mind actually to go out and find one and 'get the hang of it'!

If you do master the way to 'read' all the parts of the entries in your dictionary, and do learn the simple rules of using a thesaurus – and do refer to both regularly – your mastery of English words and vocabulary range *must* improve!

So, having gained access to a thesaurus, move on now to the thesaurus Assignments.

Assignments

1   Consider the following sentences:

a   One sure way out of the recession lies in a definite growth in the economy. This . . . . . could be achieved in a number of ways.

b   Acquiring the business to produce this growth, however, is by no means easy. In order to . . . . increased business, it is necessary to be competitive across a range of world-wide markets.

Assume that you do not wish to repeat the word 'growth' in the dotted space in *a* nor the word 'acquire' in the dotted space in *b*. Consult your thesaurus to find two suitable alternative words which would fit in *a* and *b*.

2 Follow the same approach to find appropriate alternative words for each of the dotted spaces in the following passage. The numbers beginning the dotted spaces refer to words shown after the passage to provide you with the sense of what is wanted:

'It is always a pleasure to be introduced by you, Mr Chairman, and indeed, it is with great 1...... that I stand before you all this evening to talk about improving one's English. Many experts have put forward their methods for 2...... either written or spoken English skills but there is no quick or simple route to this worthy destination. Indeed, the 3..... is sometimes full of pitfalls and often goes uphill! The person who wishes to 4...... in correct and acceptable English must possess the qualities of patience and determination. He or she must 5..... work through a progressive programme of study which will provide plenty of opportunities for practising accuracy and style. It is certainly in the 6...... of writing that progress and development are to be won.'

With the help of your thesaurus, find an alternative to the word given below which will fit in each of the numbered spaces:

1 pleasure   2 improving   3 route   4 communicate   5 patiently
6 practice

3 Using your thesaurus, find suitable alternatives for the words or phrases set in italics in the following sentences:

   a   The young girl looked extremely *agitated* as she waited for her driving test.
   b   The ballroom formation dancing team appeared *extremely lively* as they went through their routine in front of the judges.
   c   As he felt rather depressed, he was not *in a sociable frame of mind*.
   d   The chairman ran the meeting in a most *dictatorial* way.
   e   The bomb-blast left a scene of *havoc* never before witnessed in such a quiet village.
   f   From the look on her face, it was clear that she *had resented* the remark made by the angry customer.

4 Again, with the help of your thesaurus, find a suitable alternative for the following definitions (either as a single word or as a phrase – a small group of words):

youngster: when taken to mean someone young, poorly dressed and presumably fending for himself
mistake: meaning when something has gone wrong as a result of carelessness on someone's part
evil: as if in league with the devil
to be cheeky: as, for example, a child being disrespectful to adults
to voice: when, for example, speaking carefully so that each syllable is clearly understood

Chapter 5

Improve your
written English I:
nouns and verbs

Already we have used the words 'noun' and 'verb', and it has been assumed that you may already know what they stand for. However, in our carefully structured approach, it is important to make quite sure that you are sufficiently confident about both to be able to recognize a noun or a verb whenever you see one at work!

Also, before we may proceed to study how sentences are built up, we need to have established some common definitions of the labels given to different words doing different jobs.

The first and most essential of the parts of speech to examine are nouns and verbs, since, at bottom, they alone are quite capable of becoming the only components or parts of perfectly acceptable sentences:

John slept.
Night fell.
Peter was swimming.
The blow had been struck!

The noun

The word 'noun' is quite simply a naming word or label used to describe those things which have become the names of people, places, objects, parts of our surroundings, works of art, towns, and so on.

There are four different types of noun which are easily spotted and understood:

Common – the label for ordinary, everyday things.
Proper – the label for the names of people, towns, book titles, rivers, plays, films, and so on.
Abstract – the label for things which cannot be seen or touched – the label for feelings, emotions, ideas which describe processes, such as 'government', 'illness', 'poverty', and so on.
Collective – the label for identical groups of things, such as a pride of lions, a bevy of schoolgirls.

Very often – but not always – nouns are preceded by the words 'a' or 'the':

<u>A</u> man appeared over <u>the</u> horizon.
<u>The</u> sale of <u>the</u> house fell through.

The girls all wanted to become engineers.
Love is blind.
The school of whales moved into deeper waters.

As you can see, the nouns in the above sentences are:

man   horizon   sale   house   girls   engineers   love   school
whales   waters

Notice that if we write 'the' in front of a noun, we mean 'a particular one', and if we write 'a' in front of a noun, we not only mean a single one, but also 'no particular one, just any old one'. Check the sentences above again, and you will notice that some nouns are introduced without the help of 'a' or 'the':

The girls wanted to become engineers.

They did not want to become particular engineers, but engineers in general – hence no need for 'a' or 'the'. The same holds true for the whales moving into deeper waters in general. Also, notice that very often, with abstract nouns – such as 'love' – the words 'a' or 'the' are also omitted.

Properly, the word 'a' is called 'the indefinite article', and the word 'the' 'the definite article'.

The common noun

Immediately following is a list of randomly chosen common nouns to help you get the feel of what they are like:

tree   grass   dustbin   flower   weed   skin   fur   tail   fence   hill
rock   valley   mountain   window   roof   door   path   station
tower   road   motorway   car   bus   train   plane   typist
salesman   manager   butcher   postman   hairdresser   book   pencil
desk   file   shelf   paper   telephone   computer

Such a list is almost endless, for there are literally thousands and thousands of objects, tools, machines and natural plants, etc. around us, all of which are known by common noun labels.

The proper noun

The second type of noun to consider is called a 'proper' noun – we can think of it as a type of noun which is used as a label for 'one-off' things. Proper nouns identify the names of people, pets, books, films, plays, particular buildings, rivers, mountains, and so on.

The essential feature of the proper noun to remember is that it always begins with a capital letter – and if it is made up of several words, they each begin with a capital letter:

- Queen Elizabeth II   Sir Isaac Pitman   The Rolling Stones   The Prime Minister   William Shakespeare   John Smith   Patch   Susan Jones   Wolfgang Amadeus Mozart
- The Declaration of Independence   Big Ben   Westminster Abbey   Times Square   The Taj Mahal   Victoria Falls   The Amazon   Mount Everest   The Grand Canyon   The Rhine   The Sahara Desert   Palm Springs   Asia   Europe
- *She Stoops To Conquer*   *Twelfth Night*   *Gone With The Wind*   'Eine Kleine Nachtmusik'   'Muskrat Ramble'   'The Mona Lisa'

As you can see, each of the above proper nouns stands for a single person, artistic creation, place, etc. This feature of the proper noun will help you decide whether or not to give it initial capital letters.

Proper nouns stand for people or things which are unique.

Notice also in these examples that sometimes the proper noun is introduced by the word 'The'. Unfortunately, there is no rule to provide guidance here, only what has become accepted usage:

The Taj Mahal	'The Mona Lisa'
Palm Springs	Big Ben
Mount Everest	Victoria Falls

Even where the first word of the proper noun is 'The' it is sometimes omitted in prose to avoid ugliness:

The Royal and Ancient Golf Club
'I have never played at the The Royal and Ancient Golf Club.'

Also, some publishers and typists put the titles of books, plays or films into inverted commas to indicate that they are the direct quotation of the correct title. However, this practice is nowadays by no means universal, and some titles are printed in italics to distinguish them from the rest of the text, and sometimes the inverted commas are simply left out.

Even though there may be thousands of John Smiths living throughout the world, whenever we refer to one of them – who is, after all, a unique individual – we must employ initial capital letters: John Smith. But keep on your guard, for there are a number of words which look as though they ought to be proper nouns but which are, when you think carefully about them, really common nouns which do not need a capital letter:

There is still a number of *d*ukes living in Britain.

The Anglican *b*ishops met yesterday at a conference on world peace.

Ten *h*eadmasters, twelve *h*eadmistresses and three college of further education *p*rincipals formed the working party to investigate local secondary education under the chairmanship of Mr Peter Sharp, Director of Education for West Midshire.

As you can see, dukes, bishops, headmasters, headmistresses and college principals are all considered as part of larger groups and are in fact common nouns, whereas Peter Sharp, as referred to, is an individual, so both he and his job title are given initial capital letters.

The abstract noun

The term abstract here may be taken to mean 'not in the natural, physical world' and so is used to identify those nouns which are used for labels of thoughts, feelings, emotions, processes, and so on. The following list will provide you with the flavour of them:

silence sorrow anger government theory planning concentration thinking joy pleasure atheism argument kindness.

We cannot touch silence, hear pleasure, see atheism – in fact abstract nouns lie outside the realm of the five senses.

Many abstract nouns possess the following suffixes or endings:

–ness which means 'the state of': loneliness, helpfulness, blindness
–ism which means 'a system of belief or values': capitalism, socialism
–ion which describes the abstract function: taxation, administration, emigration, degradation
–ment which also conveys the idea of 'a state of': agreement, postponement, inducement

It is interesting to note that very many abstract nouns have their origins in Latin or Greek words which were used by monks, officials of the king's court and other administrators down the ages in Britain.

The collective noun

As its name suggests, the collective noun is used as a label to identify groups or collections of things:

a *school* of whales   a *flock* of pigeons   a *pride* of lions   a *team* of footballers   a *troupe* of acrobats   a *gaggle* of geese   a *pack* of hounds

Sometimes such collective nouns are used in constructions other than the 'a ... of ...'. For example, for the board of directors of a company, we may write as a sort of shorthand:

The *board* decided to go ahead with the purchase.

Other collective nouns used in this way include:

band   set   jury   squad   group   cluster

The following examples illustrate their use:

– The *team* (of athletes) was roundly beaten.
– Before reaching its verdict, the *jury* conferred for seven hours.
– The *committee* (of the angling club) changed the rules on Sunday matches.

One point to take care about is the sense of a collective noun being thought of as plural or singular:

– The jury *has* reached *its* verdict. (Singular as a united whole.)
– The jury *are* split. (Plural as divided into more than one part.)

Make sure, therefore, when using collective nouns that you form the correct part of the verb, singular or plural according to the sense you wish to convey.

The verbal noun

Though we have yet to examine verbs, it is useful in this section on nouns to include at the end a brief note on words which are nouns but which are made up from verbs – hence the title 'verbal nouns'.

Simply, they are formed from the present parts of verbs (called by grammar experts 'participles'). All we need to remember is that:

in the *present* they end in *-ing*.

If we take the verb 'to die', then we will have:

present participle 'dying'

Other verbs will give us going, beating, walking, hearing, etc.

We may use these present participles as nouns to refer to abstract (usually) ideas:

– *Dying* is always done alone.
– *The going* at Aintree is good for the Grand National.
– The First Eleven took *a beating* at the hands of Westpark Comprehensive School.

Notice that sometimes such verbal nouns are introduced by the word 'the', and sometimes not.

Me or my?

Consider:

– He never forgave me marrying his fiancée!
– My wife does not mind me going to the pub once a week.

In both the above sentences 'me' is wrongly used and should be replaced by 'my'.

Why? Because constructions in which the part of the verb called the gerund is used – it is the part ending in *-ing* or *-ed* – as a noun must be preceded by the possessive form of the pronoun:

– He never forgave *my* marrying Daphne.
– She does not mind *my* going to the pub.

By the same token the possessive pronouns:

his sleeping   *her* working   *their* arriving

should be used:

– She hated *his* sleeping until noon each day.
– He disliked *her* working full-time.
– They cheered *their* arriving in the open carriage, in spite of the rain.

'*Him* sleeping', '*them* arriving' are colloquial and to be avoided in correct writing.

Writing it right!

Assignments

1   Make a list of the nouns you can identify in the following sentences and write after each whether it is common, proper, collective or abstract:

a   Over the hilltop appeared a boy riding a bicycle which had a wicker basket over its front wheel containing a packet of groceries for Mrs. Jones.

b   His irritation evaporated upon hearing the news that the church had been saved, and with it the peal of bells he loved.

c   Last night Beethoven's 'Fifth Symphony' was the major work played at the Promenade Concert at The Royal Albert Hall.

d   He said that the problem called for careful planning and much thought.

Writing it right!

The dangling participle

A lovely name for a defective piece of usage which always seems to make one feel rather sorry for it! Here is an example:

Going down the road, the loose tile fell on his head.

In this sentence, 'Going down the road' is a present participial construction ('going' is the present participle of the verb 'to go'). Normally, in such constructions, the subject governing this participial phrase comes immediately next in the sentence. Here, what comes next is 'the loose tile'. Clearly it was not the loose tile which was going down the road, so we have a nonsense caused by the writer over-compressing his ideas. The sentence would have to be reconstructed as:

As *he* was going down the road a loose tile fell on his head.

So beware of the poor dangling participle which lacks a true subject to hang on to! Other examples of this kind of error are:

– Pouring the water out of the barrel, the missing wedding ring fell on to the ground.
– Clutching the steering wheel tightly, the car careered round the corner.
– Having missed the bus, the rain seemed even colder and wetter!

e The series of plays would be produced on Independent Television in December and a large number of viewers was expected.

f Many tourists were disappointed to discover that the Tower of London was temporarily closed for repairs.

g The Cutty Sark was one of the fastest tea-clippers to make the run from India to England in the nineteenth century.

h Henry is a duke, while Thomas is an earl. According to the rules of precedence, Henry must walk before Thomas in the procession.

2 Write down brief answers to the following questions:

a How would you define the meaning of the indefinite article?
b What makes the proper noun easy to identify?
c List four suffixes which often occur at the end of abstract nouns.
d How would you explain what a collective noun was to someone who did not know?
e Write down three examples each of a common, proper, collective and abstract noun you have met in this section.

The verb

Some unavoidable mention has been made in previous sections to the verb, for which no apology is really necessary since it is indeed so important a part of speech that early mention of it has proved unavoidable!

However, it is now time to consider the verb and its role as a part of speech in careful detail. And indeed, we shall be returning to examine its more various functions in later sections.

Essentially, the word 'verb' is used to describe those parts of speech which communicate to the reader the idea of an action or a thought process or a state of mind.

In the following examples, all the verbs (which are set in italics) express the idea of an action being carried out:

– John *cut* his finger.
– The sales manager *is dictating* his report.
– An explanatory letter *was despatched* yesterday.
– The train *will arrive* in Bristol on time.

For each of the above illustrations, a mental picture of what is happening may be readily formed. This characteristic makes it relatively easy to identify such 'action verbs' at work. Notice also in the examples above, that in order to communicate precisely when a thing happens, the verb idea is sometimes expressed in more than one word:

will arrive   was despatched   is dictating

In addition to such verbs, however, there are thousands which describe 'actions' in the abstract, and these are more difficult to spot:

– The chairman *considered* carefully the last section of the draft minutes.
– The research team *analysed* the likely cause of the accident.
– He *decided* reluctantly to accept the offer.

The verbs italicized above all convey an abstract meaning – a process of reflecting carefully upon a tricky passage of words, a logical examination of the reasons why an accident happened, a mental thought process which we call decision-making. Verbs, then, not only convey the idea of physical action, but also mental processes of thought or abstract concepts.

Writing it right!

How to easily avoid the split infinitive

If you look more closely at the above title to this piece, you will see that the infinitive 'to avoid' has in fact been 'split' by the insertion of the adverb 'easily'. And indeed, this title was deliberately written to provide an arresting example of what splitting an infinitive means – simply separating the word 'to' from the root part of the verb forming the infinitive by inserting another word or phrase. This practice is generally considered to be bad, though it must be confessed that we all split many infinitives in the spoken word:

'I was asked to quickly find you and take you to the Managing Director's office.'

Usually, the offending adverb can readily be placed after the infinitive: ... to find you quickly ...
Sometimes a more distant position is needed:

You are requested to come to the M.D.'s office *immediately*.

Remember: Generally it is better style to avoid the split infinitive unless by so doing the natural word order you desire is upset and the sequence of words feels awkward:

It's up to you to simply choose whichever one you like best!

'Simply to choose' is possible but the quoted version trips just as readily off the tongue!

Tenses

In English, as in other languages, the verb also conveys the idea of *when* a thing took place – either in the present, past or future. Thus another function of verbs is to mark down the timing of an event by expressing it in what is termed a tense.

Tenses of verbs express the idea of:

- present
- past
- future

in a number of clever and sophisticated ways. For example, consider the following sentence:

By the time you read this letter, I shall have arrived in Toronto.

The writer of the letter is in fact anticipating (at the time of his writing) an event which lies in the future – but for the letter's reader, when reading it, it will have become an event already in the past because of the time lag between the writing and the reading of the letter. All this meaning is conveyed in:

shall have arrived

and it is for this reason that some grammarians call such a tense of the verb 'the future in the past'. Other tenses shown below provide a taste of the hard and complicated work verbs do!

- The order for six gross of Christmas cards *had been processed* before the instruction to cancel it *was received*.
- Your car *is being serviced* at this very moment!
- If I *had possessed* more money at the time, I *should have* definitely *bid* even higher for the Ming vase.

Tenses of verbs are able not only to express single, completed actions, but actions which are going on continuously at the time of speaking or writing: *is being serviced*. Also, tenses are able to communicate complex ideas about actions which might have taken place if conditions had been right – in other words actions conditional upon certain factors. Notice how the meaning of each of the following sentences is subtly altered according to the tense used:

Present

simple	He mows the grass.
continuous	He is mowing the grass.

Past

simple	He mowed the grass.
continuous	He was mowing the grass.

Future

simple	He will mow the grass.
continuous	He will be mowing the grass.

Conditional

simple	He would mow the grass.
continuous	He would be mowing the grass.

The following illustrate some of the ideas which can be communicated by the use of such tenses:

– He mows the grass every week in summer.
– He is mowing the grass round the back – pop round and have a word now. (The work is being done at the time the speaker is speaking.)
– He mowed the grass only yesterday.
– He was mowing the grass when the canister dropped through next door's roof! (Again, an action carried out while the canister dropped.)
– He will mow the grass this afternoon if he knows what's good for him!
– He will be mowing the grass tomorrow morning, so he won't be able to play football. (Here the sense is 'he is due to mow the grass tomorrow'.)
– He would mow the grass if he weren't so mad about watching the tennis on television.
– He would be mowing the grass right now instead of watching television – if I had my way! (One activity here – the mowing – is conditional upon the speaker having his or her way.)

Below is a table of tenses set out so you can look carefully over the range of tenses – and therefore meanings available to you when using verbs.

Tenses of the verb

In the following table, the verb 'to type' has been set out in the various tenses it may express.

Table of verb tenses

| | **Infinitive:** to type | |
Tenses	Active	Passive
Present		The letter
simple	I type	is typed
continuous	am typing	is being typed
Past		
simple	typed	was typed
continuous	was typing	was being typed
Perfect		
simple	have typed	has been typed
continuous	have been typing	has been being typed*
Past perfect		
simple	had typed	had been typed
continuous	had been typing	had been being typed*
Future		
simple	shall type	will be typed
continuous	shall be typing	will be being typed*
Future in the past (Future Perfect)		
simple	shall have typed	will have been typed
continuous	shall have been typing	will have been being typed*

| **Infinitive:** to type | | |
Tenses	*Active*	*Passive*
Conditional		
simple	would type	would be typed
continuous	would be typing	would be being typed*
Conditional in the past		
simple	would have typed	would have been typed
continuous	would have been typing	would have been being typed*

NOTE: Those tenses in the passive form of the verb marked with an asterisk are nowadays very seldom seen.

Remember that the tenses of a verb in its active form mean that the doer of the action is 'controlling' the verb – I *typed the letter*. In the passive form of the verb, the structure of the sentence is changed so that the 'doer' takes a back seat and the message is conveyed more impersonally – *The letter was typed by me*.

One further important aspect of tenses to remember is that, though in some tenses the verb idea is conveyed in a single word: *type*, *typed*, most tenses are formed both in the active and passive with the help of the verbs 'to be' and 'to have': *have been typing*, *will have been typed*, so keep firmly in mind that a single verb idea may be expressed in as many as five words, all of which are in effect equal component parts of the verb.

HINT!

Spend a little time studying this table and checking from it the various tenses which you may have used daily unmindful of the names given to them. The benefit of spending time on this activity is that you will very soon develop the ability to establish in a piece of writing whether there is a 'fully fledged' verb within it or not, and this is important in producing correct English.

The verb: active and passive

So far, in considering the verb, we have concentrated upon those of its forms which are used when the 'doer' is carrying out the action of the verb:

– He mows the grass.
– John cut his finger.
– The research team analysed the likely cause of the accident.

In all of these kinds of verb constructions, the form of the verb is said to be in the *active voice*.

But look again at this example:

The order for six gross of Christmas cards had been processed before the instruction to cancel it was received.

If you examine this sentence carefully, you will see that it is not 'the order' which is doing the processing and nor is it 'the instruction' which is doing the receiving. In each case, the real doers of both actions have been left out of the sentence. In order to make this fully apparent to the reader, we might have added:

The order for six gross of Christmas cards had been processed by <u>the production staff</u> ...

Similarly, we might have included:

... before the instruction to cancel it was received <u>by the production manager</u>.

Thus, the characteristic of verbs used in the passive is that the real doer of the action can either be left out entirely, to be 'understood' by the reader, or included as an *agent of the action*, communicated always by the introductory word 'by':

– by the production staff
– by the production manager

In the same way, two alternative verb constructions are available to us to convey an idea of grass being cut:

active   He cut the grass.
passive   The grass was cut <u>by him</u>.

For the time being, it is enough for us to be aware of these two different ways of expressing the same idea: one, active, where the doer is firmly in the driving seat of the 'doing', and the other, passive, where the 'doing' is communicated more impersonally. Later on, we shall examine how these two different approaches affect the way in which the reader accepts information communicated in either the active or passive voice.

As well as communicating their meaning through single words or via groups, verbs must also follow further rules or conventions as they express our ideas.

Firstly,

RULE	**All verbs which express an idea in sentence form must have a number.**

This pronouncement sounds rather grand – if not pompous! All it means is that verbs used in sentences must either convey their meaning in a singular or plural way. The following examples will quickly establish this rule for you:

Singular	**Plural**
She painted the picture.	*They hung* the picture on the wall.
I am going to Bristol tomorrow.	*We shall expect* to meet you there.
It was old and broken.	*You* three *take* the bus.

The idea of number, then, simply means expressing ideas through the verb in either the singular or plural version.

Secondly,

RULE	**All verbs which express an idea in a sentence must have a person.**

In actual fact, we have all been expressing verbs in 'persons' quite happily since we first used *I, you, he, she, it, we, you* or *they* together with either a singular or plural form of the verb. The following table sets out the various persons (three in total) singular or plural in which all verbs conveying the action in sentences are expressed:

Table of persons of the verb

	Singular	Plural
First person	I type	We type
Second person	You type	You type
Third person	He, she, it types	They type

A single glance at the above table is enough to make us realize why those people using English have not experienced the need to bother unduly about person – simply because it only affects the spelling of the verb in the third person singular! In languages like French, German or Spanish, however, it changes in each person, singular and plural!

Writing it right!

Shall and will and should and would

The confusions which occur over using these words correctly stem from the fact that people forget that the future tense of the verb 'to be' is inflected – that is to say the form of the word varies depending on which person it is in:

	Singular	Plural
1st person	I shall	we shall
2nd person	you will	you will
3rd person	he, she, it will	they will

Thus the same inflexion occurs when the conditional tense is used: I should, but you would, and he, she and it would.

If you remember this, you will always get right that useful ending to letters:

I *should* be grateful if you *would* advise me as soon as possible.

This way of remembering the difference between first and second person verb forms will enable you to avoid writing erroneously:

I *would* be grateful if you *could* ...

where 'could' comes from 'can' which means to be able, which is not what is meant: the writer is not going to be grateful if the letter's recipient is physically able to do the advising by picking up a phone or typing a letter!

Remember too: 'should' can mean 'ought to' and when it does it is correct to write in the second or third person:

– You *should* go to visit your mother.
– They *should* write more often.

Likewise, 'would' can mean 'to have a definite intention', and again, this meaning causes the verb to act quite differently:

I *would* (go) if I thought it would make any difference.

In another meaning, the future tense of the verb to be, 'shall', can be used correctly in the second person when emphasis is needed:

You *shall* (i.e. not 'will') go to the Ball, Cinderella!

and, correspondingly:

I *will* not be contradicted! (i.e. not 'shall')

Summary

To summarize, then, verbs used in sentences as action words need to be expressed in either the singular or the plural and must be written in either the first, second or third person singular or plural. Also, they may appear as single words or in 'verb clusters' incorporating various tenses of the verbs 'to be' and 'to have'.

By the same token, each 'action verb' in a sentence must be controlled by a doer word properly called the *subject of the sentence.*

At this point, it is worth pausing for a moment to consider the implications of these rules you have just absorbed, for they are indeed the key to a most important skill you have now acquired!

From now on, you will always be able to tell whether a sentence has been correctly written or not by using the following checklist:

RULE	In order for a sentence to meet the established rules and conventions of grammar and syntax, it must:
	• **Possess a subject.**
	• **Include a verb which is expressed in a tense and is written in the singular or plural and in either the first or second or third person. (When a verb in a sentence satisfies these conditions, it is called a** *finite verb.***)**
	• **The consequence of these rules is that, to qualify as a proper sentence, the subject and its verb must agree in number and person:**

subject	finite verb
John (first person singular)	**slept (first person singular past simple tense).**

'John slept' therefore satisfies the rules for being a fully acceptable and grammatically correct sentence in its own right!

Of course, not all correct sentences in grammar terms are as short and simple as the above introductory example.

Subject	Finite verb	Rest of sentence
Sally	opened	the envelope.
The Inter City Express	will arrive	at Platform Three.
The windows	had been broken	during the burglary.

In each of the above examples, the essential rules for being an acceptable sentence have been met – each has a subject and a finite verb expressed in a singular or plural form.

Later on, we shall consider the ways in which the 'rest of the sentence' may be constructed.

On the matter of subjects, you will almost certainly have noticed that subjects often arrive in the form of nouns or as '*he, she, it, we,* etc., which, as a part of speech are called pronouns – dealt with in detail on page 104.

If you feel the need to, re-read this section on verbs and their functions, then work through the assignments for this section.

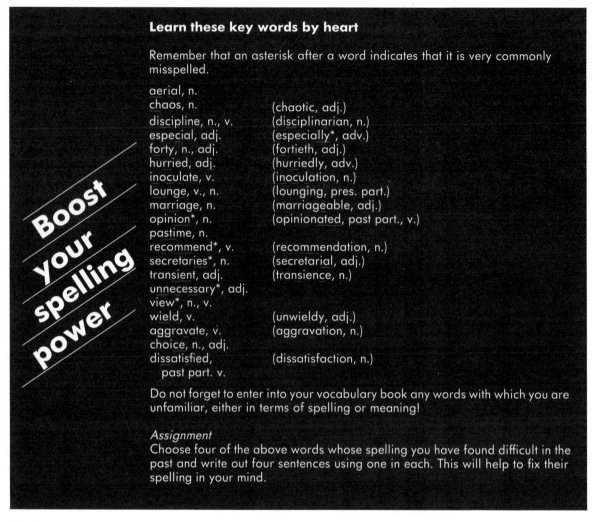

Learn these key words by heart

Remember that an asterisk after a word indicates that it is very commonly misspelled.

aerial, n.
chaos, n.   (chaotic, adj.)
discipline, n., v.   (disciplinarian, n.)
especial, adj.   (especially*, adv.)
forty, n., adj.   (fortieth, adj.)
hurried, adj.   (hurriedly, adv.)
inoculate, v.   (inoculation, n.)
lounge, v., n.   (lounging, pres. part.)
marriage, n.   (marriageable, adj.)
opinion*, n.   (opinionated, past part., v.)
pastime, n.
recommend*, v.   (recommendation, n.)
secretaries*, n.   (secretarial, adj.)
transient, adj.   (transience, n.)
unnecessary*, adj.
view*, n., v.
wield, v.   (unwieldy, adj.)
aggravate, v.   (aggravation, n.)
choice, n., adj.
dissatisfied,   (dissatisfaction, n.)
  past part. v.

Do not forget to enter into your vocabulary book any words with which you are unfamiliar, either in terms of spelling or meaning!

Assignment
Choose four of the above words whose spelling you have found difficult in the past and write out four sentences using one in each. This will help to fix their spelling in your mind.

Assignments

1   Study the sentences below and then write down either the single words or 'verb cluster' groups of words which you think are acting as the finite verbs of the sentences:

a   After the match had been concluded, both teams walked into the pavilion where they had changed and sank into the baths which had been run for them.

b   With any luck I shall be returning to London before the last tube will have left for Wimbledon.

c   The parcel should arrive by 12 p.m. tomorrow if it has been posted in Leeds on time.

d   'We shall be getting some more snow before dinner, if I'm not very much surprised,' observed the Yorkshire farmer.

e   The rain was falling steadily outside the window, as she stared into the dim light of the street. A figure in a sodden overcoat caught her eye, who was walking steadily towards her.

f   The secretary glanced at her watch and then at the pile of papers on her desk. At this rate she would not have finished them before her boss, Mr Jackson, returned. I shall have to persuade him to buy that word processor, she thought determinedly. That would save us both a great deal of time!

2   Write a brief definition of a verb being used actively in a sentence.

3   Compose a sentence containing a verb being used in the passive voice by re-arranging the following components of the sentence:

of the departed   the old church   only occasionally   by relatives was visited

4   Insert a suitable word to form part of the finite verb in the conditional tense to complete the following sentences:

a   I . . . . . go to the disco if I had the entrance fee.
b   The dance team . . . . entered for the competition by their instructor if she had felt they stood any chance of winning.

5   What specialist term is used to describe the 'by him' part of the following sentence:

The window was broken by him.

6   In the above sentence, how is the finite verb being used, actively or passively?

7   Write down how you would define the following:

a   the number of a finite verb;
b   the person of a finite verb.

8   What three essential requirements must a verb satisfy to qualify as the finite verb of a sentence?

9   Explain briefly what the job of the subject of a sentence is.

10   Write down the letter preceding each of the following sets of words which you think are proper, grammatically acceptable sentences:

a   Running down the road before the storm broke.
b   Referring to your letter of 30 June 19—.
c   As the rain had stopped, play resumed.
d   Paul slipped.
e   The coach full of holiday-makers were held up in a traffic jam.
f   Dashing round the corner.
g   Broken and smashed beyond repair.
h   Susan should have gone since it was her turn.
i   The band broke into a rousing version of 'Colonel Bogey'.
j   Despite his determination to join the police force even in view of his height of five feet six inches and his poor eyesight requiring glasses.

Now, write a brief note about each of those sets of words above which you do not consider to be grammatically acceptable sentences saying why not.

11   Below are set out two groups of words, one being subjects, the other being finite verbs. Rearrange them so that they make sense as complete sentences in the set which follows them:

Subjects	Finite verbs
building	modelled
the match	has acquired
mannequin	will be engaged
a group of words	could be heard
city of Liverpool	will take place
roar	must include
Mr Jenkins	was creaking

a   The . . . . . of the racing cars . . . . . over a mile away.

b   In order to qualify as a sentence it . . . . both a subject and a finite verb.

c   The ancient . . . . . with the broken fence . . . . . in the wind.

d   . . . . with a customer until 2.30 p.m.

e   The . . . . a world-wide reputation for the wit of its inhabitants.

f   Although delayed by fog, ... under floodlights.

g   The . . . . the costume expertly.

12   Make sense of the following passage by inserting the correct finite verbs in the appropriate spaces:

List of finite verbs: work   are aware   check   learn   have made must possess   will be expecting   form   is   know   may be   pays
Clue: one of the above finite verb clusters is separated by a word in the passage.

It . . . . . important that you . . . . . to recognize nouns easily whether as single words or in word groups because nouns . . . . . the subjects of sentences. As you already . . . . ., all sentences . . . . . at the very least a subject and a finite verb. And you . . . . . that, sooner or later, someone you . . . . . for . . . . . you to be able to write grammatically correct sentences or perhaps to correct draft letters which . . . . . not . . . . . grammatically correct. So, it . . . . . to know. . . . . . how much you know by working through the above assignments again in case you . . . . . some unspotted errors.

Chapter 6
Punctuating in English I: the full stop

Introduction

The ability to understand the ways in which punctuation marks are used in English and to make sensible decisions about how to apply the rules governing punctuation are essential skills to be mastered.

Many would-be writers of English restrict their range of writing and the impact they might communicate because they avoid using certain punctuation marks – like the semi-colon or dash – since they are basically unsure of how they should be used correctly.

If you make a careful study of the Punctuating in English sections of this text, you will discover in yourself an ability to punctuate confidently and with distinct advantage to the points you are seeking to put across.

First of all, consider the following passage, which has been set down in print just as it might have been spoken, with all the written punctuation marks omitted:

The boys name was daniel and he was always asking whats for tea mum anyway one day he broke a teacup which his mum had placed near the edge of the table and was soundly spanked for his carelessness in his room he sulked for half an hour before coming down his mind soon turned to thoughts of play however as the memory of his punishment faded.

Such a passage would be instantly understandable if spoken since the speaker would use pauses, rises and falls in his pitch of the words and particular emphases on certain words, all of which would help in conveying the meaning. However, such oral punctuation marks are not available to us when faced with the written word. Thus the need arises for a system of punctuation to be employed which will echo the punctuation marks of the spoken word. In this way, we stop at the end of the sentence a writer has written because the full-stop tells us to do so. In the above passage, as we read its unfamiliar words, we are unsure of where one sentence ends and another starts. Moreover, we find it difficult to tell when someone's speech is being directly quoted, since there are no inverted commas to help us.

Consider then, carefully, the role of each individual punctuation mark in the same passage set out for you below:

The boy's name was Daniel and he was always asking, 'What's for tea,

Mum?' Anyway, one day he broke a teacup which his mother had placed near the edge of the table and he was soundly spanked for his carelessness. In his room he sulked for half an hour before coming down. His mind soon turned to thoughts of play, however, as the memory of his punishment faded.

Notice first the two proper nouns in the passage, 'Daniel' and 'Mum', which both begin with a capital letter because they refer to two particular individuals. Also, the actual words which Daniel used are quoted and are therefore 'encased' in inverted commas. Check also the particular meaning given to the passage by the location of the full-stop after 'for his carelessness'. This has the effect of conveying that he was not spanked in his room: '. . . and he was soundly spanked for carelessness in his room. He sulked . . .' might have been the alternative punctuation.

Such a small passage, then, is sufficient to illustrate the importance of punctuation as:

- an aid to understanding a piece of written English as it is read;
- a means of avoiding ambiguity in expressing meaning, and of communicating precisely to the reader what is meant by the words selected and put into a sequence.

The range of punctuation marks in current use

The following table sets out the range of punctuation marks you are ever likely to encounter in current prose writing:

.	the full stop
,	the comma
—	the dash
-	the hyphen
?	the question mark
!	the exclamation mark
" " ' '	inverted commas (double or single)
;	the semi-colon
:	the colon
( ) [ ]	brackets
'	the apostrophe

There are, then, eleven major punctuation marks to master. A very useful tip is to collect examples of their use from your daily reading of newspapers, magazines and books and to set them down in your pocket notebook to help you to remember them. In particular, be on the look-out for those punctuation marks you seldom or never use – they are the ones to incorporate into your repertoire of punctuating skills!

The first – and indeed most essential – of all the punctuation marks is the full-stop, and so we shall start by examining it in some detail.

The full stop

In modern punctuation there are three principal uses of the full stop:

- to indicate the end of a sentence;
- to indicate that a word has been printed in its abbreviated form;
- to show (when used in a series like this . . .) that a word or section of words has been omitted from a piece of writing.

Writing it right!

Lie ... lain, lay ... laid, bear ... borne and their like!

In the English verbs which abound in our language are some whose past parts are very easily confused. It helps to make a list of them so as to learn to distinguish between them. Here are some to start you off:

- *to lie* (when it is intransitive): past tense I lay, I have lain. Example: The wounded man had lain several hours in the undergrowth before being discovered.
- *to lay* (when it is transitive and can take an object): past tense I laid, I have laid. Example: The chicken has laid an egg.
- *to bear* (when it means to carry as of a burden): past tense I bore, I have borne (with a final *e*). When to bear means to give birth to, then the final *e* still is needed in sentences like 'Mrs Jones has borne a boy'. But keep in mind. 'I was bor*n* in Wales.

Such verbs are called irregular and lists of them are to be found in most usage texts – for example:

to rise, rose, risen   to break, broke, broken

Remember in this context the difference between 'to awaken', which is intransitive and cannot take an object, and 'to wake', which can take an object:

She woke him.   *but*   He awoke.

And there is also the intransitive and transitive verb 'to wake up':

I woke up. (intransitive)
She woke him up. (transitive, object: him.)

Incidentally, there is a very useful punctuation rule to be noted and learned in the sentence with which this section starts: 'In modern punctuation'. Notice that of course it commences with a capital letter, but see also that it flows on after the colon before the bulleted sections using a small *t* for each 'to' – 'to indicate', 'to show' – and that the full stop appears after the word 'writing'. This is because the whole string of words from 'In modern . . .' to '. . . of writing' has been constructed as a single sentence, and it would therefore be incorrect to start each numbered section as,

- To indicate . . .

RULE	**The golden rule of the full stop in punctuating sentences:** **The golden rule is, quite simply, that each sentence in English must start with a capital letter and finish with a full stop.**

So obvious, you may say, as to be unworthy of my attention – but before you dismiss this rule, think about how many times your writing has driven onwards, using an endless supply of commas when it needed the discipline of shorter sentences and full stops! Here are just a few examples to illustrate this use of the full stop:

– The manager read the customer's complaint most carefully.
– Having opened the post, Sally set about identifying the most important letters.

– On the day in question, which was dark and wintry, the farmer noticed the abandoned car as he was driving his tractor into the top field.

As you can see, the first example illustrates the most common sentence structure – **subject** + **finite verb** + **rest of sentence**. Such sentences pose few problems for the writer. The second example illustrates how such a structure has been varied by beginning the sentence with a present participal construction using 'Having'. The final sentence shows a more complicated sentence – still a single sentence, but, as you will have spotted, containing three finite verbs and three subjects:

– (the day) which was
– the farmer noticed
– he was driving

So, perhaps knowing when precisely to use a full stop is not quite so simple after all!

RULE	**Another golden rule to remember is:**
	Do not use a comma when you should use a full stop!

This example illustrates the rule:

. The
– The old lady was waiting patiently for the bus, the Number Eleven eventually came into view ten minutes late.

The error shown above, where a full stop should have been used after 'for the bus' instead of a comma, is one of the most common which inexperienced writers make. A variation upon it is to use the dash instead of the full stop:

I had a lovely time at the party – Jeremy was there – he's absolutely enchanting – I could hardly believe it when he asked me to dance!

Though many of us lapse into this kind of writing in friendly, personal letters, it is not acceptable when correctness is important. The following illustrates how the message might have been better punctuated, still using a dash for the effect it can very usefully convey:

I had a lovely time at the party. Jeremy was there – he's absolutely enchanting. I could hardly believe it when he asked me to dance!

In this amended version, you will see that only one exclamation mark has been used – over-use of the exclamation mark is to be avoided like the bubonic plague since its value for emphasizing something lies in its scarcity value. Did you notice that only the exclamation mark was needed as the final punctuation mark? The dot or stop at its foot has the effect of the normal full stop so you never need to do this:

... asked me to dance!.   **Wrong**

Although the usual rule is to start each new sentence with a capital letter, there is one particular circumstance when it is necessary to introduce a word with a capital letter (other than a proper noun) in the middle of a sentence.

This is when the direct quotation of what someone said is reported in a particular way:

The boy's name was Daniel and he was always asking, 'What's for tea, Mum?'

In effect this way of quoting speech directly joins what are really two sentences into a single one.

Also, as we have learned in respect of the exclamation mark, no additional full stop is needed at the end of the sentence when a question mark is used – as shown above – at the end of a sentence.

Abbreviations

A further use of the full stop is to indicate to the reader that a word has been used in its abbreviated form. This is done by putting a full stop immediately at the end of the word:

etcetera	etc.
exempli gratia	e.g. (meaning: for example)
Mister	Mr. (note also: Mrs., Ms.)
Doctor	Dr.
Crescent	Cres.

Many dictionaries include a section which classifies abbreviations which are in common use, while others include abbreviations in the appropriate spot within the entry for words beginning with *a*, *b*, *c*, etc. Notice in the sentence immediately preceding this one that when a word which has been abbreviated ends a sentence – as here with 'etc.' – only a *single* full stop is needed.

Until about twenty years or so ago, the use of the full stop with abbreviations was widespread, but nowadays the reader is more likely to see a whole range of abbreviated words or acronyms – words formed by the initial letters of other words like BBC, ITV, NATO, etc. – printed without the use of the full stop at all:

TUC   NALGO   Dr Jekyll   Mrs Smith   pp   eg

This development was the result of a change in technology when advances in the design of typewriters and computer keyboards made the system of open punctuation in letters more attractive since typists and word processor operators needed to make fewer keyboard depressions by omitting many of the full stops which had been previously part of accepted printing and typewriting convention. The use of the full stop to indicate an abbreviated word is nowadays optional and the most important piece of advice is to remain consistent in your writing – either include them always or omit them altogether. The appearance of both sorts of punctuation is shown below with the letters a John Smith is entitled to display after his name:

John Smith, Esq., B. Sc., Dip. Ed., M.B.I.M. (closed punctuation)
John Smith Esq B Sc Dip Ed MBIM (open punctuation)

Notice that in the system of punctuation called 'open' there is a need for spacing between the abbreviation entries and that 'MBIM' is run together. You may agree that the omission of commas and full stops in open punctuation makes for a 'cleaner' appearance of the text.

Omissions

The third use of the full stop is as a set (...). When a newspaper, for example, wishes to show that a sentence or phrase has been omitted from a reproduced quotation, it will indicate it by entering a set of dots or full stops where the omission is:

'The future of the Third World countries, then, is especially worrying unless the developed nations of the world can be persuaded to make available to them increased support such as loans at small interest, technological know-how, and aid without strings whenever disaster occurs. ... Unless the Developed World's leaders make a concerted effort to produce and implement such a policy, then they will bear a heavy moral responsibility for not having done enough in time.'
    This was the message of Dr Juan Gomez, United Nations Ambassador to the Third World, speaking in New York last night.

Other marks

As a footnote to the examination of the full stop, it is worth mentioning a punctuation sign which looks like two full stops set side by side over a letter in a word:

coöperative society   Emily Brontë   preëminent

This symbol is called a diaeresis and informs the reader that, in the case of two vowels set next to one another, both are to be sounded separately – 'co-operative', 'pre-eminent'. In the case of its use after a consonant, it indicates that the vowel is to be sounded – Emily 'Brontay'. Sadly perhaps the diaeresis is very seldom seen nowadays.
    Lastly you may see in English printed matter two dots over words of German language origin:

Herr Müller   Österreich (Austria)   Lübeck

This is called an umlaut sign in German and is used to show a modified pronunciation of a vowel sound.

Assignments

1   Write down brief definitions for each of the three uses of the full stop you have learned.

2   Punctuate the following passage by inserting the necessary capital letters and full stops to make it a series of correctly punctuated sentences:

after a busy day at the office, jenny reached home closing the door behind her, she struggled to remove her soaking mackintosh as usual her cat, snowball, started to rub against her legs, letting jenny know someone else was hungry in the kitchen the remains of breakfast, cereal bowl, plate, cup, saucer and marmalade pot were just as jenny had left them in her usual morning rush following her customary evening routine jenny filled the kettle with water and plugged it in next she turned on the radio and said as usual to snowball, 'who's for his dinner, then?'

3   Add whatever punctuation you think necessary to the following:

a   the small boy shouted for the ball to be given to frank he was the team's centre-forward and idol of the small band of supporters at the gasworks end

b   after a few minutes of careful thought, the young child looked straight into its mother's eyes and asked, 'is it true that babies are found under gooseberry bushes'

4   Insert full stops where you think appropriate as you write down the abbreviated versions of the following (assuming that the convention involving the full stop is to be used):

etcetera   Post Script   et sequitur (you may need to look up the meaning of this one in your dictionary)   post meridiem   miles per hour   Doctor of Philosophy

Your writing will undoubtedly be the better for following the spirit of this golden rule on full stops!

RULE

Whenever in doubt in constructing a series of sentences, it is better to stop and start a fresh sentence rather than to write in a series of over-long sentences which stretch the reader's comprehension and increase your chances of losing your sentences' grammatical threads!

Chapter 7
Mastering spelling I:
introduction and plurals

Of all the world's many languages, English must surely rank among the most irritating when it comes to spelling!

Certainly it has caused a great deal of heartache, anger and indeed sore bottoms and hands in generations of school-children who have laboured mightily to master its quirks and baffling eccentricities, often under the supervision of unsympathetic school-teachers!

Furthermore, the problems associated with spelling the English language are no respecters of persons – famous statesmen, actors and indeed writers have struggled to master the organization of alphabetical letters into correct sequences to form words which are deemed to be correctly spelled.

Nowadays, however, society is much more informed about some of the problems which are associated with spelling difficulties and a more sympathetic approach has evolved. The problems of those people, for example, who suffer from dyslexia – a complaint where the sufferer finds difficulty in putting down letters in the correct order, so that 'dog' may be written 'dgo' – are much better understood.

Much more fortunate than the dyslexic are those who possess a form of photographic memory where they can see the spelling of a word or phrase in their mind's eye set down, black on white, just as if they were reading the words from a page in front of them. Other people who cannot achieve this kind of recall can 'see' the correct spelling of a word by writing various versions of it down on a piece of scrap paper and deciding which one is correct. This process matches the written version against the correct version stored in the writer's memory.

Most of us, however, just have to consult the dictionary on many occasions to be sure, especially since our memories sometimes play tricks and because we may need to spell a word we have not met often enough for it to be firmly etched upon our memories.

Getting rid of the guilt!

Some people load themselves with guilt about their inability to spell, as if it represented some dire shortcoming in themselves of which they should feel ashamed. Of course, no one can sensibly defend the lazy writer who is content to 'have a stab' at a spelling or who is content to wallow in a mire of misspelling simply because he or she cannot be bothered to learn how to spell correctly. Nevertheless, a needless sense of guilt about one's difficulty with spelling only serves to hold up progress, and a lack of confidence in oneself is no basis for mastering anything. So let's get rid of any lingering feelings of personal inadequacy from the start of these Mastering Spelling sections.

The future in the past tense

There are no particular problems here except when some writers go in for 'overkill'!
   Consider:

   I should have asked him to have left the party at once.

Wrong! The future in the past tense is wrongly used. All that is needed is the simple infinitive:

   I should have asked him (i.e. I ought to have asked him)
   to leave the party at once.

Remember too:

   I would have included you in my group if I had known you wanted to accompany us.

Not:

   I would have included you in my group if *I would have known* you wanted to accompany us.

   This is **wrong!**

Writing it right!

The illogical history of spelling

Until the early seventeenth century spelling was very much a hit or miss affair where English was concerned. As we have already discovered, right from the Norman Conquest until the arrival of the Tudor kings and queens in the sixteenth century, English was in the melting-pot, so to speak. Moreover, there were in the Middle Ages of England (indeed there still are today) a number of very different dialects in Great Britain, each with its own individual set of vocabulary and way of spelling a particular version of a word. Furthermore, right up until the Victorians introduced education for all in the nineteenth century, the vast majority of the British existed with an oral culture – in other words, they could neither read nor write, and therefore spelling correctly was hardly an essential skill to be mastered!

It was not until scholars called lexicographers or dictionary compilers began in the seventeenth century to set down in book form the meanings of words in alphabetical lists, that the variety of spellings of identical words began to settle down in favour of a single, universally accepted spelling. Unfortunately, there did not exist at this time any logical, consistent rules for spelling. Consider the pronunciation of the following, for example:

plough   cough   rough   through   thorough

Here no less than five quite different pronunciations are served by the *-ough* spelling!

Alternatively, the following words illustrate how varied can be the ways in English in which an identical sound may be spelled:

p<u>ee</u>k   p<u>ea</u>k   p<u>iqu</u>e   shr<u>ie</u>k

The -*eek* sound above has four vowel variations as well as consonantal alternatives. If we added words of foreign origin, like 'sikh' and 'batik', we should have six!

Again, why is it that someone may be '*fitt*ed' for a suit, but is said to have 'benefited' from a legacy? Why should someone make a refe*rr*al about a refe*r*ence? Why should a baron s*ei*ze his chance to bes*ie*ge his enemy's castle?

As these brief examples illustrate, the spelling of words in what is deemed their correct form in English, has upon occasion very little to do with logic or a rational approach.

For this very reason, if you do possess any lingering feeling that the ability to spell properly is a skill with which all the people you know were born and that you somehow missed out because of some personal shortcoming, you can quite simply put it out of your mind from now on. Virtually everyone has some difficulty with spelling some English words if they are honest. Certainly some are lucky in that they have a developed visual memory for the appearance of words, but barring physical handicaps, everyone has the capacity to improve, provided they are prepared to work at it on a daily basis.

And indeed, the return on such an investment of mastering spelling is very extensive and lasts a lifetime. It may open career doors which previously you may have considered firmly locked, like becoming a secretary or word processor operator. Or it might provide the assurance needed to progress to a supervisory or management post where a lack of confidence in your writing ability may be what holds you back. Or it may be nothing at all to do with work, but may open the door in your leisure time to reading across a wider range of books, magazines or journals with increased enjoyment.

In my view, English is such a rich and glorious language that it deserves to be spelled correctly, in the way that a painted masterpiece deserves to be maintained with love and care.

In the Mastering Spelling sections which follow, the emphasis has been placed on examining in detail those particular areas which cause especial spelling problems, and to providing wherever possible rules to be learned as a constant help, or if not 100 per cent rules, the guidelines which deal with the majority of cases. If there is no help of this nature, then you will simply be advised – 'When in doubt consult your dictionary!' (And with English spelling, we may sometimes conclude that those seventeenth-century dictionary compilers were on to a good thing in devising such an essential tool which each writer of English has had to buy in every generation since!)

Spelling plurals

A good place to start with spelling is with plurals. Fortunately the vast majority of English words form their plural form simply by the addition of an *s* to their singular form:

boat/boats government/governments hill/hills

However, there are exceptions to this simple rule.

RULE	**Words ending in**
	-ss, -x, -ch, -zz, -tch, -sh, -s* in the singular add -es to form their plural.
	* unless it is the final letter of a word of Latin origin like basis, where the plural is bases, the i being dropped.)

Examples:

pass/passes box/boxes fuzz/fuzzes patch/patches wish/wishes
atlas/atlases

Note that with such a plural rule, the word in question is almost certain to have a single vowel preceding the ss, x, zz, etc. and that very often, the words are of one syllable.

A small group of words exists in current English whose origins go back to the Saxon and Nordic languages of 1500 years ago. In such languages, the endings of nouns or naming words were different according to how they were used and many had a plural ending of -en. There are some words which have retained this plural form today:

child/children ox/oxen man/men woman/women
brother/brethren (used in some particular contexts)

Other words with such a pronounced change in their plural form are:

mouse/mice louse/lice

Words ending in y in the singular

The next group of words which very largely conforms to a rule comprises those which end in y. The vast majority of such words form the plural by dropping the y and adding -ies:

secretary/secretaries lady/ladies country/countries baby/babies
melody/melodies lullaby/lullabies

RULE	**Where a word ends in y preceded by a consonant drop the y and add -ies to form the plural.**

However, if the letter immediately preceding the y is a vowel, then the plural form is likely to be correctly achieved simply by adding an s:

valley/valleys delay/delays play/plays honey/honeys
abbey/abbeys toy/toys

Words ending in o in the singular

The next group of words to examine are the ones which end in o in their singular. Here there is really no rule of any significance, and you will just have to consult your dictionary whenever in doubt. Here are some common ones where the plural is made either by adding simply an s or an es:

hero/heroes alto/altos potato/potatoes piano/pianos
tornado/tornadoes soprano/sopranos tomato/tomatoes silo/silos

Words of foreign origin

Words which often cause difficulty are those which have arrived from foreign languages and found a place in everyday English. Sometimes they retain the foreign language plural form, and sometimes they have become fully anglicized and simply add an *s* to the singular. In a typically English way, they may sometimes be used in the plural in either form! Examples include:

formula/formulae, formulas stadium/stadia, stadiums alga/algae
stimulus/stimuli bureau/bureaux

It may be fairly considered that today where two plurals exist the use of the foreign language version of the plural of such words has largely become fussy and pedantic.

-fs or *-ves* plurals

A few words exist in English which end in *f* in the singular and have optional plural forms:

dwarf/dwarfs, dwarves scarf/scarfs, scarves
handkerchief/handkerchiefs, handkerchieves

Sometimes, however, their plural *has to change to -ves*:

leaf/leaves knife/knives sheaf/sheaves

Again, whenever in doubt, check in your dictionary!

Singular as plural

Lastly, just a few words either have no plural form, or we tend not to use it in certain contexts:

chicken fish deer sheep corps swine

HINT!

One of the best ways of improving your spelling of plurals (other than regular dictionary checks) is to make a note in your notebook of any unfamiliar plural forms you meet in your newspaper, magazine or library book reading. This will help you commit them to memory and to remember them when you need to.

Assignments

1 Write down the plural form for each of the words shown below. First, attempt those you are confident about to reinforce your confidence. If there are some which you are not sure about, consult your dictionary and then write down their correct plural form. This will help you to remember them for next time – and there is almost certainly going to be a next time!

adversary miss abbess soprano wharf cutlass belly chief
tumulus fungus dynamo hoof opus axis virtuoso turkey
batch menu negro valley sheaf

2   Write down the singular form of the following using the same approach as suggested in **1** above:

heroes   dwarves   bureaux   brethren   bases   formulae   fuzzes messieurs   anthologies   cupolas   corps

Consult your dictionary whenever you need to, and check the meaning of any words you have not met before while you are at it!

Chapter 8
Improve your written English II: the adjective

Now that you have a clear understanding of the parts played by nouns and verbs in forming sentences, it is most appropriate to consider a further part of speech whose main function is to extend the meaning of the noun:

RULE	**Adjectives extend the meaning of nouns (or other adjectives)**

The following sentence illustrates this important function:

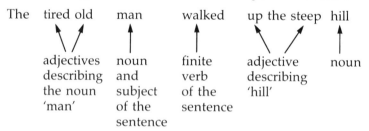

The tired old man walked up the steep hill

adjectives describing the noun 'man'

noun and subject of the sentence

finite verb of the sentence

adjective describing 'hill'

noun

As the above sentence shows, adjectives play a major part in extending the meaning of ideas – putting flesh here on to the bare idea of *'The man walked up the hill.'*

The adjective

Though it is not particularly important to remember their names or individual functions, there are five types of adjectives which grammarians have thought it worthwhile to identify separately:

1	those which describe	*Descriptive*
2	those which point out or identify	*Demonstrative*
3	those which pose questions	*Interrogative*
4	those which indicate possession	*Possessive*
5	those which indicate how many	*Quantitative*

Examples:

- *Descriptive:* good   bad   green   bright   heavy
- *Demonstrative:* this   that   these   those
- *Interrogative:* what   which   whose

- *Possessive:* my   his   your   our   their
- *Quantitative:* three   forty-two   few   many   some

The describing adjective

There are literally thousands and thousands of descriptive adjectives to be found in current English. Those listed below will provide you with just a taste of their flavour and variety:

the *busy* shopkeeper   a *tall* building   an *aluminium* window-frame   the *green* bicycle   *fat* seals   a *lovely* day   a *cutting* remark   *bankrupt* stock *driving* rain   *broken* fingernail   *three* pennies   the *noisy* room   *precious* moments   a *special* offer

As you can see the adjective in each of the above examples is telling us more about the noun it describes – not just any finger-nail but a *broken* one, not a wooden window-frame but an *aluminium* one.

You may have noticed two words in the examples which looked like verbs – *driving* and *broken*. In fact they come from the verb infinitives *to drive* and *to break* but can be used as adjectives when in what is called the present or past participle form.

RULE	**Present participle parts of the verb are words ending in *-ing*. These often act as adjectives:**

Present participle parts of the verb are words ending in *-ing*. These often act as adjectives:

the *strolling* holiday-makers   the *winding* road
the *turning* wheel   the *running* water

Past participle parts of the verb are words ending mostly in *-ed* except where verbs change in the past like 'break/broken'. They also often act as adjectives.

the *smashed* vase   a *blistered* foot   the *mended* fence   the *typed* report

Examples:

– His secretary put the *typed* report on Mr Jenkin's desk.
– The *strolling* holiday-makers filled the sunny esplanade.
– A *blistered* foot can be very painful.

While the most common location for descriptive adjectives (and in fact any adjective) is immediately in front of the noun it describes, sometimes in English an alternative construction is used after the verb *to be* or other verbs:

– The train was *crowded*.
– His life had been *free and easy*.

In such cases the simple test is to ask what was crowded? The train was crowded. Life had been free and easy. If the answer is a noun in the sentence, then the words are adjectives.

The demonstrative adjective – the one that points out

Simply, there are four:

this hat   *that* box   *these* shoes   *those* shirts

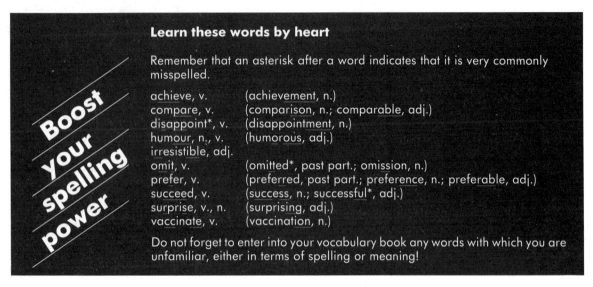

Boost your spelling power

Learn these words by heart

Remember that an asterisk after a word indicates that it is very commonly misspelled.

achieve, v.   (achievement, n.)
compare, v.   (comparison, n.; comparable, adj.)
disappoint*, v.   (disappointment, n.)
humour, n., v.   (humorous, adj.)
irresistible, adj.
omit, v.   (omitted*, past part.; omission, n.)
prefer, v.   (preferred, past part.; preference, n.; preferable, adj.)
succeed, v.   (success, n.; successful*, adj.)
surprise, v., n.   (surprising, adj.)
vaccinate, v.   (vaccination, n.)

Do not forget to enter into your vocabulary book any words with which you are unfamiliar, either in terms of spelling or meaning!

Their function is to draw particular attention to a person or object. Sometimes they are used without the inclusion in the sentence of the nouns to which they refer:

– I don't like *those* (shirts).
– I'll take *these* (shoes).
– She will use *that* (box).
– You can wear *this* (hat).

However, as we shall see in more detail later on page 106, when the nouns to which such words refer are omitted, then words like *this*, *that*, *these* and *those* stand in place of them and are called demonstrative pronouns.

The interrogative adjective – the one that asks a question

Interrogative adjectives are used in sentences which ask questions:

– *Which* film would you like to see?
– *Whose* coat is this?
– *What* dessert would you prefer?

The same words have the same functions in a sentence even when the direct question has been turned into a statement:

– I did not discover *which* film she wanted to see.
– I have no idea *what* impulse made him quit his job.
– It does not matter *whose* coat it is if it fits you!

Again such interrogative adjectives may be used (without the nouns they refer to) as pronouns, as we shall see later.

The possessive adjective

As its name suggests, the possessive adjective is used to show ownership or at least possession of something:

my desk   *your* comb   *his* umbrella   *her* lipstick   *its* tail   *our* house
your (plural) car

Remember that with *your*, the sense may refer to a single or plural ownership, and the good writer makes sure that there is no uncertainty on this score in the reader's mind.

The quantitative adjective – the one which shows 'how many'

Adjectives which either show a specific quantity:

three ties   *two hundred and forty-six point four* grams   *fifteen* trees
one million voters

or which indicate a general or even vague notion of number:

several people   a *few* spectators   *some* birds   *many* tickets

are called interrogative.
   Other interrogative adjectives are:

each   single   all   no   every   most

Examples:

– Not a *single* valuable has been recovered since the burglary!
– *All* schoolboys go through a rebellious phase.
– *Each* dress is stocked in several popular sizes.

A word on adjectives and good style

Properly used, adjectives contribute a wealth of meaning and detail to a piece of writing. Yet the adjective is one of the most overworked parts of speech in the English language. Consider the following passage, where adjectives have been deliberately heaped upon the nouns they modify to show you the tedious effect this has:

The old, grey-haired, dirty tramp walked up the hot, dry and dusty road until he reached the brow of the hill, sun-baked, exposed and featureless, shimmering in the heat of the merciless unforgiving summer sun. Before him he saw, nestling in the fold of the hidden, remote and tree-covered valley an expanse of fresh water which formed a rippling, green, rush-covered, ornamental lake.

Just count all the adjectives you can identify in this passage totalling sixty-three words. Now work out the ratio of adjectives to all words used!
   Of course, this example has been deliberately overloaded with adjectives to make a point.

HINT!

Using adjectives: a golden rule!
When using adjectives, above all choose the most effective you can for the particular context – and use them sparingly. It is much better style to find nouns and verbs which convey the meaning you wish to communicate.

The above example, stripped of all its adjectives might be written thus:

The tramp walked up the road until he reached the brow of the hill which shimmered in the summer's heat. Before him he saw in the valley an expanse of water in the form of a lake.

Taking the advice of the Golden Rule to heart, the passage might be written like this:

The grimy tramp trudged up the road, sweltering in the noonday heat until he reached the brow of the hill, which shimmered beneath a baking sun. Before him, nestling in a valley, an ornamental lake lay rippling through the green of many trees.

Verbs like *trudged* and *shimmered* convey a strong sense of tiredness or bright light, while fewer adjectives, like *grimy*, *sweltering* and *baking* impart the feeling of intense heat and layers of dirt. Similarly, the nouns have been chosen for their effect upon the reader: *tramp*, *road*, *heat*, *brow*, *hill*, *sun*, *valley*, *lake*, *trees*. Notice that all the nouns are short and simple words which convey their meaning easily and directly.

The next time you have to write a passage of prose, take the time to think more about the words you are using – whether nouns, verbs or adjectives and try to choose only those best suited to the task you want them to carry out.

Writing it right!

Few and less

Generally these two words cause little bother – 'a few scraps', 'less cold than last winter', 'few candidates failed', and so on.

But the use of the comparison does sometimes cause problems.

Remember that when the individual parts of the group standing for either 'few' or 'less' can be identified individually, then the correct word is 'fewer':

There were *fewer* spectators at yesterday's game than at the previous home match.

Here the use of the word 'less' would be inappropriate in:

There were *less* spectators … **Wrong!**

Where, however, the idea expressed is of a single entity like water in a bucket, then 'less' is correct:

There is *less* water in the reservoir this autumn because of the dry summer.

Assignments

1 Write down each of the words being used as adjectives in the following sentences:

a After a rushed meal, the holiday-makers climbed into the double-decker bus and resumed their slow journey up the winding passes of the Swiss alps.

b An icy wind howled through the broken window and rattled the dust-covered cups and plates on the abandoned Dutch dresser.

2 Opposite are assembled a group of various types of adjective. Put them into appropriate sets under the following headings:

Describing Pointing out   Questioning   Possessing Showing quantity
        (Demonstrative) (Interrogative)   (Quantitative)

straight   our   every   its   some   those   sharp   two   which
their   most   what   shining   few   all   whose   that   huge
mended

3   Write down the names of those two parts of the verb which may be used as adjectives. What suffixes do they generally have?

4   Identify the adjective in the following sentence:

The crowd, which was enormous, was assembled to see the match.

5   In the section on adjectives, mention was made that adjectives can sometimes modify the meaning of other adjectives. Which adjectives are working in this way in the following sentence:

I like the bright blue jumper, but Sally prefers the dark brown pullover.

6   What advice would you give a would-be writer on using adjectives to best effect?

Chapter 9
Punctuating in English II: the comma

Of all the punctuation marks used in writing English, the comma is almost certainly the most difficult to use well! So you will need to pay particular attention to the advice given in this section. One of the main reasons why writers find the comma a demanding punctuation mark to use stems from its wide range of functions – sometimes simply to provide a 'breathing space' in the flow of ideas, sometimes to affect quite extensively the very meaning of a sentence.

The comma as an aid to meaning

In many ways the comma in writing may be likened to the sense pause in spoken English. It provides a momentary pause so that the reader may absorb what has been conveyed before continuing to take in the next part of a piece of writing:

The news in the letter came as a totally unexpected shock, since she had made up her mind to leave him.

Here the comma obliges the reader to pause, and increases the drama of the second part of the sentence.

Methodically, he tore the letter into small pieces, threw them into the blazing fire, picked up the poker and broke each glowing ember of the notepaper into tiny fragments.

In the above sentence five principal ideas are expressed in a connected sequence, each centring upon the rejected lover's actions. Firstly all was done methodically, the letter was torn up, thrown upon the fire and totally destroyed with the aid of the poker. Each of these ideas is separated – the first four by the use of the comma and the last one by the use of 'and'. The effect of interrupting the flow of the narrative by the comma in this way is to make the actions slow and deliberate, so we can see that the comma not only plays a part in conveying meaning accurately, but also in contributing to the effect upon the reader of a piece of writing.

To reinforce the concept of the comma aiding meaning, try to piece together the meaning of the following passage, set down without the commas it needs:

Having been cleared for landing the plane circled down its main flaps braking on the icy snow-filled air blocking out the sky with its black lumbering mass roar of engines and piercing landing lights.

The above passage illustrates how much we take the comma for granted in rendering a long sentence that much easier to digest and understand:

Having been cleared for landing, the plane circled down, its main flaps braking on the icy, snow-filled air, blocking out the sky with its black, lumbering mass, roar of engines and piercing landing lights.

Even so, from the point of view of good style it would be better to avoid using so many commas by dividing the sentence in two:

Having been cleared for landing, the plane circled down, its main flaps braking on the icy, snow-filled air. It blocked out the sky with its black, lumbering mass, roar of engines and piercing landing lights.

In the above form the passage also provides a good example of the relative strengths of the comma and full stop, where the latter provides just that little more of a pause.

Guidelines on the comma and sentence sense

- When you are writing always consider carefully whether a comma is needed to provide a pause between sense groups of meaning or whether a full stop would better indicate the break between two distinct ideas.
- Avoid the temptation of allowing your sentences to go on for too long and to 'pepper' them with commas which may in fact interfere with the ready communication of your ideas. The golden rule is: whenever in doubt, stop and start a new sentence.

With the second guideline in mind, consider the following example:

The bent, old man stooped, picked up the box of matches, half full of charred, used match-sticks, opened it with shaking, gnarled fingers, trying to grip a single, unused match, from among the confusing pack, his hands white and shrivelled in the cold, damp air of the basement room, where his cat, its fur fluffed out against the cold watched his every move.

As a helpful exercise, rewrite this passage, removing as many commas as you can while retaining its sense and spirit. Also, see what you can do to get rid of any unnecessary adjectives and if you want to refashion it by changing the number of sentences, fine! You will find a version at the back of the book to compare yours with – after you have produced it!

The comma at work

Bearing in mind the above guidelines on using the comma effectively, consider now the following examples of the comma at work in a variety of roles:

Separating items in a list

A very common use of the comma is to separate items into a list:

– An inspection of her purse revealed three credit cards, two five pound notes, seventy-five pence in coins, a first-class stamp, an old receipt for a pair of mended shoes, a business card and three library tickets.
– John, Mary, Susan and Bill all passed the English examination.

As you can see, commas may be used to separate either groups of words or single words – in the case of the second example, the names of people. Notice that the introduction of the last item in the list which is introduced by the word 'and' needs no comma:

. . . a business card_and three library tickets.
. . . Susan_and Bill all passed the English examination.

In just the same way, the comma can be used to separate much longer groups of words in a list. Such longer groups of words which contain a subject and finite verb are called *clauses* when linked together in one long sentence and they are dealt with in detail on page 93. For the time being, however, just concentrate on the positioning of the commas in such passages:

The policeman slowly opened his notebook,_licked the tip of his pencil and began to write deliberately, while the poor motorist shuffled uncomfortably from one foot to the other and a group of onlookers began to form on the pavement,_just in front of the now twisted halt sign.

Notice in the above example that the rule followed is just the same – commas at the end of each item in the list except for the final 'and'. But, in this example, a further piece of information has been added – 'just in front of the now twisted halt sign'. This late addition needs the extra comma, and has been deliberately left until last for comic effect.

Introducing a modifying word at the beginning of a sentence

Another very common use of the comma is to provide a pause after a word beginning a sentence which changes or reinforces either what has just been written or what is coming next:

This shortcut in making puff pastry is used frequently by professional chefs. *However,* it is not recommended for beginners.

Notice that the use of *however* here is to prepare the reader for a contrasting statement to qualify what has just been stated. Other such 'checking' or 'holding' expressions which may be used to start sentences in this way are:

Nevertheless,_ Even so,_ Still,_

Other expressions may be used to introduce a sentence which reinforces what has just been written:

The damage you have done has caused a great deal of inconvenience. *Moreover,* the compensation will not begin to pay for the loss of use of this indispensable machine!

The introduction of the second sentence by the word *moreover* prepares the reader for what will be a reinforcing statement adding to the impact of the first. Other such words which produce the same effect are:

Furthermore, Indeed, Certainly,

Sometimes such expressions may be used to good effect with commas in the middle of sentences:

His excellent result was, *moreover,* quite unexpected!

Here the effect is to add extra emphasis on the last part of the sentence. Further examples are:

– The rather pathetic attempts of the old burglar were, *however*, doomed to failure since he knew nothing about modern alarm systems.

– Sir Archibald Blenkinsop attended meetings infrequently. He was, *nevertheless*, excellent company when able to do so and will be sadly missed.

Separating an inserted phrase or clause in a sentence

Sometimes ideas are 'pushed' into sentences by authors as if by way of an afterthought and commas are needed to maintain the original construction of the sentence:

– They left the safety of the log cabin, *despite the grim weather forecast*, to keep to their schedule and rendezvous with the fresh dog-team and new provisions.

– Fred Larkin, *Nettlebury's fast bowler*, caught his captain's request and set off to bowl from the Dog and Duck end.

– They drove slowly up the long drive and the manor house, *covered in unsuspected ivy*, looked dark and forbidding.

In the above illustrations, the insertions of:

despite the grim weather forecast   Nettlebury's fast bowler   covered in unsuspected ivy

have the effect of interrupting the normal structure of the sentence and are therefore bracketed off by commas.

Sentences where a dependent clause precedes the main clause

Firstly, don't worry about the title above – clauses of this nature are dealt with fully on page 117 and the entry regarding them and the comma is included here for the sake of easy reference at a later stage of your development. For the time being, just absorb the effect of the writing given the inclusion of the commas:

– Although the fog had become dense with the fall of the air temperature at dusk, the drivers still careered madly along the motorway.

– After she had made the final touches to the portrait, she stepped back and considered her artistry with a smile of satisfaction.

Unfortunately, in such sentence constructions in English there is no rule governing the introduction of a comma, and the following examples show the effect without one:

– If I were you I most certainly would go!

– As the radiator was damaged beyond repair the tourists were stranded.

A rule of thumb is that the length of the two components of the sentence will govern the need or not to separate them by a comma. If the use of a comma helps to convey meaning and to aid the balance of the sentence then it is sensible to use one.

Commas after present and past participles

When an idea is included as part of a sentence by using either a present or past participal construction, then a comma is frequently employed to aid the communication of meaning:

– Having paid for the repairs to the radiator, the tourists were able to resume their journey.
– Driven to desperation by the thought of missing the Cup Final, he decided to raid his small savings to purchase a ticket he could not really afford.

Commas in direct speech

When direct and indirect speech together form a single sentence, then a comma is used to separate them:

– 'I don't think I shall go to the theatre after all,' said Jack.
– 'Of course you are perfectly free to make an official complaint,' warned the factory supervisor, 'but you must be prepared to accept the consequences.'

Notice in the first example that the separating comma comes *inside* the second set of inverted commas:

'. . . after all,' said Jack.

And notice also in the second example, that where the indirect speech (warned the factory supervisor) interrupts the direct speech, then the second comma comes *before* the re-opening inverted commas:

warned the factory supervisor, 'but you must . . .'

Also remember that when a question mark or exclamation mark con-clude
the direct speech in the middle of the sentence, no other mark of punctu-ation is needed:

– 'How do you know?' asked his mother.
'Leave this office at once!' shouted the manager.

And, neither is a capital letter needed for the word introducing the indirect speech: *a*sked his mother   *s*houted the manager.

Separating letters etc. in closed punctuation

One form of punctuating the names and addresses of the recipients of letters in correspondence layout is called 'closed punctuation'. This requires full stops and commas to be shown as follows:

P. Wilkinson, Esq., M.A., Cert. Ed., F.B.I.M.,
Head of Business Studies Department,
Chester Polytechnic,
Wirral Way,
Chester,
Cheshire.   CH12 3CP

Defining and non-defining relative clauses

Despite this dreadful title, there is an important use of the comma to be learned which has to do with the use of ideas introduced by the words 'who', 'which' and 'that'.

Consider the following:

– The man who was drinking a pint of stout was the one being sought by the police.
– The man, who was drinking a pint of stout, was the one being sought by the police.

Not much difference in the meaning of either of the above examples you may be excused for concluding. But, the omission of the commas in the first sentence defines the wanted man as the one – the only one – who was drinking a pint of stout. Thus the clause which introduces the idea 'who was drinking a pint of stout' needs no commas since it is a defining relative clause. In the second example, however, it is simply an additional piece of information included for descriptive effect and does not define the wanted man in the sense of being the only one drinking the stout. Therefore it is separated by commas like any other insertion into the structure of a sentence.

HINT!

What to avoid in using commas effectively
- **Avoid using too many adjectives in front of nouns which need to be separated by the use of the comma:**

The heat from the burning, merciless, drifting sand blistered their feet as if their boot leather was made of cardboard.

Try to find a single better adjective to convey the meaning:

searing sand   or   scorching sand

Or convert one of the adjectives into an adverb:

The heat from the scorching sand $\left\{ \begin{array}{l} \text{mercilessly} \\ \text{relentlessly} \end{array} \right\}$ blistered ...

- **Remember that you do not need a comma before the final 'and' in a list:**

Mix the flour, eggs, milk and butter into a stiff pastry.

- **Write more, shorter sentences instead of long, rambling ones linking too many ideas together with commas. This will help you to communicate your ideas more easily and promptly.**
- **If your sentence's meaning seems perfectly clear without the comma – then leave it out!**

Assignments

1 Insert commas and/or full stops where you think appropriate in the following:

a before pulling away look behind for pedestrians or oncoming vehicles signal your intention check your rear-view mirror and avoid causing other vehicles to slow down as you move off
b the charges he faced included impersonating a gas board official breaking and entering resisting arrest and forty-two other offences he had asked to be taken into consideration
c the defence counsel insisted that despite the case against him he was basically a man of good character
d 'the trouble with you' he said angrily 'is that you never think before you speak'

e there is good reason however to believe that she may have been able to pass on the message before she was captured

f even so by following the instructions carefully you will be able to set up the equipment yourself

g though they had been duly warned of the inevitable consequences of their actions they still went ahead with their plan to kidnap the chief constable as part of the university's rag week

h if you go she will want to go too

i the chairman's office which was situated on the top floor was reached by a private lift

Chapter 10
Mastering spelling II: vowel sounds

Whenever the word 'vowel' is referred to, we tend usually to think of the famous five: *a, e, i, o, u,* pronounced, *ay, ee, eye, oh, you*. Yet the truth of the matter is rather less simple, since the *Concise Oxford Dictionary* (seventh edition) lists some thirty-one distinguishable vowel sounds!

ā	as in (fāt) = fate	eɪ	ō	as in (gōt) = goat	əʊ
ă	as in (făt)	æ	ŏ	as in (gŏt)	o
a	as in (*agō'*)	ə	*o*	as in (flă'g*o*n)	ə
ah	as in (bah)	ɑ	oi	as in (boil)	ɔɪ
ār	as in (fār) = fare	eə(r)	ōō	as in (bōōt)	u
âr	as in (fâr)	ɑ(r)	ŏŏ	as in (bŏŏk)	ʊ
aw	as in (paw)	ɔ	oor	as in (poor)	ʊə(r)
ē	as in (mēt) = meet	i	ôr	as in (pôrt)	ɔ(r)
ĕ	as in (mĕt)	e	ow	as in (brow)	aʊ
e	as in (tō'k*e*n)	ə	owr	as in (sowr) = sour	aʊə(r)
ēr	as in (fēr) = fear	ɪə(r)	ū	as in (dū) = due	ju
êr	as in (fêr) = fur	ɜ(r)	ŭ	as in (dŭg)	ʌ
er	as in (tā'k*er*)	ə(r)	*u*	as in (bō'n*u*s)	ə
ī	as in (bīt) = bite	aɪ	ūr	as in (pūr) = pure	jʊə(r)
ĭ	as in (bĭt)	ɪ	See ṅ (under 'Consonants'	
i	as in (bā's*i*n)	ə	above) for French nasalized	
īr	as in (fīr) = fire	aɪə(r)	vowels.	

In the course of this section the approach will be to concentrate upon those vowel sounds which cause the most difficulty when spelled.

The *ay* sound

Some words possessing the *ay* sound spell it as a long *a*:

hate   mate   pale   may   rake

But there are a number of different spellings which sound identical:

gate/gait   straight/strait   sail/sale   way/whey   slay/sleigh
wade/weighed   vale/veil   lane/lain   rain/rein/reign

The most frequent 'sets' in which you are likely to encounter the *ay* sound spelled are:

- as *-ay-* particularly in verbs which then have past tenses spelled *-ayed*, e.g. played
- as *-ai-* many nouns have the *-ai-* spelling:
  maid   tail   sail   gait   waiter
  and many verbs too: waive   train   claim
- as *-ale* pale   sale   whale   tale   bale
- as *-ate* mate   state   crate   plate   abate
- as *-eigh-* weigh   sleigh   (not so frequent)

The best way to learn to spell those *ay* sounds you have not yet mastered is to collect sets of those words which are spelled in the same way and which sound identical:

pail   tail   rail   mail etc.   weight   freight   reign   deign
sale   pale   fate   plate   crate   rein   vein   veil   tray   clay
display

Another good way to fix such spellings firmly in the mind is to set together the words which sound the same but have different spellings. Such words are called homophones:

rain   reign   rein   way   whey   weigh   slay   sleigh   fate   fête
grate   great   gate   gait   vale   veil   straight   strait

As a rule of thumb, keep in mind that the most likely spellings for the *ay* sound are: long *a*, *-ai-*, *-ei-* and *-ay-*.

The *eye* sound

The first variation for this vowel sound is, as you might expect, the long *i*:

bīle   dīne   mīme   customīze   whīte   wīre

A particularly helpful spelling guideline worth mentioning here is the effect of the single or double consonant on the pronunciation of words. For example, a long *i* sound (or any long vowel sound) is most frequently followed by a single consonant, and a short one by a double consonant:

whīning   wĭnning   tīling   tĭlling   smīler   mĭller

This effect of the double consonant on the length of the vowel sound will often help you to spell a word correctly if you know how to say it!

The most common spellings of the *-i-* (long *i*) sound occur in these groups of letters:

-ice   *-ide*   *-ile*   *-ime*   *-ine*   *-ise*   *-ite*
slice   decide   pile   sublime   dine   devise   finite

See how many words you can think of under these headings.

Another way in which the *eye* sound is commonly spelled is with the *-igh-* variant:

slight   higher   mighty   nigh   sigh   tight

Very common in this group are those words ending in *-ight*:

bight   fight   light   might   night   right   sight   tight

The letter *y* is often used in English for the *eye* sound:

sty   dry   sly   pyre   style   myopic   scythe   bicycle

And finally, almost inevitably in English spelling, come the 'best mixed' versions:

aisle   isle   die   sleight

However, if you consider the possible variations for the *eye* sound, almost all of them are to be found in either the *-i-* long *i* sound, the *-igh-*, *-y-*, variants, and this narrows the field considerably.

Again, it is good practice to collect in your notebook via your reading those versions you have not previously met and to commit to memory those homophones you are likely to need:

die/dye   bite/bight   slight/sleight   site/sight/cite   aisle/isle/I'll
stile/style   wine/whine

Learn these key words by heart

Remember that an asterisk after a word indicates that it is very commonly misspelled.

absorb, v.	(absorption, n.; absorbent, adj.)
acquaint*, v.	(acquaintance, n.)
breathe, v.	(breath, n.)
bureau, n. -eaux pl.	(bureaucracy, n.)
category, n.	(categoric, adj.)
centre/center, v., n.	(central, adj.; centering, v.; centred, v.)
deficient, adj.	(deficiency, n.)
desire, v., n.	(desirable, adj.; desirous, adj.)
eliminate, v.	(elimination, n.)
emphasize, v.	(emphasis, n.; emphatic, adj.)
equip, v.	(equipped, v.; equipment, n.)
feasible, adj.	(feasibility, n.; unfeasible, adj.)
February, n.	
genius, n.	(geniuses, pl.)
grammar, n.	(grammatical, adj.)
honour, v., n.	(honourable, adj.; honorary, adj.)
horrendous, adj.	
incident, n.	(incidental, adj.; incidence, n.)
incipient, adj.	
lively, adv.	(livelihood, n.)

Boost your spelling power

Do not forget to enter into your vocabulary book any words with which you are unfamiliar, either in terms of spelling or meaning!

The *ow* sound (as in 'slow')

For the writer with a spelling problem, the *ow* sound presents a challenge, since there are quite a number of ways in which the *ow* sound may be spelled differently as the following chart illustrates:

- as a long *o* gō sō pōlite sōlō tōtal cōlon
  tow sow mow low row minnow own slow
- as -*ow*- oat stoat goat boat moat coat float
- as -*oat* coke joke yoke choke smoke awoke
- as -*oke* (note here: folk-song pronounced 'foke-song', and the word ochre,
  pronounced 'oker')
- as -*oe*- doe foe hoe roe heroes toe
- as -*oa*- oast coast roast toast goad toad road
- as -*ough* dough though (note also: bureau cocoa)

Fortunately as you grew up you will have learned a very large number of such variants without realizing it. Nevertheless, this is a vowel sound you may need to consult your dictionary about more frequently than others.

The *ooooh* sound (as in 'moon')

The *ooooh* sound is most frequently spelled like this:

- as a double *o* moon boot tool booth stoop
- as -*ue* blue clue sue rue pursue
- as -*ew* threw crew stew brew
- as -*ough* through
- as -*u*- prune (seldom)

The *you* sound

Closely linked to the *ooooh* sound is the *you* sound which adds a 'yuh' to the front of it. Most frequently this sound is made by the letter *u* beginning a word.

- as *u*- utilize unity unique useful
- as *eu*- euphemism euphonium euphoria
- as -*ew* stew knew mew few

and note the following:

hue revue due view ewe dune tune beautiful

The *air* sound

The *air* sound tends to be spelled in one of these ways:

- as -*air*- fair pair lair bairn cairn hairy fairy
- as -*ear* tear wear bear pear
- as -*are* rare fare care stare prepare parent

Also to be on your guard for are:

*ae*rate *heir* *where* *ga*rish mal*a*ria

The *auw* sound (as in 'scowl')

This vowel sound comes most frequently in these spellings:

- as -ow- bow owl bowel jowl scowl allow
- as -ou- bout rout scout mount nous mouse tout
- as -ough bough slough plough sough

The *aaaah* sound (as in 'father')

One of the problems associated with spelling this sound lies in the difference of the spoken *aaaah* sound in different parts of the country and regions of the world. In southern England, for example the word grass is pronounced 'grahss' while in more northern parts, the pronunciation would rhyme with 'lass'.

The *aaaah* sound, then with such reservations in mind may be spelled:

- as long -a- part tart father path
- as -ea- hearth heart
- as -au- laugh draught

The *oy* sound (as in 'boil')

This you will encounter most frequently:

- as -oi- devoid soil goitre poison boisterous
- as -oy- boy soya voyage coy destroy (but notice: buoy)

The *aw* sound (as in 'awe')

The following are the most likely variations you will meet:

- as -aw- caw awful gnaw prawn awning drawl
- as -augh- daughter slaughter taught caught
- as -ough- bought fought nought ought
- as -au- applaud cause saunter haul
- as -all- hall falling stall

The *ur* sound

This sound also includes quite a few variants, the most common being:

- as -ur- curt further burn blurt burble
- as -ir- dirt girdle girth mirth swirl stir
- as -er- fern tern alert disperse pertinent
- as -ear- dearth earth earn yearn pearl
- as -or- worse worth word wort

The *ire* sound (as in 'fire')

The three most commonly occurring variants are:

- as -ire- dire fire irate entire (notice that when the -ir sound occurs at the end of a word it frequently is followed by a silent *e* which makes the *i* sound long)
- as -yre- byre lyre pyre
- as -iar- liar friar

And notice:

drier higher choir quire pariah

The short vowel sounds

The short vowel sounds like *igh, ogh, ugh, agh*, etc. tend to cause less trouble where spelling is concerned:

- *igh* sounds hit bill dip sin hiss
- *agh* sounds bat man patter trap
- *ogh* sounds bottom pot volley cotton
- *ugh* sounds cub mutter puss stuffing
- *yuh* sounds just junta young

But keep in mind words like:

rough tough enough mother among constable etc.

Conclusion

As you will have realized by now, this section on vowels has shown just how wide is the variety of vowels sounds, and how varied too the ways in which identical sounds may be spelled.

The best approach to tackle and to conquer the problem presented by this wide range of sounds and alternative spellings is to work out a consistent plan and to stick to it.

Most recent research has indicated that the best way to improve your ability to spell such vowels sounds is to assemble as you go along word clusters which embody identical vowel and spelling sounds and letter sequences. To start you select an anchor word in the area which you know well and can spell:

HINT!

How to develop spelling clusters

Anchor word   earth (representing the *ur* sound)

Extension words   dearth   hearse   pearl   earthenware
Anchor word   concede (representing one of the *ee* sounds)

Extension words   procedure   secede   recede   accede

Such word clusterings can also be used as triggers to recall:

'but, supersede and proceed'

or 'eam, but um, pearl but to 'come a purler' and so on.

By building up such spelling groupings in one's head, the correct spelling is being reinforced all the time and the exceptions to such groupings are also readily called to mind.

Next, the writing down of an unfamiliar spelling helps to fix it in the mind and the sequencing of the letters as the word is written – preferably a number of times – is also absorbed and retained by the brain.

Let these watchwords prompt you to carry out the actions they urge:

Read it!   The more you read, the more often the words you find difficult to spell will be photographed on your retina and carried into your brain.

Write it!   The more frequently you write a new word down, the sooner you will be able to recall it from your long-term memory on request.

Say it!   The more often you incorporate it into your selection of words you use regularly, the sooner you will feel comfortable with it, and build the bridge between the word's sound and its written appearance.

Summary: most commonly occurring vowel sound spellings

- the long *a* sound as in 'may'

-a-	-ai-	-ei-	-ay-
mate	maid	weighed	displayed

- The long *e* sound as in 'seed'

-ee-	-ie-	-ei-	-ea-	-e-
deed	siege	seize	reveal	concede

- The long *i* sound as in 'pine'

-i-	-igh-	-y-	-ei-	-ie-
wipe	sight	dye	sleight	died or vie

- The long *o* sound as in 'go'

-ow-	-oa-	-oe-	-ough-	-eau-
tow	goat/moan	toe	dough	bureau

- The long *you* sound as in 'usual'

-u-	-eu-	-iew-	-ew-	-ue-
unity	euphonium	review	yew	hue

- the long *oooh* sound as in 'moon'

-oo-	-ue-	-ew-	-ough-	-u-
balloon	clue	stew	through	prune

- The *air* sound as in 'fair'

-ai-	-ea-	-are-
pair	wear	snare

- The *ow* sound as in 'cow'

-ow-	-ou-	-ough-
sow	about	bough

- The *aaah* sound as in 'father'

-a-	-ear-	-augh-
path	hearth	laugh

- The *oy* sound as in 'boy'

-oi	-oy-
spoil	deployed

- The *aw* sound as in 'crawl'

-aw-	*-augh-*	*-ough-*	*-au-*
prawn	daughter	bought	haul

- the *ire* as in 'fire'

-ire-	*-yre-*	*-yer-*	*-igher-*
spire	lyre	dyer	higher

- The *ur* sound as in 'hurt'

-ur-	*-ir-*	*-er-*	*-or-*	*-ear-*
spurn	dirt	alert	worth	earn

RULE

Some rules and guidelines for spelling vowels

- **Unless the word is of foreign origin, the vowel sound *you* is always formed after the consonant *q* by *u*:**

quite   quilt   quiver

- **The letter *i* usually comes before *e*, except after *c*:**

ceiling   conceit   deceive

but beware of other identical sounds:

conceal   recede   scene etc.

- **When a vowel sound is pronounced long, then very often it is followed by a single consonant:**

mātey   mătted   hōping   hŏpping

and likewise, when pronounced short, by a double consonant.

- **Very common vowel sounds among suffixes as the ends of words are:**

-ary -ery -ious -ous -ion -ience -ient -ible -able -ful -ist

Some have an identical pronunciation, so whenever in doubt, consult your dictionary!

- **The spellings of commonly occurring prefixes and suffixes are given on pages 101 and 114.**
- **Inside words, the most commonly encountered double vowel sequences are:**

ae ai ay ei ie ee eu eau oi oy ough oo

- **Vowel sounds do not occur very commonly at the ends of words, and double vowels very seldom. Those you will meet, however, are:**

-ia -ae -au -eau -io

- **Identical pairs of vowel letters tend only to occur as:**

ee oo

Assignments

1 The *ay* sound: write down four different words which illustrate four different ways in which the *ay* sound may be spelled.

2 The *ee* sound: fill in the blanks – each one represents a letter – in the words shown below to complete their spelling and to illustrate different examples of the way the *ee* sound may be spelled.

pl_ _d   to persuade or beg
proc_dure   way of doing things
exc_ _d   go beyond go over
formul_ _   directions or instructions for, say, making something
fr_ _ze   paper decoration on a cake, or decoration round a wall
s_ _ze   grab hold of

3 Write down five words which illustrate five different ways of spelling the long *o* sound as in 'go'.

4 Write down the other word (or words) which sound exactly like the one given. Example: bare/bear, way/whey/weigh:

isle   bore   bale   beer   earn   dew   pair   fate   faint   review
vale   vain   new   taught   wine   liar   straight   slight   sole

5 Write down seven different words which include the letters *ough* pronounced differently each time!

6 Write down four words illustrating the different ways the *aw* sound may be spelled.

7 Complete the following. Each dash represents a letter.

sl_ _ _ _ter   to kill
b_ _ _ _ _   purchased
h_ _ _   to pull along
a_ _ing   shade erected over a window
g_ _ _   to chew at (as a dog chews a bone)

8 Troublesome spellings: write down the word which fits the following definitions.

    a   a four letter word meaning one who inherits
    b   a four letter word meaning a row of seats, say, in a stadium, or a level on a multi-level wedding cake
    c   a seven letter word meaning a bill for goods purchased
    d   a foreign word of six letters meaning office

9 Make up a cluster group of words for each of the following 'anchor words' and make sure they share the same vowel spelling as that part of the anchor word underlined:

r<u>ei</u>n
f<u>ough</u>t

10 False friends: the definitions a to f below describe a particular word. Write it down and then next to it write the false friend which sounds identical but which is spelled differently, e.g. in charge of a college: princip<u>al</u>, false friend: princip<u>le</u>.

    a   to convince someone to do something
    b   to follow someone
    c   the organization which runs a town or county
    d   the barrister who prosecutes or defends in court
    e   not moving
    f   letter-paper and envelopes

Chapter 11

Improve your written English III: the adverb

Adverbs generally have the important job of extending the meaning of verbs. Like adjectives they can be classified in a list according to the jobs they do. This list is interesting but not vital in terms of committing it to memory. What *is* important is that you develop the ability to recognize an adverb when you encounter one so that you are in a position to make a judgement on whether it is really needed or whether it might make for better style if a more descriptive verb were used on its own.

Types of adverbs	Examples: words and phrases
Of time	soon tomorrow next month
In what way	slowly fast carefully
Where	nearby on the chair down the road
To what extent	too quite very never
Why	So For this reason As a result

There are some other types of adverb which need not concern us at the moment. Let us now consider how the types of adverb listed above modify finite verbs in sentences. In fact what adverbs quite simply do as their part in the setting down of ideas is to add on extra meaning – most often to verbs:

- **When**
  I shall go.
  I shall go *tomorrow.*
  　　　　next Friday.
  　　　　when I feel like it.
- **How**
  The train pulled in.
  The train pulled in *slowly.*
  　　　　　with a screech of brakes.
- **Where**
  John is studying.
  John is studying *upstairs.*
  　　　　in the garden.
  　　　　where he won't be disturbed.

- **To what extent**
  This soup is hot!
  This soup is *very* hot!
  　　　　　extremely hot!
  Notice here that the adverbs 'very' and 'extremely' are this time modifying the adjective 'hot'.
- **Why**
  I am upset. I shall not go.
  I am upset. *For this reason* I shall not go.

Writing it right!

Double trouble with comparatives!

Some people tie themselves into knots when using the comparative form of words:

hard
harder (comparative)
hardest (superlative)

As you know, the comparative is formed by adding 'er' on to the end of the root word, 'hard' in this case.
Don't fall into the trap of adding an additional comparative by using the word 'more' as well:

The batsman hit the next ball *more harder* than the previous one. **Wrong!**

The same mistake can occur when using the superlative form:

That was the *most funniest* film I have ever seen! **Wrong!**

Solution? Simply omit the word 'more' or 'most'!

As we have already seen, adverbs can, on occasion, modify the meaning of adjectives. They can also modify the meaning of other adverbs:

– She decided to return home *very* quickly.
– He put his suggestion to the meeting *quite* forcefully.

One important point to keep in mind about adverbs is that they very often – but not always – end in *-ly*:

happi*ly*　grand*ly*　disappointed*ly*

but: He was running *fast*.
　　 The marksman aimed *low*.

So do not make the mistake of adding *-ly* on to a word which is already an adverb, rather check if it is acting as a word or expression modifying the meaning of the finite verb.

A note on adverbs and good style

Like adjectives, adverbs should be used sparingly. The lazy writer tends to pile up adverbs after verbs just as he does adjectives before nouns:

The peasant woman lifted the wheatsheaf *slowly, carefully* and *rhythmically*.

Much better is to choose a single adverb to encompass such ideas;

The peasant woman lifted the wheatsheaf *laboriously*.

Indeed, an approach often to be preferred is to select a verb which conveys more precisely the required meaning:

– They *walked hesitantly* down the dark tunnel.
– They *edged* down the dark tunnel.
– Her eyes *shone brightly* as she *ran lightly* towards him.
– Her eyes *sparkled* as she *skipped* towards him.

A similar approach is suggested when adverbs are used to add to the meaning of adjectives:

– Her behaviour was *extremely good*.
– Her behaviour was *exemplary*.

Again the same is true for adverbs modifying other adverbs:

– He mended his favourite fishing rod *very carefully*.
– He mended his fishing rod *meticulously*.

Thus this section upon adverbs may also be used as an example of what the text has been urging so far:

- It pays to extend your working vocabulary so as to have access to other words with which to vary and improve a sentence's style.
- It helps to know and be able to recognize various parts of speech at work so as to be able to criticize their effectiveness and to replace them or modify them consciously, so that *you* are in control of what you are writing.
- A more conscious awareness of the style of what you write will certainly aid you in making it more effective and thus help you to achieve your aims more readily.
- A knowledge of grammar and usage need not be dull and academic, but can be of direct assistance to you in your efforts to write more interestingly and effectively.

Writing it right!

Only trying to help

There are some words – and 'only' is one of them – that can alter the whole meaning of a sentence depending on where they are located in it:

a I only hit him once.
b I hit him once only

In a, the meaning implied is that in spite of several attempts, the speaker managed to land only one blow, while in b the meaning is that only a single blow was launched and that was all that was needed.
So always take care with the placing of words like 'only' or 'quite', since they tend to modify or affect the meaning of the word which immediately follows them.

Assignments

1 Make a checklist of the five types of adverb you have now mastered.

2 Adverbs can occur in sentences as single words, and as groups of words. True or false?

3 Write down the word/words acting as adverbs in the following passage:

Slowly the salesman could sense that his very detailed sales presentation was having an effect upon Mr. Johnson. He saw him nodding cautiously, in a friendly way. The salesman altered his approach then and made the final point which would clinch the sale:

  'You can rely on me, Mr Johnson. I'll have them delivered here by tomorrow and you can stack them high and sell them cheap because of their low price!'

4 Make a list of all the adverbs you can think of in five minutes which do not end in -*ly*.

5 We know that adverbs can extend the meaning of verbs. What other parts of speech can they give extra meaning to?

6 Write down a brief note on how to use adverbs to best effect in a piece of writing.

Chapter 12

Punctuating in English III: inverted commas and quotation marks

Inverted commas are the sign or code in punctuation for telling the reader that what lies between them is direct speech – those words set down exactly as they were spoken. Inverted commas are used like a set of brackets to distinguish in a piece of prose writing what was actually said, and what was reported, or what represents the author's views on the subject. Sometimes direct speech only lasts for a single line, sometimes for a whole paragraph. Sometimes two or more people converse in a dialogue. Whatever the pattern of direct speech being recorded by a writer, it is important for him or her to know how to present it to the reader according to established conventions.

Indeed it is important for everyone who reads to know how to interpret correctly the punctuation for direct speech.

You may have been one of those primary school-children for whom the task of remembering what inverted commas looked like was made easier by referring to them as 66s and 99s. For indeed this is just how they do look in many typescripts. However, today a number of modern typewriters, daisy wheels, dot-matrix printers, etc., have adopted what looks like two top halves of an exclamation mark to signify inverted commas. Moreover, some publishers only use single inverted commas instead of two as the mark for inverted commas, as in this book. For many writers, however, inverted commas will always be 66s and 99s, while single inverted commas are restricted to signifying a quotation of some well-known verse or proverb.

- Double inverted commas

  "Excuse me," interrupted the young woman sitting in the first row. "Are you saying that you reject the argument that the works of Shakespeare were written by Francis Bacon?"

- Single inverted commas
  'Hey you!' he shouted. 'That's my bag you're taking!'

- Quotation marks

  I always hated that proverb: 'Neither a borrower nor a lender be!'

Rules for using inverted commas

No matter what form inverted commas take, the rules for using them correctly are the same:

1   Inverted commas enclose *all* those words – including their punctuation – which are the direct speech:

"I don't know why she became so upset. Perhaps she knew him or perhaps not. Anyway, I'm sure she'll get over it," said the nurse.

As the above example illustrates, all the spoken words set down in writing are enclosed by the inverted commas, even though they run into several sentences, which are themselves normally punctuated. Notice that the final comma of the direct speech comes before the second half of the inverted commas. Notice also that the following word 'said' in the reported speech section of the example begins with a small *s*. There is never any need for a capital letter which introduces the reported speech 'tag' in such a way.

2   Sometimes, to vary the way in which direct speech is conveyed to the reader, the reported speech comments – 'said Jim', 'remarked Julie', 'shouted Fred', etc. – are set down in the middle of a passage of direct speech:

"If we do go," replied Julie, "we shall have to catch an early train."

Notice in the above example the precise locations of both the commas, particularly the one which finishes the reported speech, which comes before the re-opening of the inverted commas. Check too the use of the small letter *w* for 'we' which continues the direct speech. A capital letter is not needed since the direct speech is all one sentence as the writer has reproduced it:

"If we do go, we shall have to catch an early train."

However, the writer could decide to make such direct speech two sentences, in which case a capital letter in the second sentence would be required:

"Fair enough, we'll catch the early train," replied Jim. "*B*ut you'll have to listen for the alarm-clock at four thirty tomorrow morning!"

In such a construction, all the words from 'Fair enough' to 'replied Jim', are deemed to be one sentence – hence a small *r* for replied.

3   In the final punctuation of a direct speech sentence before a connecting piece of reported speech, the correct punctuation is:

- either a full stop   by itself   "... until tomorrow." He left ...
- or a comma   by itself   "... until then," said Jane.
- or a question mark   by itself   "... with me?" asked Bill.
- or an exclamation mark by itself   "... and stay out!" cried Jean.

Never use them together like this:

"..........,?" "..........!."

4   When the same speaker is the speaker of a succession of connected sentences in a single passage, only one pair of inverted commas is needed to open and close the direct speech – provided that there are no 'he saids' or 'she replieds' or 'he continueds' inserted anywhere. If a speaker's remarks span more than one paragraph, then the convention is to re-open the direct speech marks at the beginning of the new paragraph to remind the reader.

5   A further convention is that whenever a fresh speaker speaks, then the direct speech is delivered on a fresh line:

– "I say, Jemima! That's an absolutely gorgeous dress you're wearing!" gushed Cynthia.
– "Oh, do you really think so?" replied Jemima, enjoying being the centre of attraction. "It's just a little something I found in the King's Road, darling."

6   On the other hand, a mixture of the same speaker and reported speech continues down the normal line progression of the paragraph:

"It's so peaceful here," sighed Mark. Above him the sun shone through the over-arching branches of the beech trees in a ripple of yellow and green. "I could stay here for ever!" he said dreamily.
"You don't really believe that, do you?" responded Hilary. "You'd be bored out of your mind within a week!"

Notice also in the above example that a further convention is to indent – that is move several spaces to the right-hand side of the page – the first direct speech word of a new speaker.

Employing quotation marks

Early in our study of punctuation, we learned that the proper nouns of books, plays, films, place-names and so on are displayed with initial capital letters:

Babes in the Wood   St Mark's Square   Pitman New Era

In some printing circles it is customary to give titles a single quotation mark:

The programme 'Down Your Way' has been a firm favourite with radio listeners for many years.

Notice also how a quotation is dealt with inside direct speech:

"I was lucky to get two circle seats for 'The Marriage Of Figaro'."

It is a good idea to employ conventions such as 1 to 6 above even when you are writing in longhand, so as to reinforce them in your memory. Bear in mind, however, that nowadays there is a great deal more type-setting/editorial freedom than there used to be in the matter of indicating direct speech and quotations – sometimes, for example, a title may simply be set in italics to distinguish it from the rest of the text, and the advent of interchangeable golf-ball and daisy wheel typeheads has made it much easier for typists and compositors to vary the printed appearance of text in eye-catching ways.

Assignment

Punctuate the following passage:

the party was proving to be as boring as laura had anticipated in the corner by the hi-fi silenced some two hours previously by a spilt harvey wallbanger arthur spiggot and marcia ferndrop were indulging in their annual duel of name dropping and literary insults what did you think of sinclair's new novel wind across the saltflats asked arthur as an opening move i thought it overrated and a considerable disappointment compared with his earlier work cruise along the wind replied marcia disposing of a seven hundred and forty-three page novel in seventeen crisply delivered words of dismissal really responded arthur surely you must have missed its delicate similarities with grimthorpe's march of the walrus now there's a masterful attack on modern-day values if you like humph grunted marcia admitting no such thing actually i'm off the modern novel nowadays she observed with a sniff they seem to attract too many intellectual snobs i say spluttered arthur digesting the insult with a mouthful of sour spanish white wine you're surely not including me in that remark are you i mean to say i've always believed that the modern novel should communicate with the working class you wouldn't recognise a member of the working class in the middle of the crown and anchor public bar on a saturday night concluded marcia as she moved across the room with the confidence of one who has just achieved a second round knockout

Chapter 13
Mastering spelling III: consonant sounds

Consonant sounds are easier to learn to spell correctly than vowel sounds – there are fewer of them in English! The *Concise Oxford Dictionary* lists some twenty-six, excluding the Scottish *ch* sound as in 'loch'.

However, one of the major spelling problems with consonants is being able to tell whether the consonant sound is being represented by a single or double letter.

su*mm*ers all-co*m*ers be*gg*ar re*g*ular
la*m*ent co*mm*and a*ss*ist a*s*ide

The other major problem is knowing whether the consonant sound is being made, say, by an *s* or a *c*, by an *f* or a *ph*, by a *k* or a *q*, by an *s* or a *z*, since very often such letters stand for identical sounds:

*s*cience *c*ite *s*ight ba*ck* pla*q*ue
mi*s*ery mi*zz*en (mast) la*tch* atta*ch*

Again, we must heap our irritation and frustration on those long-gone dictionary compilers – if only to get rid of it somewhere!

However, there are some crumbs of comfort to be had. For example, the *kuh* sound, is very commonly spelled *-ck*, especially at the ends of words. *F* for *fuh* is far more frequent than its Greek counterpart *ph*. Incidentally, the *ph* consonant sound is nearly always found as part of prefixes or suffixes of Greek origin:

*ph*oto *ph*obia *ph*otograph

So the spelling of consonants does have some handholds to start climbing with.

Guidelines on doubling up consonants

As a rule, neither prefixes nor suffixes affect the spelling of the base words on to which they are joined:

active: *hyper*active *re*active *inter*active
natal: *ante*natal *post*natal
human: human*ist* human*ism* human*ity*

However, there are some that do:

Prefixes *il- im- in- ir-*

Examples:

Base word	**With prefix**
*mo*vable	*imm*ovable
*mo*dest	*imm*odest
*l*egible	*ill*egible
*l*ogical	*ill*ogical
*n*umerate	*inn*umerate
*r*egular	*irr*egular
*r*ational	*irr*ational

Such doubling up of the consonants as shown above only occurs, however when the first letter of the base word is the same as the second letter of the prefixes listed above. By contrast consider:

| *p*ossible | *imp*ossible |
| *a*ctive | *ina*ctive |

Also, the prefixes *il-* and *ir-* rarely occur unless in front of a word starting with an *l* or an *r*.

Where two vowels are put next to each other by the addition of a prefix, they are sometimes hyphenated:

anti-aircraft   pre-emptive

But not always: cooperative

Often the prefix and the word become welded together for ever:

triangular   biopsy

The use of the hyphen is also sometimes encountered in words like:

trans-ship   sub-branch   counter-revolution

Still engaged in mastery of the doubling up problem, let us now consider suffixes. The ones which tend to cause problems are:

Suffixes *-ed -ing -er -est -y -able*

One very useful rule to remember is that with words of one syllable, ending in a consonant preceded by a vowel, the final consonant is doubled whenever a suffix is added to it which begins with a vowel:

wi*n*/wi*nn*able   sto*p*/sto*pp*able   we*t*/we*tt*er/we*tt*est   ru*n*/ru*nn*ing

This rule remains true when the suffix is a single *y*:

fu*n*/fu*nn*y   spo*t*/spo*tt*y   gu*m*/gu*mm*y

The rule does not work (alas!) for words of more than one syllable:

listen/listened   quiet/quieter   break/breakable

However, another rule which does work on the subject of doubling up is for words ending in *-ful*. To turn these into adverbs then simply add *-ly*:

beautiful/beautiful*ly*   grateful/grateful*ly*

Also, for words already ending in *y*, simply drop the *y* and add *-ily*:

happy/happily   sorry/sorrily   merry/merrily

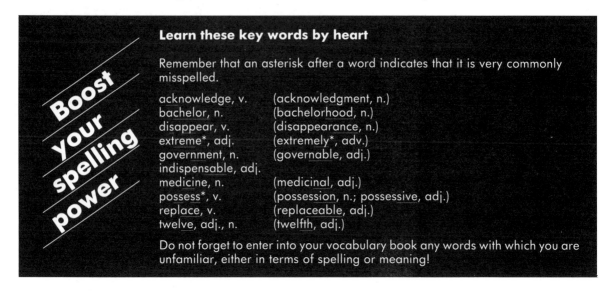

Boost your spelling power

Learn these key words by heart

Remember that an asterisk after a word indicates that it is very commonly misspelled.

acknowledge, v.   (acknowledgment, n.)
bachelor, n.   (bachelorhood, n.)
disappear, v.   (disappearance, n.)
extreme*, adj.   (extremely*, adv.)
government, n.   (governable, adj.)
indispensable, adj.
medicine, n.   (medicinal, adj.)
possess*, v.   (possession, n.; possessive, adj.)
replace, v.   (replaceable, adj.)
twelve, adj., n.   (twelfth, adj.)

Do not forget to enter into your vocabulary book any words with which you are unfamiliar, either in terms of spelling or meaning!

Care, however, must be taken with words ending in *e* when suffixes are to be added. In most instances, the final *e* is dropped:

argue   arguing   argument
insure   insurance
advise   advisable
white   whiter   whitest
active   activist
medicine   medicinal

But, there are some exceptions which must be carefully learned:

move   can be either movable or moveable
like   can be either likable or likeable
change   changeable
love   loveable
live   liveable
mile   mileage
acre   acreage

Make sure you note such words down in your pocketbook and revise them from time to time, until you have them committed to memory.

Notice also that words ending in an *e* generally drop it when the suffixes *-ly* and *y* are added to make them adverbs:

terrible/terribly   interminable/interminably   due/duly

and words already ending in *y* tend to drop it and replace it with an *i*:

dry/drily   happy/happier   giddy/giddier

Bear in mind with the above guidelines on the doubling up of consonants that these are the most common pairs of consonant letters you are likely to encounter:

-bb-   -dd-   -gg-   -ll-   -mm-   -nn-   -pp-   -rr-   -ss-   -tt-

Consonant sounds to distinguish between

The *sssss* sound

This *sssss* sound may be spelled in the following ways:

- as a single *s*: history   paste   aspic
- as a double *ss*: pass   assign   useless
- as a *c* followed by a vowel: conceal   concede   certain   practice
- as an *sc*: science   miscellaneous

But notice words like conscience pronounced 'konchuns'.

The *sh* sound

The *sh* sound as in 'shush' also comes in a variety of forms:

- as *sh*: rubbish   shoe   hashish
- as a single *s*: censure   surety
- as *t* followed by a vowel: station   repetitious   spatial
- as *sch*: schedule (not very often encountered)
- as *c* followed by a vowel: delicious   special
- as part of a sound signified by an *x*: noxious (pr. 'nokshush') (not very often encountered)
- as a *ch* in words of French origin: chalet   chateau   nonchalant

The *ch* sound as in 'church'

- as a *ch*: church
- as a *t* followed by a vowel: conscientious   pretentious
- as a *t* followed by a *u*: overture   tumultous   tempestuous
- as *tch*: pitch   thatch   match

The *juh* sound as in 'judge'

This sound has a number of variants:

- as a *j*: jumper   justice   jerk
- as a soft *g* followed by an *e* or a *y*: geography   garage   acreage
- as *dj*: adjudicate   adjourn   adjective
- as *du*: reduce   adduce   induce
- as *dge*: judge   fudge   hedge

The *eff* sound

- as a single or double *f*: puffing   fit   fashion   snuff
- as *ph*: photograph   phobia   graphic
- as *ough*: rough   cough   tough
- as *augh*: laugh   draught

The *jzuh* sound as in 'leisure'

This sound, like an *s* and a *j* said together occurs mainly as either a single *s* or a single *z* followed by a vowel:

pleasure   leisure   measure   seizure   vision   azure

It can also be spelled with the soft *ge* sound as in mirage   barrage.

The *kuh* sound

This sound also may be spelled in a number of different ways:

- as *ck*: ba*ck*   du*ck*   ja*ck*et
- as *qu*: pla*qu*e   li*qu*or   s*qu*id   *qu*ire
- as *ch*: stoma*ch*   *ch*ianti   a*ch*e   *ch*aracter
- as a single k: too*k*   hoo*k*   mista*k*e   brea*k*
- as a single *c* (usually to start words): *c*oat   *c*ombat   *c*areer
- as *cqu*: a*cqu*aint   a*cqu*ire   a*cqu*isitive (usually *acq*- starts)

Double troubles!

Inevitably there are some words which cause particular problems in the 'doubling up dilemma' with consonants. A good number are listed below for you to study from time to time as a means of internalizing them:

a*cc*o*mm*odation   a*cc*idental   a*cc*ess   a*dd*ress   a*gg*ressive   a*gg*ravate
a*pp*arent   a*ss*ent (but n.b. ascent)   co*mm*i*tt*ee (but commitment)   co*mm*emorate   co*mm*ence   collaborate   corroborate   corrupt
co*nn*oisseur   disa*pp*ear   de*ss*ert (when the last course of a meal is meant)   di*ss*ent (but n.b. also descent)   di*ss*atisfied   emba*rr*ass
exce*ss*   exa*gg*erate   gra*mm*ar   i*ll*icit   i*ll*egible   i*ll*egal   inte*ll*igent
interrupt   interrogate   irrelevant   irreverent   necessary   occur (but occurred and occurrence)   occasion   occidental   omit (but omi*tt*ed and omission)   para*ll*el   professor   profession   po*ss*ess   permi*ss*ion
permi*ss*ible   pa*ss*ion   refer (but referral and referred)   u*nn*ecessary
underrate   woo*ll*en   who*ll*y

Of course, there is not much point in just studying lists of words – those above have been set down to draw to your attention some of the words with double consonants which frequently cause difficulty – a much better way of adding such words to your own 'list of words I can spell confidently' is to use them at the earliest opportunity. So if the list contains some you know you tend to stumble over, jot them down in your notebook and set out to use them somewhere, somehow tomorrow!

RULE	**Summary of rules and guidelines for spelling consonants**
	• **No English word other than in slang (spiv) ends in *v* or *j*.**
	• **In general terms, the addition of a prefix or a suffix to a base word does not alter the spelling of the base word – except for single syllable words ending in a consonant preceded by a vowel where the final consonant is usually doubled.**
	stop stoppable etc.
	Also, as we have found, some words drop a final *e* when a suffix is added.
	• **Words ending in *y* usually change it to an *i* when the *-ly* suffix is added:**
	beauty/beautiful merry/merrily
	• **Words ending in a single *l* usually keep it when the *-ly* suffix is added:**
	usual/usually accidental/accidentally

- Base words of more than one syllable ending in *e* usually drop the *e* when a suffix is added:

agile/agility   determine/determination

- The prefixes *il-*, *im-*, *in-* and *ir-* have the effect of doubling the consonant in such words like:

illegitimate   immediate   innocuous   irregular

- Check in your writing for the 'double trouble' words and collect them in your spelling repertoire – words like:

ascent/assent   decent/descent/dissent   holy/wholly
desert/dessert   accede/exceed

- Make up whenever you can, jingles or rhymes for remembering the spelling of words with consonant problems like:

Committee – double *m*, double *t* double *e*!
Add a *d* to dress for address

- Always remember – there is never any spelling prize for a wild or even inspired guess! Whenever in doubt:

Look it up in your dictionary!

Assignments

1   Write down the four prefixes beginning with the letter *i* which have the effect of creating a double consonant spelling need when linked to certain base words. When you have done this, write down for each two words as examples.
2   What is the general rule about the spelling of base words when either prefixes or suffixes are added to them?
3   What generally happens to words ending in *y* when the suffix *-ly* is added to them? Can you think of any exceptions?
4   What is the rule about adding suffixes to words of one syllable which end in a consonant preceded by a single vowel?
5   Does the rule for **4** above work with words of more than one syllable?
6   Write down for each of the following the different ways that the sound may be spelled:

sssss   sh   ch   kuh   juh   eff   jzuh (as in 'leisure')

7   Complete the spelling of the following words where each _ represents a single letter:

pl _ _ _ _   a decoration or ornament which is hung on a wall
a _ _ _ _ _ _ _ance   someone you know
a _ _ _ _ _odation   where you may live
ref _ _ _ _ _   made mention of
i _ _ _ _ _ble   not able to be read
u _ _ _ _ _ _ _ _ry   not needed
o _ _ _ _ _ed   happened
pro _ _ _ _ _r   runs a university department
d _ _ _ _ _t   last course of dinner
o _ _ _ _ed   left out

8 What vowel usually follows a soft *g*? Write down three examples.

9 What rules cover the consonants *q* and *j* in English spelling?

10 Write down the homonym or homonyms (words which sound the same but are spelled differently) for each of the following:

ascent baron council decent cord guerilla lightening need palate shake weather holy practice draught arc nave

11 Can you think of a guideline which helps you to know whether a consonant sound in a word of more than one syllable should be spelled with a single or double consonant (i.e. with a single or double *m*, *n*, *t*, etc.)?

12 Add as many words (up to ten) as you can to form a cluster group around the anchor word 'leisure' which contain the *jzuh* sound – the same sound as the *s* in 'pleasure'.

13 Do the same for the following anchor words and the sounds indicated:

a	acquire	the *kuh* sound of the *acq*
b	gracious	the *shush* sound of the *-cious*
c	science	the *sss* sound of the *sc-*

Chapter 14

Improve your written English IV: simple and not so simple sentence construction

From me to one to you!

A particularly irritating misuse of the person – first, second or third – occurs when a writer forgets which person he is using within a single construction. For example:

The older *one* gets, the more *you* value the comforts of home.

Here, the writer uses both 'one' and 'you' in a single sentence which requires the same pronoun for both parts of the construction:

– the older *one* gets ... the more *one* values ... *or*
– the older *you* get ... the more *you* value ...

Similar mistakes can occur in using the first person 'I/me' and we/us' in single constructions:

I am pleased to advise you that *we* are able to supply the following information.

In letters, it is better practice to stick right through to 'I' if you have the authority to write on behalf of an organization. Using 'we' can often appear pompous, especially if 'I' has been used elsewhere within a paragraph.

A quick revision

So far the main features of grammar and syntax which you have covered are:

- *Parts of speech*: The noun, the verb, the adjective, the adverb and the parts they play in constructing ideas in sentence form.
- *Sentence structure*: The role of the subject of a sentence as naming word which controls the action of the finite verb. The role of the finite verb in the sentence as the word (or word group) which communicates the action of the sentence.
- *Agreement*: The finite verb must be expressed in a tense, and agree with its subject in number and person if the sentence is to be grammatically correct.
- *Basic components of a sentence*: At the very least, a grammatically written sentence must contain a subject and a finite verb.

- *The term 'phrase'*: A phrase is a group of words which does not contain a finite verb. Phrases are very often introduced by prepositions, which are considered in detail on page 131.
- *The term 'clause'*: A clause is a group of words which occurs within a sentence, but which does contain both a subject and a finite verb. Clauses are dealt with in detail on pages 117–122.

Reminder on simple sentence structure

Firstly, in labelling terms, simple sentences fall into two basic parts:

The subject	The predicate
Bill	snored
Bill	snored loudly
Bill	snored loud enough to wake the dead!

As the above examples illustrate, the word predicate just simply means 'everything which is not the subject'.

Secondly, simple sentences which generally begin with the subject take on very often this kind of structure:

Subject	Finite verb	Rest of sentence
The tired manager	looked	at the clock on on the wall.

What makes up 'the rest of the sentence'?

It is now time to consider what can make up that part of a sentence's structure which has been called 'the rest of the sentence' for the sake of convenience. At this point it is essential to be clear that only simple sentence structures are being examined and that a working definition of a simple sentence is:

RULE	**Working definition of a simple sentence** **A simple sentence is a group of words containing only one subject governing one finite verb.**

The 'rest of the sentence' in simple sentences may take a number of forms:

The sky is blue.

Here as you can now well see, there is a subject – the sky, the present tense of the verb 'to be' as the finite verb and the adjective 'blue' acting as the rest of the sentence, and adding a focus of meaning to it. The author might have written such an idea at much greater length, but still using his words adjectivally:

The sky is a lovely shade of turquoise blue.

Here the single adjective 'blue' has been transformed into a much more poetic adjectival phrase! As you can see, the phrase embodies much more information, all of which in this case is extending the meaning of the word 'sky'.

Just as phrases in sentences can act in an adjectival way, so they can act as adverbs:

– He listened *cautiously*. (adverb)
– He listened *in a cautious frame of mind*. (adverbial phrase)

The single word adverb of manner 'cautiously' is here turned into an adverbial phrase which is telling the reader more about how 'he' listened.
Here are two more examples:

- Adjectival phrase: The prisoners became *sullen and moody*.
- Adverbial phrase (of time): You will escape *before tomorrow's sunrise!*

The object as the rest of the sentence

So far we have examined sentences with subjects and finite verbs. Now we must consider the role of the object in a sentence.

RULE	**Working definition of an object in a sentence** **An object in a sentence is the person or thing to whom or which the action of the sentence is directed: the object 'receives' the action of the subject.**

Subject	Finite verb	Object
John	broke	the window

Here it is clear who (subject) broke what (object).

These are further examples:

Subject	Finite verb	Object
The mailroom clerk	opened	the letters and parcels.
The clumsy cleaner	has dropped	the priceless Ming vase.
A group of children	will be sitting	important examinations.

As you can see in each of the above examples, an object can be either a single entity or several – a vase, letters and parcels or examinations. What they have in common is that they all receive the action of the subject – here expressed by means of a finite verb which is in the active voice. What happens when the voice of the verb becomes passive we shall see later.
You will also almost certainly have noticed that the above examples have all been constructed upon the basic approach of:

Subject + finite verb + object or + rest of sentence.

This can become very boring, however, in a succession of simple sentences, but is the way in which we learned to write at primary school:

We went to the beach. The sun was shining. I played with Spot. He chased the ball. It was fun!

Such short simple sentences would soon tax the patience of an adult reader looking for more variety, extended meaning and different pace and rhythm in a passage of writing. As an illustration, consider the following sentences:

Subject	Finite verb	Object
The senior typist	operated	the word processor.

| Ken Jones | won | the important roofing contract. |
| Their centre-forward | scored | the winning goal. |

The addition of an introductory adverb phrase can transform such sentences:

- In the new, purpose-built suite the senior typist operated the word processor.
- After lengthy negotiations, Ken Jones won the important roofing contract.
- With an unexpected scissors kick, their centre-forward scored the winning goal.

As you can see, the use of such adverbial phrases to introduce simple sentences not only provides useful additional information, but also makes the message of the main part of the sentence more interesting since the reader is kept waiting a little for the communication of the main subject plus finite verb part of the message. An element of suspense is therefore possible:

Despite all his most careful training and preparation, he lost the heavyweight championship of the world.

In order to provide variety in a passage of prose writing, the adverbial phrase could be tacked on to the end of a sentence:

- Ken Jones won the important roofing contract after lengthy negotiations.
- The senior typist operated the word processor in the new, purpose-built suite.

Here the effect is to impart the main message first and to add on a bit of extra meaning for the reader afterwards. As a result, the emphasis is thrown upon the typist operating the word processor rather than upon its new location.

The following two passages will further illustrate the importance of varying the construction of sentences in a passage in order to obtain and keep the reader's interest.

Passage 1
The crowd was waiting expectantly. The Band of the Royal Marines was due. The Band turned into the square. There was an increasing excitement in the crowd. The bandsmen's uniforms looked brand new. Their instruments gleamed in the morning sun. The Drum Major raised his mace. He then dropped it smartly. The band instantly stopped playing. They all dropped their instruments to the rest position simultaneously.

By combining some of the ideas expressed in separate sentences above into longer, single sentences, the pace of the information provided is quicker and the absence of full stops assists a smoother flow of the description which echoes the marching entrance of the band until it stops playing instantaneously:

Passage 2

The crowd was waiting expectantly for the arrival of the Royal Marines' Band. Amid increasing excitement, the Band turned into the square. The bandsmen's uniforms looked brand new and their instruments gleamed in the morning sun. After raising his mace, the Drum Major dropped it smartly. The Band stopped playing instantly and dropped their instruments to the rest position simultaneously.

What has given the second passage more interest and made it more mature in style terms is the compression of the same ideas – either into phrases:

– for the arrival of the Royal Marine's Band
– Amid increasing excitement
– After raising his mace

or, as you will undoubtedly have noticed, into longer sentences linked together by the word 'and':

– The bandsmen's uniforms looked brand new *and* their instruments gleamed in the morning sun.
– The Band stopped playing instantly *and* dropped their instruments to the rest position simultaneously.

What this second passage has, in fact, introduced us to is the idea of what the grammarians call the **compound sentence**. Simply put, this is a sentence which contains more than one subject and more than one finite verb. In fact what were sentences in their own, separate right in Passage 1 have been converted into two clauses linked by the word 'and' in Passage 2.

RULE	**Working definition of a compound sentence** **A compound sentence is one which is made up of more than one clause, so that it contains two or more subjects governing two or more finite verbs – divided into clauses.**

Compound sentences tend to be constructed as follows:

- They link together equally important and main ideas by a succession of linking words like 'and', 'but', 'next' 'and then' etc., which are termed coordinating conjunctions.

A further type of sentence which may be constructed is called **complex**.

RULE	**Working definition of a complex sentence** **A complex sentence is one in which a main clause is linked to a dependent clause by means of a subordinating conjunction. Note: sometimes a single complex sentence may contain several main clauses linked to several dependent clauses.**

Examples:

Main clause	**Dependent clause**
He put his raincoat on	*because** it was raining outside.
They were in a depressed mood	*even though** their team had won the match.

*Subordinating conjunctions introducing dependent clauses.

Summary

As we have discovered, the whole tone and impact of a simple sentence can be changed by the addition of descriptive phrases and by where they are located – either at the beginning or end of the sentence.

Simple sentences can be used to convey meaning directly and quickly because their structure is easy to absorb. However, adult readers are able to cope with more than a single idea per sentence and so simple sentences are often turned into compound or complex ones by joining them together by link words such as 'and', 'but', 'then', 'next' or 'because', 'even though', 'although', etc. These linking words which are used to connect clauses are another part of speech which are called **conjunctions**, which are examined in detail on page 117.

In sentence structure terms, we have learned so far that the 'rest of the sentence' can be made up from either adjectival or adverbial words or phrases or can consist of an object which is receiving the action of the finite verb.

Lastly, we have seen how the conscious elimination of full stops which punctuate short sentences and the conscious joining together of ideas into compound and complex sentences can quicken the pace of a piece of writing and render it more mature and not so 'young' in the effect its style has upon the reader.

Assignments

Quick revision

1 What are the basic components needed in a sentence to make it grammatically acceptable?

2 Define (*a*) a phrase and (*b*) a clause in terms of the grammatical components each possesses.

3 'The rest of the sentence' – of what may it be made up?

4 Write down your brief definition of a simple sentence.

5 How would you explain to someone unfamiliar with grammar and usage what an object was in a sentence? Write down your explanation as briefly and simply as you can, and include two or three examples to clarify your main points.

Sentences and style

6 What would you say was the general effect upon a reader of beginning a sentence with an introductory phrase (perhaps an adverbial one) before setting down the subject + finite verb part of the sentence?

7 And what contrasting effect by putting the same such phrase after the subject + finite verb which begin a sentence?

6 and 7 supplementaries: Compose a sentence for **6** and for **7** which illustrate the two effects in your opinion, and compare yours with those supplied in the Answers Section.

8 Define in your own words briefly what (*a*) a compound sentence is, and (*b*) a complex sentence. Then compose one for each which satisfies your definition.

9   What is the name given to parts of speech which link clauses together?

10   Rewrite the following passage to make it more mature and interesting to the reader by combining its ideas into fewer sentences. See if you can transform a sentence into an introductory or closing phrase and then link it to another sentence. Check whether you can join two sentences into one by using a conjunction and fewer words overall. Try to make your version more 'alive' and less 'dead' than one given below:

The development of the microprocessor or silicon chip occurred in the late 1960s. It brought about much change in the office equipment business. The first silicon chip for commercial use was manufactured in the USA in 1971. The company which made it was called Intel. It was about the size of a postage stamp, and about as thick as a piece of card. It did not take long after 1971 for office equipment manufacturers to realize the potential of the microprocessor. It was tiny but embodied a powerful memory. The memory was able to control the production and distribution of large amounts of information. It did this by means of micro-computers and word processors. These new pieces of office equipment were soon small enough to sit on the tops of desks. Larger companies by the early 1980s began to 'network' office equipment. The term 'network' means to link together items of equipment to enable them to communicate together. A word processor could provide text for a photocopier. The photocopier could read it optically. It could then produce documents in multiple copy form. Or, a computer could design a set of plans. These plans could be transmitted to, say, a building site thousands of miles away by a facsimile transmitter. The microprocessor has revolutionized the working lives and leisure habits of millions of people.

Chapter 15

Punctuating in English IV: question and exclamation marks

It is helpful to examine the question mark and exclamation mark together, since both form alternatives to the full stop, and importantly, both have the same force as the full stop.

In just the same way as the full stop, both mark the end of a grammatically complete sentence:

– 'Where are you going? Do you have permission to leave early?'
– 'Stop at once! You'll regret this intrusion I assure you!'
– Have you ever stopped to ask yourself why you read the newspaper delivered to your front door each day?
– The 21st March, the first day of spring! Enough to make anyone's heart soar after the sort of winter we've just endured!

As the above examples illustrate, question marks and exclamation marks are equally at home either within direct speech or as part of what are two journalistic excerpts. Notice that the question mark within the direct speech does away with the need for any other punctuation other than the closing inverted comma at the end of the quotation, and, in fact, replaces completely the function of the full stop. The exclamation mark, as you can see, has the effect of making what has been written seem more interesting and unusual, since we have become conditioned as readers to the idea that anything which ends with an exclamation mark must be particularly noteworthy, dramatic or exciting. Yet – simply because of the over-use of the exclamation mark in advertising and persuasive writing – its impact is nowadays reduced. As a result of our over-exposure to it, we tend to disregard its insistent plea to 'Look at me! What I'm punctuating is important!' This is why you should use exclamation marks sparingly so as to maximize their effect in your own writing.

The question mark at work

Remember the following essential guideline:

RULE	The question mark is used as a punctuation mark to show that a direct question has been asked – whether in direct speech enclosed within inverted commas, or as part of a passage of prose writing which needs no inverted commas.

When employing the question mark with direct speech, always keep in mind that the question mark replaces any other punctuation, and that although it signifies the end of a grammatical sentence within the direct speech, it is not followed by an initial capital letter in any immediately following reported speech:

'Whatever shall I do?' asked the owner of the flooded house.

In the same way, the question mark (and the exclamation mark for that matter) need no other or additional punctuation when they occur at the end of a line in a passage of direct speech dialogue:

'What do you think of the show so far?'
'Not a lot!'

In a piece of straightforward writing which may occur in either a newspaper, journal or magazine, writers are fond of posing to the reader a question which they then proceed to answer themselves. Such questions are called rhetorical questions – a rhetor originally meant someone like a debator. The following example illustrates the use of the rhetorical question:

At this busy time of year with a host of jobs to do before Christmas, how does the busy housewife cope with the problem of bored young children on holiday from school who are at the same time over-excited at the approach of Santa Claus? The answer may well be to invest in Toybox's pre-Christmas activity kit for children between 6 and 10 years old.

Sometimes the authors of novels seek to create a mood of tension and uncertainty by using the question mark in a piece of descriptive writing. Thus:

Should she admit her guilt? Or should she try to brazen it out? Should she simply pack her bags and get as far away as quickly as possible? One look at the lifeless body staring up at her with sightless eyes made up her mind for her. With an unexpected coolness, she threw a few essentials into an overnight bag and slipped noiselessly out of the apartment door.

Points of uncertainty which are statements

One of the most frequently encountered errors in the use of the question mark is in using it when what has been written is in fact a statement and not a question:

I wondered whether I should tell her or not?   **wrong**

Here the writer is repeating as a statement for the benefit of the reader what he wondered. So a full stop is the appropriate mark of punctuation.

Similarly, a problem of whether or not to include a question mark can occur when a direct question is reported by someone else:

• Direct speech question

'Should I visit Fraser's in Bristol tomorrow?' the salesman asked his district manager.   **correct**

• Speech or reported speech version

The salesman asked his district manager whether he should visit Fraser's in Bristol on the following day.   **correct**

As you can see, the question of the direct speech has been turned into a statement in the reported speech and therefore no question mark is needed – the writer is simply stating what the salesman said at a particular point in time.

Another error that sometimes creeps into question mark use in relation to reporting something that was said occurs when the two different types of writing are wrongly mixed:

- Direct speech version:

'Julie, shall I buy you a ticket for the play as well?' enquired David.   **correct**

- Reported speech version wrongly including direct speech:

David asked Julie shall I buy you a ticket for the play as well?   **wrong**

- Correct reported speech:

David asked Julie whether he should also buy her a ticket for the play.

correct

HINT!

Tips for using the question mark correctly

- **Always ensure, when using the question mark within inverted commas that it comes immediately before the closing inverted commas and stands by itself:**

  'Where did I put the tin-opener?' asked Jim's mother.

- **Remember, as the above example shows, that in the first word of the reported speech (or tag showing who said the direct speech – here 'asked') there is no capital letter needed to start 'asked', even though it does come directly after a complete sentence. However, remember that an initial capital *is* needed if the speaker carries on in direct speech:**

  'Where did he go? What did he say?' shouted Chris anxiously.

- **Never be tempted to put two or three question marks together in an effort to strengthen their effect:**

  'You don't mean to say he actually won????'

- **Avoid posing too many rhetorical questions in a piece of writing as this tends to irritate the reader, who cannot get back at you directly:**

  What is the answer to this problem? Nobody really knows. Can it be avoided with a modicum of care? Only if every sensible precaution is taken. What can the individual do about it? Fortunately there are books in libraries which deal with this sensitive and delicate issue.

- **Remember that direct questions become statements in reported speech needing no question marks.**

  – 'What shall I do with this broken chair?' asked the cleaner.
  – The cleaner asked what he should do with the broken chair.

The exclamation mark at work

Much of what we have learned about using the question mark correctly applies also to the exclamation mark – especially in terms of direct speech.

Essentially the exclamation mark is used to 'exclaim' something, whether it is a dramatic confession, a shouted warning or an expression of anger. It is also employed by writers to convey emotion or sarcasm to the reader or to imply that what is being uttered is not to be taken at its face value. In fact

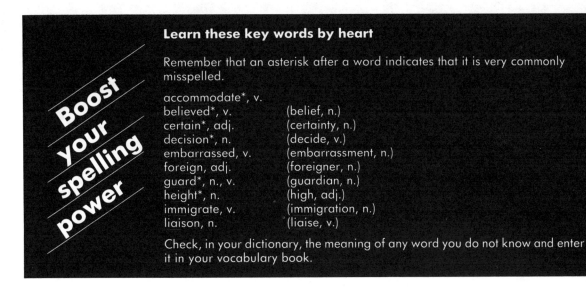

Learn these key words by heart

Remember that an asterisk after a word indicates that it is very commonly misspelled.

accommodate*, v.
believed*, v.   (belief, n.)
certain*, adj.   (certainty, n.)
decision*, n.   (decide, v.)
embarrassed, v.   (embarrassment, n.)
foreign, adj.   (foreigner, n.)
guard*, n., v.   (guardian, n.)
height*, n.   (high, adj.)
immigrate, v.   (immigration, n.)
liaison, n.   (liaise, v.)

Check, in your dictionary, the meaning of any word you do not know and enter it in your vocabulary book.

Boost your spelling power

there are quite a number of different uses to which the exclamation mark can be legitimately put, as the following examples illustrate:

– Only three out of the one hundred people surveyed gave the right answer!
– Before them white torrents of water fell in beautiful cascades at least three hundred feet into the misty valley below!
– Oh, so you mean to say that you took this mighty decision all by your pretty little self!' he sneered.
– 'What style! What elegance! What poetry in motion!' gushed the portly proprietor of the dancing school as he careered round the floor with Miss Peabody.
– 'Shut up if you know what's good for you!' barked the bank robber.
– This simple precaution will certainly help you to avoid all the unpleasantness of holiday tummy!

HINT!

Tips for using the exclamation mark correctly

- Above all, do not debase the value of the exclamation mark in your writing by using it too frequently. Sometimes the absence of the exclamation mark where one might be expected allows facts or simple description to speak for itself much more effectively:

    Of the eight hundred and sixty-two Allied prisoners of war sent to the camp during its three years of operation, only twenty-four survived.

- Follow the rules for the question mark when you are using the exclamation mark in direct speech – additional commas or full stops are not needed, and the first word of any immediately following reported speech does not need an initial capital letter:

    'Oh no you don't!' shouted the guard.

- Be sure of what effect you are seeking before reaching out for an exclamation mark from your 'punctuation tool kit' – simple full stops often make the point unaided. While we may have become used to the strident tone of advertising writing:

    Freedom! That's what the new Eagle convertible offers you!

—Super whiteness! The new formula action of Spume brings a starburst of dazzling white to your washday blues!

Such similar tones can look pretty silly in a more down-to-earth context

Fantastic! That was her response to the fourth year's project on the food value of the potato!

A better version might be:

She thought that the fourth year's project on the food

	excellent	
value of the potato was first-rate	+.	(simple full stop)
	most creditworthy	

- Unless you are writing the 'balloon speech' remarks of characters in comic strips or conveying the destruction of whole galaxies (POW!!! SPLAT!!! BLAM!!!) avoid the temptation to use more than a single exclamation mark at a time!

Assignments

1 Punctuate the following sentences correctly and include any question marks or exclamation marks you think appropriate.

   a   how do you like your steak cooked sir enquired the waiter
   b   just show it the frying pan briefly answered the american with a grin
   c   get your lovely tights and stockings here theyre guaranteed theyre a bargain theyre going fast shouted the street trader to the passing christmas shoppers
   d   i asked the price of a return ticket to edinburgh
   e   what are the consquences of acid rain foresters all over europe can show you the cost in dead and dying precious trees
   f   get out shrieked juliet in a fit of rage and dont come back
   g   she posed the question of what should be done about the unsold copies of your garden in winter by jack green
   h   going away this easter here are some tips to make your visit more fun for you and more bearable for your hosts

Chapter 16
Mastering spelling IV: list of prefixes

A large number of the prefixes used in English today stem from either Greek or Latin. Whether or not you ever studied these languages, it is extremely helpful to know what the prefixes mean and how they are spelled. A particular benefit from this investment comes in making an intelligent guess (whenever a dictionary isn't handy) about the meaning of a long word deriving from Greek or Latin.

Browse through this list of prefixes and pay particular attention to those which you have not previously met. Use this page as a quick reference page to refresh your spelling and as a guide to general meaning. From now on pay close attention to the words you encounter with prefixes and make sure you really do know what they stand for.

Prefix	Meaning	Examples
a-, ac-, ad-	to, towards, in addition to	advance accept
ab-	off, away from	abrupt abbreviate
ambi-	of both kinds	ambidextrous amphibious
ante-	before, in front of	antenatal antepost
anti-	against	anti-aircraft antidote
arch-	chief, foremost	archbishop arch-enemy
be-	covered with (archaic)	bestrewn bedecked
bi-, bin-	of two	bicycle binary
bio-	about life, living things	biology biochemistry
circum-	around, round	circumnavigate circumference
com-, con-, cor-, co-	with, together	compute consign corroborate
contra-	against	contradict contraceptive
di-, dis-	away from, not	divest disbelieve
duo-	of two	duet duologue
e-, ex-	out of, away from	egress exit exodus
geo-	of the earth	geography geometry
hyper-	extremely, very	hyperactive hypersensitive
il-, im-, in-, ir-	not	illegal immoral irregular
inter-	among, across	interstate interrupt
intra-	within	intravenous intradepartmental
intro-	towards, into	introduce introverted

Prefix	Meaning	Examples
mal-	bad, wrong	maladjusted malign malpractice
mis-	not, wrongly, badly	misjudge misbehave
mono-	one, single	monorail monoplane
non-	not, none	nonentity nonexistent
ob-, oc-, of-, op-	in the way of, open	obstacle occlude oppose
per-	through	permeate pervade
phil-	lover of	philatelist philosophy
photo-	to do with light	photograph photosynthesis
poly-	of many	polytechnic polygamous
post-	after	postmortem postpone
pro-	on behalf of, for	protect propose
psycho-	of the mind or soul	psychoanalyst psychologist
se-	apart, without	secede separate
semi-	of a half	semicircle semi-detached
sub-	under, beneath	submarine subterranean
super-, supra-	above, beyond	superimpose supranational
syn-	together, like, as	synthesize synchronize
tele-	from a distance	telescope television
theo-	of gods	theology theocracy
trans-	across, through	transport trans-ship
tri-	of three	tricycle triangle
ultra-	very, extremely, beyond	ultrasonic ultraviolet
un-	not	unsound unusual
uni-	of one	unify university unisex

Many of the words formed from such prefixes have come down to us almost unchanged from their original Latin or Greek:

	Literally
contradict	to say against
antenatal	before birth
interrupt	to break into
philology	love of words or language
television	pictures from afar
theocracy	government by the gods
unilateral	on one side only

Once you are familiar with the spelling of the above prefixes and their meaning, and take an interest in the many abstract words which stem from the Latin or Greek, then a host of often difficult words will become much easier to understand, to remember the meaning of – and, most important – to add to your working vocabulary!

Assignments

1 Choose fifteen of the above prefixes (not all the easy ones!) and find two words for each – not from the given examples of course – which incorporate the prefix.
2 Browse through the entry for each prefix in your dictionary and see what words are listed under them.
3 Supply the correct word for the following definitions. Clue: each contains one of the prefixes listed above.

a   a collector of matchboxes
b   to leave a country for good
c   speaking only in single, short words
d   many-sided shape
e   someone who photographs well is said to be . . .
f   a hater of women
g   able to use either hand equally well
h   an instrument for 'listening at a distance'
i   to break away from as did the Southern States from the Union in the American Civil War

To solve these you may have to ask around your friends or relatives or to scan through your dictionary if you think you know what the correct prefix is!

Chapter 17

Improve your written English V: pronouns

As their name suggests, pronouns stand 'on behalf of' nouns. In speech and writing we often use them as a quick, 'shorthand' means of referring to previously mentioned nouns:

Noun	Subject	Finite verb	Noun object
The	fielder	returned	the ball.

Pronoun subject		Finite verb	Pronoun object
He		returned	it.

As you can see from the above illustration, pronouns can also act in sentences as subjects or as objects.

Types of pronoun

There are several different kinds of pronoun to which the grammarians have given names to act as convenient labels. In this section we shall examine them and the roles they play in sentences to aid the communication of meaning.

Personal pronouns

Logically enough, the personal pronoun provides an alternative way of referring to people previously mentioned either by their names or occupations, etc.

Personal pronouns exist in each of the three persons singular plural:

	Singular	Plural
First person	I	we
Second person	you	you
Third person	he, she, it	they

You will see these versions of the personal pronoun when it is acting as the *subject of the sentence*. However, when it is acting as the *object of the sentence* it becomes:

	Singular	Plural
First person	me	us
Second person	you	you
Third person	him, her, it	them

Similarly, when the personal pronoun is indicating possession, it will appear as:

	Singular	Plural
First person	mine	ours
Second person	yours	yours
Third person	his, hers, its	theirs

The following illustrations show the personal pronoun at work in each of these three ways:

–*She* loves *him* but *he* doesn't love *her*.
– 'Is this coat *yours*?'
– 'No, *it's mine*!'
– '*It* was given to *us* by *them*, so *it* is clearly *ours*!'
– 'Oh, why doesn't *he* ask *them* to give *her* the wretched coat back if *it* really is *hers*.'

The reflexive pronoun

Sometimes what we want to express means showing that a particular action returns upon its originator:

– She cut *herself* on the knife.
– He threw *himself* into his work.

Such pronouns ending in *-self* are called reflexive, reflecting as they do the action of the doer back on to him or herself:

- Singular: myself   yourself   himself   herself   itself
- Plural: ourselves   yourselves   themselves

Note: there are no such words (except in dialect) as:

hisself   meself   theirselves

Interrogative pronouns

Interrogative pronouns ask questions:

Who are you, if I may ask?
Which would you prefer?
Whom did you wish to see?
What do you want?
Whose is the Rolls Royce?

Relative pronouns

The relative pronoun is so named because it relates back to the noun to which it refers. Relative pronouns comprise:

who   whom   which   that

Examples:

– The man *who* was in naval uniform looked very distinguished.
– This is the house *that* Jack built.
– The crowd cheered the horse *which* came last because it had gamely finished the course.

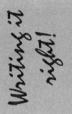

Is it who or which?

Briefly and simply, keep 'who' and 'whom' for people and 'which' for things. Remember that the word 'that' is used sometimes to stand for both:

The table that stood in the hall.
The girl that had red hair.

At this point you should re-read the section on defining and non-defining relative pronouns in the comma section on page 62.

Demonstrative pronouns

Such pronouns 'point things out' or 'demonstrate' where they are etc. The demonstrative pronouns are:

this or *that* in the singular and *these* or *those* in the plural.

Examples:

– I prefer *these* to *those*.
– Do you want *this* or *that*? Make up your mind!

Indefinite pronouns

Sometimes in writing we wish to convey a vague idea of quantity or extent instead of, for example, writing 'two' or 'three' or 'five thousand'. This being so, we use what are called indefinite pronouns:

few   some   little   many   several   any   none   more   less

and so on:

– Only a *few* attended the meeting.
– I don't want *any*, thank you.
– I examined *several* but *none* came up to standard.

Is it 'who' or 'whom'?

One way of choosing the correct alternative is to know enough grammar to be able to deduce whether the 'who' or 'whom' is acting as the subject (who) or object (whom) of the sentence or clause – and you now have this ability!

Who is that? (subject)
Whom did you see? (object)

Another helpful way which needs no grammar is to try replacing the word 'who' or 'whom' with 'he' or 'him' or 'she' or 'her' or 'they' or 'them'. Whichever one fits, then insert the following:

he   she   they = who
him   her   them = whom

Example:

He is the man who(m) I saw. NB   I saw him (not he)
   so 'whom' must be correct – and it is!

Pronoun assignments

1 Set out below is a series of sentences which contain one or more pronouns representing each type illustrated above. Identify and write down each pronoun you find in each sentence and state what type you think it is.

a I like her and she likes me.
b It is mine and certainly not yours!
c Who saw the old lady collapse?
d You owe us more than you owe them.
e She hated herself afterwards for the words she had said.
f Whom do you wish to call for interview?
g I like this. Which do you prefer?
h Many are called, but few are chosen.
i The report which he drafted was long and complex.
j That is the car that I saw breaking the speed-limit!

Chapter 18
Punctuating in English V: hyphens, dashes and brackets

These three punctuation marks have been grouped together partly for convenience – because the dash and brackets sometimes share a similar function – and partly to ensure that you become quite clear in your mind about the difference between the use of the hyphen and the dash.

The hyphen at work

Essentially the hyphen and the dash symbols look exactly the same, which is probably the cause for confusing their quite different uses. They appear above the line and look like this –. In printed matter the hyphen '-' is usually made shorter than the dash '–'.

The best way to remember the hyphen is as a coupling just like the one used to join railway waggons together, for that is what the hyphen does. It joins either two words or two parts of words together. In the first instance, the two words joined together by a hyphen are so linked to provide a distinct and composite meaning:

cricket-bag   double-barrelled   hand-towel

In such words the joint meaning has become so fused together that to all intents and purposes words linked by a hyphen may be considered as a single word. Indeed, over the centuries many words in English started as two, were then hyphenated and finally became a single word:

a black bird   a black-bird   a blackbird

Sometimes hyphens are used to join not two but three words:

man-of-war   master-at-arms   vis-à-vis

Another use of the hyphen is to join words together where the first word completely changes the meaning of the second:

semi-detached   bi-weekly   non-aggression

Unfortunately there is no clear rule or guideline to help us decide which words are hyphenated and which 'fused' into a single word:

antifreeze   antenatal   biannual   semicircle   postgraduate

Much seems to have depended on popular usage, that old maker of words, or the way people prefer to set a word down which dictionary compilers subsequently acknowledge and follow.

A further use of the hyphen which printers and typists often use is to link those parts of a single word which become separated when the word begins at the end of one line and carries over to the next:

The damage caused to the portable radio was undoubtedly the result of faulty packing.

Everyone whose job it is to produce the printed word in various forms learns a series of rules relating to this practice:

Words should not be divided in the following cases:

1   Words of one syllable should not be divided, e.g. brought, crouched.
2   Numbers and sets of figures should not be divided, e.g. £500.65, 14 × 12 m.
3   Abbreviations should not be divided, e.g. UNESCO, O & M.
4   The last word of a paragraph should not be divided.
5   When the division of a word would lead to misunderstanding, e.g. sip-hon, it should not be divided. (Adapted from *Universal Typing* by Edith Mackay, Pitman Publishing)

Also, when words are divided at line ends, sensible rules apply for making the break at the end of syllables or component parts of words:

mis-understanding   spill-ing   down-cast etc.

It is worth including in this section another use of the hyphen. It is not often seen and must be used with care to avoid errors of syntax.

We don't want any second- or third-rate applicants.

Notice that both 'second-rate' and 'third-rate' are words which are hyphenated. This is because in such sentence constructions as the one illus-trated, for the sake of economy, the writer has omitted the inclusion of the 'rate' part of second-rate, since it is implied and repeated in any case a little later in the sentence. However, the hyphen is still required after 'second'.

Finally, the hyphen is sometimes used in print to convey a stutter or a hasty torrent of words:

– 'I d-d-don't know what you m-m-mean!'
– ''Scuse-me-please-sir-can-I-go-to-the-toilet-now?'

The dash at work

The job done by the dash is quite different from that of the hyphen. It is used mainly to inform the reader that a group of words has been 'tacked on' to a previous group as a kind of afterthought, or to show that a group of words has been inserted again as a sort of last minute change of structure in a sentence:

– 'Drop the newspaper into your grandmother's on your way home from school – oh, and don't be late back!'
– His major weakness – and one which cost him dearly in his business dealing was his impetuous nature.
– The solution – if indeed it may be deemed a solution – is to attempt to get your money back as quickly as possible.
– 'In view of the vandalism in the bicycle sheds, there will be no Founders'

Day holiday this term – and the trip to the Science Museum next week is cancelled!'

As you may have noticed in the second example, the use of hyphens to separate an insertion in a sentence is a punctuating function which may also be carried out by means of commas:

His major weakness, and one which cost him dearly in his business dealings, was his impetuous nature.

As you can see, the dash is the stronger punctuation mark visually, and probably causes the insertion to have an increased impact upon the reader. It is therefore a matter of personal judgement whether in such instances you decide to employ dashes or commas.

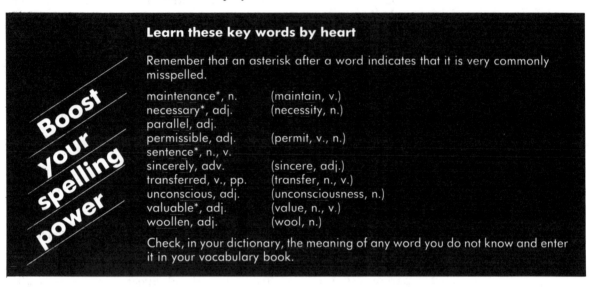

Learn these key words by heart

Remember that an asterisk after a word indicates that it is very commonly misspelled.

maintenance*, n.	(maintain, v.)
necessary*, adj.	(necessity, n.)
parallel, adj.	
permissible, adj.	(permit, v., n.)
sentence*, n., v.	
sincerely, adv.	(sincere, adj.)
transferred, v., pp.	(transfer, n., v.)
unconscious, adj.	(unconsciousness, n.)
valuable*, adj.	(value, n., v.)
woollen, adj.	(wool, n.)

Check, in your dictionary, the meaning of any word you do not know and enter it in your vocabulary book.

Some writers fall into the trap of using the dash as a substitute for the full stop or comma in a kind of jerky and undisciplined way, with the result that every idea seems to have been supplied as an afterthought:

'Lovely of you to come, Samantha – and what a lovely dress! – Must have cost Tommy a fortune – Do come into the drawing room – This is Samantha everyone – Tommy's latest!'

The use of the dash in the above example might of course be justified as a means of depicting a gushing and affected hostess at a fashionable London dinner party. Unless you are seeking such similar effects, however, keep your dashes in check for more prudent and sparing uses!

In quite a different style and tone, the following piece illustrates how irritating the misuse of the dash may become when it halts, slows and generally obstructs the flow and structure of a series of sentences which thus become unnecessarily complicated:

The Treaty of Versailles – allowing for the fact that the Allies at the end of the First World War were all for extracting huge war reparations from Germany – was later seen by many historians as one of the causes of the rise of Nazism in Germany in the 1920s. The bitter pill of Versailles – after the fall of Paris in

1940 – no doubt prompted Hitler to insist that the very same railway carriage be used some twenty-two years later for the signing of the surrender of France – crowning the German blitzkrieg – it was even placed on exactly the same spot in the forest of Compiègne where the Franco-German armistice had been signed on 11 November 1918.

Brackets at work

In the printing of books and typescript outside of scientific and mathematical subjects, brackets generally appear thus: ( ). They are only used in single pairs and never thus: (( )).

As their name suggests, brackets are principally employed to separate some expression or group of words or set of numbers, etc. from the rest of a piece of writing. The reason may be to include a reference for the reader's assistance, to make an aside to the reader in the course of a piece of description, to add an afterthought into a sentence or for other similar reasons:

– The Treaty of Versailles (pages 21–38 refer) had a profound effect upon post-war Germany.
– The grimy urchin seized the fallen brooch (and few would blame him in his circumstances) and took off down the street as if pursued by devils!
– Take the mixture in its saucepan off the hot-plate (remembering to switch it off carefully) and put it on one side until it has cooled to about 25°C.
– The First Eleven to represent the School in the cricket match against the Old Boys will be:

J. A. Tompkins (Capt.)
P. W. Carter
N. Cricklewood
. . .
R. T. Jones (Twelfth Man)

– She turned to the washing-up reluctantly and entirely without enthusiasm (for the family had still not accepted her despite all her efforts to please).
'Goodness me! Are you not finished yet?' asked Mrs Coppesly in a light yet chiding voice. 'We'll never be ready at this rate!'

You will have noticed in the above examples that the insertions marked by the brackets did not start with a capital letter in the first word. The construction of the sentences is such that the additional information bracketed off forms part of the overall sentence and the final full stop occurs *after* the second bracket. However, there is nothing to stop a writer putting a fresh sentence in brackets if he so desires:

Tomkins did some slow and methodical gardening around his crease. (In his experience this never failed to upset the opening bowler.) Having thoroughly rattled the bowler, he looked up, smiled and assumed an eager 'ready' stance.

In punctuation terms, the usual rule is that the customary punctuation of the sentence follows the second bracket. However, in the example above, where brackets enclose a separate sentence the full stop occurs more naturally *inside* the second bracket. The effect of using brackets in the above illustration is to make the reasons for Tomkins's manoeuvres more of a conspiracy or secret shared between writer and reader – the brackets act as a kind of screen behind which the writer utters confidences away from the open flow of his normal prose.

Sadly perhaps, the use of brackets by contemporary writers seems to be declining. Often writers prefer to separate additions or insertions or asides by using commas or, more infrequently, dashes. Usually dashes and brackets create much longer and stronger pauses and brackets are more easily seen to be indicating that what they enclose may be of a secondary importance in the flow of a passage of prose. It is therefore a matter of using your own judgement on whether to select commas, brackets or dashes. A good way of building up your expertise in this area is to collect effective examples from your everyday reading and to record them in your notebook as guidelines to follow.

HINTS!

Guidelines for using hyphens, dashes and brackets

- **Unless you are absolutely certain, always check in your dictionary to see whether two words (or three) are connected by a hyphen or appear correctly as separate words, or as a single word.**
- **If you are using dashes in the same way as brackets, don't forget the second dash at the end of your insertion and avoid the slip of substituting a comma for it.**
- **You do not need to use dashes and commas in a kind of overkill:**

  'Excuse me, – I've come without my watch, – is it eleven o'clock yet?' (Omit the commas.)

- **The same rule applies to brackets – they work perfectly well on their own!**
- **Punctuate the group of words within the dashes or brackets normally, but remember that the punctuation relating to the sentence as a whole comes outside the brackets:**

  He slammed the textbook shut (knowing deep down that he had no hope in the following day's examination).

- **Many words which were earlier hyphenated are now being run together:**

  cooperative   photoelectric   antenatal

  so be on your guard and keep your dictionary handy as well as reading your newspaper or magazine with an eye for such trends.

Assignments

1 Rewrite the following sentences by punctuating them as you think appropriate. Bear in mind that in some instances you may have to join together as a single word what has been set down as two!

a the children had a wonderful time at the fairground they had goes on the big dipper the merry go round the roller coaster and the helter skelter

b she sat in the waiting room of the ante natal clinic as usual she felt the nausea of morning sickness and hoped the check up would not take too long

c the learner driver took the round about too fast and only just managed to stop at the traffic lights the instructor made him do a three point turn in a cul de sac and then asked him to reverse into a narrow side street

d 'i say is the stage manager there asked the play wright knowing full well that he was off the set having his lunch i want to make some changes to the furniture in front of the back drop the plaster of paris statue is too near the front of the stage

e   the china display in effect the whole display area needs to be dis-
mantled and given an out and out cleaning.

f   seeing how thoroughly the customs officials were examining the suit
cases of every returning holiday maker albert began to worry about his five
hundred cigarettes not to mention the camera wrapped up in his dressing
gown his two bottles of brandy and the brand new wrist watch which
seemed to be burning a ring around his wrist

g   having bottled your elder berry wine leave it for at least three months
longer if you can avoid the temptation to try it and you will have a wine well
worth the effort spent in its making

Chapter 19
Mastering spelling V: suffixes

A number of spelling problems occur because of the similar – or even identical – sounds of some suffixes. It is therefore particularly important to memorize when certain suffixes are encountered whether they are *-ible* or *-able*, *-ery* or *-ary*, *-ant* or *-ent* endings for example. Collecting such 'terrible twins' as:

depend*ant*/depend*ent*   station*ery*/station*ary*   coun*sel*/coun*cil*   princi*ple*/princi*pal*

and knowing the differences in their meaning as well as their spelling is extremely worthwhile and should be seen as a definite investment of your time!

The following checklist of suffixes is by no means exhaustive, but aims to provide you with a list of the more commonly occurring suffixes for you to study and absorb:

Suffix	Meaning	Examples
-able	to be able to, to be	disposable moveable
-age	in a state of	storage bondage
-al	possessing the qualities of	legal adjectival
-ant	one who is	attendant dependant
-ar	having the characteristics of	perpendicular circular
-arch	chief, supreme, etc.	monarch oligarch
-ary	in a state of	stationary imaginary
-ast	one who is	gymnast
-ate	displaying the qualities of	considerate desperate
-craft	having the skill of	witchcraft parentcraft
-dom	domain or country of	kingdom sheikhdom earldom
-ed	past participle of regular verbs	walked hoped
-ee	one who owes a duty	lessee employee
-en	one who is	warden
-ence	state of	silence
-ent	state of being	resident dependent
-ery	having characteristics of	finery pottery
-ette	small version of, diminutive	cigarette vignette
-ful	full of	beautiful hopeful
-gram	to do with writing	telegram epigram

-graph(y)	also to do with writing or the producing of images	telegraph holograph
-hood	state of	boyhood womanhood
-iac	one who is, having the characteristics of	maniac hypochondriac
-ial	having the qualities of	beast = bestial
-ian	one who is	historian guardian
-ible	able to be	defend = defensible combustible
-ic	having the qualities of	horrific terrific
-ics	subject or study of	mechanics photographics
-ide	forming or denoting	bromide sulphide
-iant/ient	in a state of being	transient expedient deviant radiant
-ier	the 'more than' comparative	holier jollier
-iest	the 'most' superlative (see also *-er* and *-est* forms)	holiest jolliest
-ience	also in a state of	patience conscience
-ing	present participle of verbs	going swimming
-ion	of, part of, doing	action reduction
-ish	sort of	bluish whitish
-ism	belief, concept	atheism deism
-ist	one who is	atheist communist
-ity	in a state of	superiority
-ious	having the characteristics of	conscious specious
-ive	possessing qualities of	suggestive possessive
-less	not having, without	faithless doubtless
-logue	forming of talk	monologue dialogue
-ly	in a . . . way	prettily slowly
-ling	small version of	duckling yearling
-monger	dealer or trader in	fishmonger warmonger
-ment	in a state of	argument statement
-ness	having the quality of	goodness badness
-ock	little version of	hillock bullock
-oid	showing the form of	planetoid humanoid
-ology	the study of	geology theology
-or	one who does or is (see *-ess* for feminine suffix)	collector actor actress
-ose	in a state of	comatose morose
-osis	possessing the condition of	psychosis osmosis
-ot	one who is	despot patriot
-sion	state of	vision passion
-some	having the quality	wholesome handsome
-tion	having quality of	motion interruption
-ure	having the quality of being	engravure portraiture
-wise	in the manner of	clockwise
-ways	in the direction of	sideways lengthways
-ware	made of, to do with	silverware earthenware kitchenware
-wards	in the direction of	homewards northwards
-y	in a . . . way	chirpy funny

You will have noticed from the above list that most of the suffixes which we use are added on to the ends of words for the following reasons:

- to make a verb into a noun: move, movement
- to make an adjective into a noun: good, goodness
- to make an adjective into an adverb: slow, slowly
- to make a noun into an adjective: beauty, beautiful

Also, a number of the suffixes which are used to make nouns produce what are in fact *abstract* nouns – nouns which convey the meaning of emotions, states of being, ideas:

government   impatience   wastage   fusion   dualism

RULE	**Remember the basic rule that generally the adding of a suffix on to a base word does not change the spelling of the base word.**

Assignments

1   Without referring to the checklist (unless desperate!) write the meaning of the following suffixes:

-graph   -logue   -ology   -oid   -ics   -arch

2   How many different words can you form from the following base words by using suffixes from the checklist above?

(to) deceive   (to) tolerate   (to) help   (to) examine

3   Write down for each of the following suffixes two of your own words – that is avoid using examples from the checklist. You may of course consult your dictionary in case of need:

-ible   -ary   -ience   -ism   -ure

4   Complete the spelling of the following by adding the appropriate suffix:

leg_ _ _ _   able to be read
read_ _ _ _   well worth reading
depend_ _ _   one who relies on another
depend_ _ _   in a state of depending on something
dia_ _ _ _ _   conversation between two or more people
conduct_ _   one who conducts
less_ _   one who pays rent on a leasehold property

Chapter 20

Improve your written English VI: subordinate conjunctions and clauses

A quick revision

So far we have seen the simple sentence at work in the general shape of:

Subject + finite verb + rest of sentence
(Comprising: adverb/adjective
extensions or the direct
object)

Examples:

– The intruder/advanced/in a cautious manner.
– The sunset/was/a beautiful red.
– Debbie/typed/the letter.

We have learned that such sentences are called 'simple' in that they possess only one subject and one finite verb controlling the action of the subject.

In addition, however, we soon recalled how dull a collection of such sentences can be when strung together and how two or more ideas may be combined into a single sentence, where what would be sentences in their own right if standing alone become clauses of equal weight when linked together by words like:

and   but   then   next   yet   or

and the pairs:

both . . .   and   (n)either . . .   (n)or

These are coordinating conjunctions linking main clauses together.

RULE	**Remember the definition of a clause is that it contains both a subject and a finite verb.**

Examples of compound sentences made up of equal main clauses:

– He felt very tired *and* he looked urgently for the motel.
– You danced well, *but* you need to practise your reverse turns.
– First baste the bird well *then* put it in the oven at 250°C.

Note in the last sentence that the subject 'you' in the opening clause has been left out, but is 'understood' to be there. When orders or instructions are given in this way, the finite verb – here 'baste' – is said to be in the imperative which comes from the Latin word to order.

- She was hungry *yet* she was still determined to reduce her calorie intake.
- *Either* you finish your tea directly, *or* you will certainly not go to the pictures this evening!
- *Both* the floor was polished *and* the chairs were dusted.
- Hurry up *or* we shall be late!

As the above examples illustrate, compound sentences can be constructed by linking together with the help of conjunctions (the word conjunction does in fact mean to link together in Latin) ideas which might otherwise be expressed as short simple sentences capable of standing alone. The point of joining them together as we discovered was to create more interesting patterns of expression which adults could still absorb readily and which avoided the dull simplicity of a string of single subject plus single finite verb sentences.

The subordinating conjunction

There is one further area of the conjunction as a part of speech for us to examine which will also extend our ability to contruct interesting sentences.

The idea of 'subordinating' in the title of this section need not daunt us – all it means is that a particular conjunction is employed to join an idea to another where one is a main idea or clause and the other is dependent upon it or subordinate to it for its meaning.

For example, if we wrote:

Because he had grazed his knee.

we should only puzzle our reader. The reason being that we have no idea what the incomplete statement above is driving at. It is in fact *dependent* upon something else to communicate its meaning:

Johnny was crying   *because* he had grazed his knee.
Main clause   Dependent clause

The main clause 'Johnny was crying' is extended by linking a subordinate or dependent clause to it which tells us the reason why. Further examples:

- It started to rain   *although* it had been sunny and bright in the morning.
- You are likely to catch cold   *if* you go out without an overcoat on.
- The boy gave himself a large helping   *as* he was first in the queue for school dinner.
- I cannot remember   *whether* I left my umbrella in the office or on the train. (Notice here that 'or' is linking a further phrase on to the subordinate clause introduced by the conjunction 'whether'.)
- You might as well help   *since* you have finally decided to turn up!

Checklist of subordinating conjunctions

Introducing the idea of:

- *Time*: when before after until
  I will see you *before* you go.
- *Place*: where (whence archaic)
  He showed me *where* they live.

- *Manner*: how
  The teacher explained *how* I should draw the example.
- *Reason* why   because   as   since
  He ran *because* he was frightened.
- *Modifying main idea*: though   although   even   though   however   whatever
  He was determined *although* he was small in stature.
- *Setting a condition*: if   unless
  He will be angry *if* you don't apologize.
- *Purpose or result*: so   so that   in order that   with   the result that
  – He rose early *in order that* he might study for his exams before going to work.
  – He prepared well *so* he passed all his examinations.
- *Linking a description or extension*: who   which   that
  – There is the man *who* asked to see you.
  – I'd like to see the house *which* is finished.
- *Introducing a subject or object clause:* that   what
  – *That* he was an excellent painter was never in doubt. (Subject.)
  – No one ever discovered *that* he had been in prison. (Object.)

(Notice in each of the examples the *whole* clause introduced by 'that' is acting as the subject or object of the sentence.)

The above checklist is by no means exhaustive, but it does include those subordinating conjunctions which you are likely to meet most often.

It is not necessary for us to delve deeper into the grammatical terminology of subordinating clauses, except to notice the following. Subordinating conjunctions can link to main clauses dependent clauses which convey either an adverbial, adjectival or noun meaning. In other words they can quite simply carry out in a more sophisticated way the jobs which phrases can do or sometimes individual words.

Examples:

Adverbial:	I will wait *until you arrive*. (Time)
Adjectival:	The couple loved the garden *which was large and shady*. (Relative clause describing 'garden'.)
Noun subject of sentence	*That you were unaware of the possible effects of your behaviour is no excuse.* (Notice that the whole of the noun clause introduced by the conjunction 'that' might be replaced by the pronoun 'it'!)

What is *much more important* is to be able to make use of your general knowledge and understanding of the grammatical role of conjunctions and clauses in your own writing, so that you can achieve a desired effect more consciously and deliberately.

The first thing to notice is that complex sentences comprising a main clause with one or more dependent clauses can be used in two distinct ways. Either the main clause can come first, followed by one or several subordinate clauses, or a subordinate clause can precede a subsequent main clause. Deliberately all the examples so far given have been constructed as:

Main clause + subordinate clause (or clauses)

Now consider the effect upon a sentence's style of beginning with a subordinate clause:

After they had taken a lengthy and closely argued recess, the jury took their seats again in court and the foreman announced their verdict of not guilty.

Writing it right!

'As or like'

The confusion over using 'as' or 'like' in writing may be readily overcome by checking the part of speech the desired word must be in the chosen sentence.
For example, the word 'as' is used in introducing clauses in sentences and functions as a conjunction:

She did *as* she was told

Sometimes the use is combined into 'as if' or 'as though'.

He walked *as if* if he had hurt his left leg.

Whenever 'as' is being used as a conjunction, it is wrong to use 'like' as an alternative:

                as
– He walked li~~ke~~ if he had hurt his left leg.

           as
– She did li~~ke~~ she was told.

The word 'like' is more often than not used as a preposition:

– She paints like Peter.
– The ball hit the goalkeeper like a bullet.

Here the conjunction 'after' introduces a subordinate clause (adverbial of time) to create a distinct mood of tension and suspense before starting the main clause, where the key words 'not guilty' are subtly left until the very end!
If the sentence were to be written as:

Not guilty was the verdict delivered by the foreman of the jury upon its return to court after it had taken a lengthy and closely argued recess.

the chances are that the reader would skip over the rest of the sentence after having taken in the key words 'not guilty' at its very start.
Further, in a paragraph of writing, the ability to change the structure of complex sentences provides the writer with many opportunities to vary his sentence constructions and thus to maintain his reader's interest:

Was there still time? *Until* he had glanced at his watch he had thought so, *but* now he wasn't so sure. The border guards would be changing in another two or so minutes *so that* the precious seconds gained from the cold and weariness of the present guards would be lost. *Although* it seemed that Karl would not now come, Ritchie stayed huddled in the shadow of the pine trees, *as if* he were made of frozen pinewood himself. In the distance he suddenly heard a faint yet definite cry of screech owl. Karl was coming over!

In the above paragraph, a studied mix of long and short sentences – simple and complex – has been strung together in order to obtain a particular effect. At the very opening and close of the paragraph, it is the short sentences which convey most impact – whether of time running out, or the prelude to an imminent and dangerous border crossing, probably of a spy or secret service agent – just because they are short and sharp.

The middle section of the paragraph mixes complex sentences which either begin with a subordinate clause or a main clause. The effect of putting such variations side by side helps to make the writing interesting and aids the feeling of tension by ensuring that key words or phrases occur at the right intervals.

It may well be that the gifted author creates such writing without considering at all consciously what the basis in grammar or syntax is of his style and its impact. However, for those of us still aspiring to become another Ian Fleming or Frederick Forsyth, a study of the way that sentence structure aids the conveying of meaning and tone is still very helpful!

Same word – different part of speech!

By now it will not have escaped your notice that sometimes the same word can act as a different part of speech, depending on how it is being used:

that – As a demonstrative pronoun. (I'll have *that*.)
    – As a subordinating conjunction. (After a most careful search there was no doubt *that* the masked raider had completely disappeared.)

Some other words which can stand as two different parts of speech are:

who   which   his   what

Summary

The subordinating conjunction introduces a subordinate or dependent clause which relies on a main clause for its meaning to be made clear. In style terms, different effects can be created by composing sentences in constructions such as:

- Main clause + subordinate clause
- Subordinate clause + main clause, or
- Subordinate clause + main clause + subordinate clause

Assignments

1   Write down briefly what the job of a conjunction is.
2   Conjunctions have been divided in this text into two kinds. What are they? Provide a list of examples of each which you can readily recall.
3   Explain briefly what the difference is between a simple sentence and a complex sentence and what main different effects each is likely to have upon the reader in terms of conveying meaning and in terms of impact.
4   Rewrite the following passage by connecting the series of short sentences with appropriate conjunctions.

It was hot. The heat was dry. Unlike the dripping humidity of the swamps they had climbed up from. They had managed to escape from the furious tribesmen. They reached a shady plateau. They sank down exhausted from their climb. They had no rations or blankets. This did not seem important in the rush to escape from the brandished assegais of the Zulus. They had forgotten the first rule of survival. It was always to carry on your person the basic tools of survival. Hopelessly they looked around for some sticks to rub together to make a fire. They were unsuccessful and tired. This led to angry words. A sudden roar in the dusk brought them instantly back to their need to survive – if only until morning.

5   Join the following clauses together to make a single sentence by using appropriate conjunctions:

. . . . . he was under age, he strode confidently up to the bar . . . . . he ordered a double whisky . . . . . the bartender promptly poured without any concern at all!

Can you say which of the clauses of the single sentence above is the main clause?

Chapter 21
Punctuating in English VI: the semi-colon and colon

Both the semi-colon and colon are extremely useful punctuation marks and yet many writers tend to avoid employing them because they are unsure of the ways of introducing them correctly into their writing. This section aims to banish such uncertainties for good!

You will almost certainly be familiar with the appearance on the page of the semi-colon and colon:

semi-colon   ;   colon   :

In fact, throughout this text you will have seen the colon at work introducing examples just as it is in the above sentence. Basically both the semi-colon and colon are used in punctuation to provide a pause or stop for the reader to aid him or her in making sense of the writing or to help in creating a particular stylistic effect such as suspense, or a deliberate pause for the sake of heightening a contrast.

In ranking order of strength of pause or stop the list would be as follows:

Most strong ↑ full stop
colon
semi-colon
Least strong ↓ comma

The semi-colon at work

The main function of the semi-colon to be kept in mind is that it is employed when a writer wishes to create a sequence of ideas made up of several clauses – usually connecting main clauses – as a single sentence, rather than writing a series of separate sentences or connecting them by conjunctions. The only yardstick by which to measure the effectiveness of such a piece of punctuation is to consider whether the desired effect is better achieved by means of semi-colons, full stops or the introduction of conjunctions.

– He checked feverishly through the heap of bank statements; he then re-checked the list of suppliers to whom he owed money; beyond all doubt, he was bankrupt!
– He checked feverishly through the heap of bank statements. He then re-checked the list of suppliers to whom he owed money. Beyond all doubt, he was bankrupt!

He checked fervishly through the heap of bank statements *and* then re-checked the list of suppliers to whom he owed money, *but* beyond all doubt, he was bankrupt!

Though in each of the above examples the three essential stages are distinct, the less definite pause of the semi-colon has the effect of making the passage read quicker and you may think that the semi-colons better convey the sense of frantic searching than the stronger full stops. In this sense, only the preference of the writer and reader can decide which is more effective since each of the punctuation approaches is grammatically correct.

An important constructional point to bear in mind is that for the use of the semi-colon to be effective, each of the clauses separated by semi-colons must be clearly related and connected, and generally share the same subject. The following use would be inappropriate:

Tom wrote down the date in his diary; not everyone is able to cope with the demands of sitting public examinations.

Here the two ideas expressed in the clauses are totally unconnected and even if separated by a full stop would strain the reader's ability to perceive any sequence linking them. So, remember that, as the semi-colon represents a lighter pause than the full-stop, the ideas thus separated must be closely linked, usually via a shared subject and content.

Notice the connection, however, in the following example which, though not including a shared subject, does closely connect by means of the expression of cause and effect:

The time limit of Prime Minister Neville Chamberlain's ultimatum concerning the territorial integrity of Poland expired with no response from the German Reich; the Second World War had started.

Generally the use of the semi-colon does away with the need to include the linking conjunction:

– One after the other, the car-thief tried each of the keys on the large ring in the Jaguar's lock <u>but</u> it made no difference, the door remained firmly locked.
– One after the other, the car-thief tried each of the keys on the large ring in the Jaguar's lock; it made no difference, the door remained firmly locked.
– Every guest at the dinner-party had played a part in making Christopher feel thoroughly ashamed of his treatment of Susan, <u>although</u> each later denied it during the police enquiry.
– Every guest at the dinner-party had played a part in making Christopher feel thoroughly ashamed of his treatment of Susan; each denied it later during the police enquiry.

In the first example, the use of the conjunction 'but' to link the two clauses has the effect of allowing the rhythm of the sentence to flow on quickly. The substitution of the semi-colon forces the reader to pause and so places more emphasis on the information of the second clause. In such instances the effect is to give the content of the words after the semi-colon much more status – but make sure in your writing they deserve it!

The second example illustrates the same kind of effect. Here the use of the semi-colon instead of the comma and 'although' again forces a break and a pause and throws greater emphasis upon the general behaviour of the

Writing it right!

Due to or owing to

There used to be a fuss about only putting a noun after 'due to' in sentences such as:

The train was late due to fog.

Today, however, there is really no difference in established usage between:

due to   owing to   because of

The advice is therefore to use whichever expression you feel best suits the context:

The game was cancelled – *due to* poor light.
– *owing to* the riots at the pavilion end which carried on until the police arrived.
– *because of* the sad death of the Prime Minister.

dinner-party guests which was to avoid becoming involved in something unpleasant.

A further use of the semi-colon is similar to that of the comma – it may be employed to separate items in a list. Whereas with the comma such items are usually short nouns or word groups, those separated by semi-colons tend to be longer and often take the form of entire clauses:

Set upon leaving him for ever, she carefully considered what she should pack into the suitcase she had flung on to the bed; the thermal underwear, practical if unfeminine, would prove essential in Morecambe in winter; the heavy tweed skirt given to her by her mother last Christmas was warm and comfortable; the brushed cotton shirts would do better than the eye-catching but insubstantial silk blouses; the creamy-white Arran sweater was a must. Careless of what she had forgotten, she swiftly zipped the suitcase together and left the bedroom without a backward glance.

In such a piece of writing the use of the semi-colon to punctuate the list of items packed in the suitcase helps the reader to concentrate upon each item individually by slowing down the pace of the paragraph. They also help to create the effect of measured, methodical packing at a time when a highly emotional decision has just been reached and assist the author in creating a tone of irony – 'she' thinks very carefully about her future clothing needs when we might expect her to fling almost anything into the suitcase without much thought.

Where full stops or semi-colons are concerned as possible punctuation marks between what may be either individual sentences or clauses linked to form a single sentence, it is a matter of the individual writer's decision – your decision – on what to use. This section has aimed to show you how to use the semi-colon with various effects which are not obtained by means of the full stop. All you now need is the confidence to go ahead and use semi-colons, and this you can soon gain by practising your skills in the assignments set at the end of this chapter!

The colon at work

In the writing of the eighteenth and nineteenth centuries the colon was used

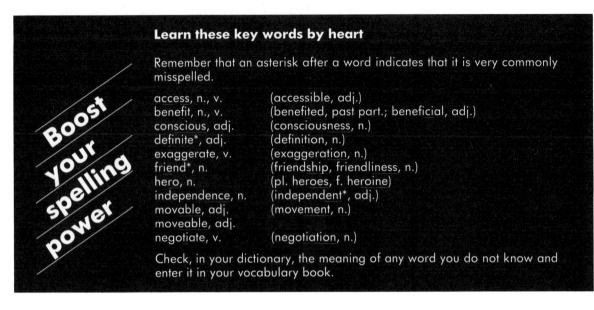

Learn these key words by heart

Remember that an asterisk after a word indicates that it is very commonly misspelled.

access, n., v.	(accessible, adj.)
benefit, n., v.	(benefited, past part.; beneficial, adj.)
conscious, adj.	(consciousness, n.)
definite*, adj.	(definition, n.)
exaggerate, v.	(exaggeration, n.)
friend*, n.	(friendship, friendliness, n.)
hero, n.	(pl. heroes, f. heroine)
independence, n.	(independent*, adj.)
movable, adj.	(movement, n.)
moveable, adj.	
negotiate, v.	(negotiation, n.)

Check, in your dictionary, the meaning of any word you do not know and enter it in your vocabulary book.

as a punctuation mark in ways very similar to those of the semi-colon outlined above. In the following passage, Jane Eyre is seeking to exchange one of her belongings in return for something to eat in a baker's shop:

I entered the shop: a woman was there. Seeing a respectably dressed person, a lady as she supposed, she came forward with civility. How could she serve me? I was seized with shame: my tongue would not utter the request I had prepared. I dared not offer her the half-worn gloves, the creased handkerchief: besides, I felt it would be absurd. (*Jane Eyre* by Charlotte Brontë, Penguin Books)

There is a definite admiration due to a writer who can create such crystal clear writing which yet manages to convey Jane's sense of shame and embarrassment by means of the studied use of the colon and the comma!

Nowadays, however, this particular use of the colon as a pause mark just short of the full stop has fallen – sadly – into disuse and in terms of the balance and the lucid flow of Charlotte Brontë's prose readers of its twentieth-century counterpart are undoubtedly the losers!

The colon is seen today, however, as a means of introducing a list within a piece of writing:

The customs officer deliberately placed the discovered items of contraband upon the long table: twelve Swiss watches, a Japanese Canon camera, eight solid gold rings, three bottles of liqueur and what appeared to be a bag of cannabis resin.

Another use of the colon you cannot have escaped while working through this book is to introduce a quotation or example which is often centred in the middle of the page or indented within a prose paragraph:

Perhaps the most telling of John Donne's poetic insights occurs in one of his sermons:

Any man's death diminishes me because I am involved in Mankind; And therefore never send to know for whom the bell tolls; it tolls for thee.

Here Donne is at pains to communicate the fellowship of all human beings, where the death of one directly affects the quality of existence of all the rest.

In a similar way, the colon may be employed within a single sentence to introduce a quoted proverb or extract from literature, or by the same token in business, for example, a quotation from an operations manual:

One of the most irritating proverbial expressions I have ever come across is: 'Neither a borrower nor a lender be'!

I am writing to point out to you the defect in your installation manual which states: 'Before inserting the screws it is necessary to ensure that the panel is aligned properly.' In my experience of trying to erect the desk, it is impossible to align the side panel in question until the screws have been inserted, by which time it is impossible to correct any leaning of the whole piece, one way or the other, away from the perpendicular!

The colon is further employed to introduce a list – say of names or parts – set out one above the other:

The following countries are signatories to the treaty:

    Australia
    Belgium
    Canada
    Denmark
    Eire
    etc.

In a similar way the colon may be used to introduce lists of, say, book titles, films, famous people and so on, whether they are set out subsequently down the page or follow on laterally in the course of a normal paragraph.

HINT!

Tips on using semi-colons and colons

- Remember that a semi-colon is generally used to provide a stop between clauses which form part of a sentence in order to create a number of effects, such as:
  - to create pronounced contrast in what is said before the semi-colon as opposed to after it;
  - to give greater emphasis to what is said in the clause after the semi-colon;
  - to separate various clauses in a long sentence which have been put into a list.
- Usually there needs to be a close similarity between the matter before the semi-colon and that after it. Often both clauses divided by the semi-colon share an identical subject:

  We all tried valiantly to resist their fast bowler; in the event we lost by ten wickets!

- If the clauses separated by the semi-colon do not share the same subject, then there needs to be a close relationship between the clauses in terms of their meaning or a sequence of events, etc.:

  – Outside, the clock struck eleven; they knew they had precisely thirty seconds before the next patrol of the nightwatchman.
  – In the wings the chorus stood ready for the finale; on the stage the soprano and tenor were locked in a seemingly endless duet; in the auditorium almost all the audience had long since fallen asleep.

- Before deciding upon semi-colons, commas or full stops, think carefully which form of punctuation will best create the effect you desire. If you can, write down the sentence as a trial go first and then see what it looks like as well as how it reads.

- It is generally good advice to avoid using a semi-colon immediately before a subordinating conjunction like:

  because   as   if   when   although   where etc.

- Usually individual words or phrases in a list required to be separated by commas rather than semi-colons:

  Dispiritedly she considered the household chores which needed to be done that day: ironing the shirts, cleaning the bathroom, tying up the daffodils and vacuuming the downstairs lounge.

- Consider whether a colon or a dash is more appropriate to mark the introduction of a piece of information:

  –He put his hand in his jacket pocket for his passport – he must have left it at home!
  –He put his hand in his jacket pocket for his passport: it wasn't there!

  In the latter example, the colon is perhaps the best punctuation mark to employ in order to obtain the extreme contrast desired.
- Remember the special use of the colon to introduce quotations, lists, a series of titles or names, etc., either within the conventional layout of sentences or to begin a list going vertically down the page.
- Do not use either the semi-colon or colon to separate ideas which are better expressed as separate sentences:

  On the bridge the captain scanned the horizon anxiously looking for that most dangerous phenomenon, the solitary iceberg. Meanwhile in her first class cabin, Mrs Ponsonby slept on oblivious of his cares.

Assignments

1   Rewrite the following sentences by including either a semi-colon or colon where you think appropriate:

a   laugh and the world laughs with you weep and you weep alone

b   the time had passed for second thoughts he shot his right arm up in the air and volunteered to join the mission

c   the following is standard procedure to be observed on hearing the fire alarm sound close all windows shut all doors without locking them leave all your belongings behind and walk without rushing to the nearest fire exit

d   have you ever come across that old but true saying dont kill the goose that lays the golden egg

e   jenkins screwed up the letter into a ball he threw it over the parapet into the murky river that was definitely the end of the whole wretched business

f   you have a simple choice either you own up of your own accord or i report you

Chapter 22
Mastering spelling VI: silent letters

One of the most – if not the most – irritating features of English spelling occurs in those words which include letters which are printed and form part of the word but which are not sounded. Such silent letters are almost like parasites, doing little or nothing useful but causing no end of trouble!

The worst of the 'species' is undoubtedly the silent letter which may begin some words:

*p*sychology	*p*salm	*w*hole	*k*nead
'sikoloji'	'sahm'	'hole'	'need'

The following checklist includes the most commonly occurring words which include silent letters. One of the best ways to master the spelling of such words is to learn them in groups which share a similarity. In each group or batch the silent letter has been italicized. Bear in mind that the checklist is by no means exhaustive, and always take the trouble to jot down in your notebook any new word you meet which has a silent letter – you can always check its pronunciation in your dictionary if you are not sure:

b de*b*t de*b*tor inde*b*ted clim*b* lim*b*

c ac*c*quaint ac*c*quaintance ac*k*nowledge ac*c*quire ac*c*quisition ac*c*quittal

d Remember that one form of the *juh* sound is made up of *dg*: mi*d*get fi*d*get ga*d*get etc.

e usually the last letter of a word. Clue for spotting it: the preceding vowel is almost always long: lath*e* bath*e* swath*e* scyth*e* blyth*e*

g *g*naw *g*nat *g*nome *g*nu *g*narled

h *g*herkin *g*hetto *g*houl *g*host *g*hastly
ex*h*aust ex*h*ume ex*h*ibit ex*h*ort
w*h*ack w*h*ale w*h*arf w*h*at w*h*ether w*h*ere w*h*en
w*h*ip w*h*ist w*h*irl w*h*isk w*h*eedle
(and some imported words: *h*ors d'oeuvre yog*h*urt)

k *k*nack *k*napsack *k*nap *k*nave *k*nead *k*nee *k*new
*k*night *k*nickers *k*nit *k*nife *k*nob *k*nock *k*not *k*now

m *m*nemonic (it means a word or phrase coined as an aid to memory)

n   Remember those words which finish in m*n* where the *n* sound is virtually silent: condem*n*   dam*n*   etc.

p   Two prefixes to keep in mind are *pneu-* and *psycho-*:
*p*neumatic   *p*neumonia   *p*neumonic   *p*sychology *p*sychosomatic   *p*sychiatry
And the silent *p* of recei*p*t

ph   Remember too the *eff* sound spelled *ph*:
ne*ph*ew   *Ph*oenician   tele*ph*one etc.

w   S*w*ord   play*w*right   (all the wrights: ship*w*right   wheel*w*right etc.)   *w*riggle   *w*rench   *w*rist   *w*rath   *w*rap   *w*rench *w*rong   *w*rite   *w*reckage   *w*reak   *w*ren   *w*restle   *w*rinkle *w*hole   *w*hore

Silent letters in foreign words: tournique*t*   soubrique*t*   si*g*nor messieur*s*   au fai*t*   *s*cimitar

Assignments

1 Set out below are a number of definitions of certain words which contain a silent letter. The total number of letters making up the word are shown as a number. Write down the word being defined:

a   Manipulating dough when making bread: 5

b   Found not guilty by a jury: 8

c   Someone you know but not as well as a friend: 12

d   When you feel you owe something to someone you are 8 to them.

e   Illness affecting the lungs: 9

f   Curved sword: 8

g   The bark of an old tree may be: 7

h   Dig up a body from a grave: 6

i   To beat eggs into a mixture is to 5 them.

j   Italian for mister: 6

k   Write down three words, each one displaying a different type of silent *p*.

l   This time do the same for the letter *h*.

m   Where in the spelling of a word are you most likely to find: silent *k*'s silent *g*'s?

n   Which letter of the alphabet most frequently follows a silent *w*?

Chapter 23

Improve your written English VII: prepositions and interjections

Prepositions seem in print to be small, relatively humble looking words yet they perform a multitude of important linking duties, by joining one sense group of words to another to convey a particular and often extremely precise meaning:

He first saw her *at* six twenty-three *in* the bus station.

Generally, prepositions act as links between sense groups of words in sentences. They establish relationships between one group of words and another such as *where* in terms of location:

The old man was sitting *on* a bench *in* the park

or *when* in terms of time:

I should be home *before* six *in* the evening.

Often, the preposition can form a link in an abstract relationship:

There was bad blood *between* the two farming brothers.

Prepositions frequently used

This list is not all inclusive but will identify the more commonly occurring prepositions for you:

in, out up, down from, to above, beneath over, under before, after till/until across, through, between like at, on, with, by for, of past into, on to

The sense groups introduced by prepositions tend to be either phrases:

in a towering rage   after the Lord Mayor's Show   at a total loss etc

or they may introduce single words:

by accident   past midnight   for ever

When they introduce clauses, they are then acting as conjunctions:

before the last dance was played

Here it is useful to note the difference in correct usage, where 'like' may be used to introduce a single word or phrase:

like John   like the previous secretary

but 'as' is used to introduce clauses:

I wanted to dance *as* they did in 'Singin' in the Rain'.

Prepositions and case

One rule of grammar that is important to absorb and remember – and one which will save you from a number of common errors in your writing – is that prepositions are followed by words which go into the accusative. At this point it is helpful to recall the cases in English: nominative, accusative, possessive and dative. Set out below as an aid for revision is a table of the cases of the personal pronoun:

RULE	The cases in English for the personal pronoun							
	Singular					**Plural**		
Nominative	I	you	he,	she,	it	we	you	they
Accusative	me	you	him,	her,	it	us	you	them
Possessive	mine	yours	his,	hers,	its	ours	yours	theirs
Dative	to me	to you	to him,	to her,	to it	to us	to you	to them

Until now, it has not been necessary to dwell upon the idea of case in our study of grammar, but in order to understand the role of the preposition and its effect upon the words it controls it is necessary to add this straightforward concept to your general understanding of grammar at work. Simply, the nominative case is said to be the one in which subjects of sentences are expressed:

– *Peter* hit the goalpost.
– *He*   hit the goalpost.

Both 'Peter' and 'he' in the above sentence are in the nominative case. Objects of sentences, however, are said to be in the accusative case:

Peter   kissed   *Mary*.
He   kissed   *her*.

Both 'Mary' and 'her' are objects in the above sentence and are said to be in the accusative case. When we wish to show that there is a sense of possession in an idea:

The cat licked *its* paw. (i.e. the paw it possessed)

the pronoun adjective introducing paw – 'its' – is said to be in the possessive case. For people we would refer to *his* or *her* or to *our* or *your* in the plural to show possession.

The dative case (where dative simply means 'given') is said to be the one in which indirect objects are expressed:

Mary gave a black eye *to Peter*.

Here, the black eye is the direct object (said to be in the accusative) and 'to Peter' is the indirect object (said to be in the dative). Thus in the example:

She gave the black eye *to him*

to him is said to be dative.

Now in English, a lot of this does not matter very much, since many words – particularly proper nouns – look exactly the same in whatever case they appear:

–*Peter* opened the office door. (Subject, nominative)
–The door swung back and hit *Peter*. (Object, accusative)
–Mary borrowed *Peter's* pen. (Possessive case – shown by use of
   apostrophe)
–She later returned it *to Peter*. (Indirect object dative case)

What *does* matter, however, in good and acceptable writing is being able to put pronouns especially into their correct case when used after prepositions. Consider the following sentence:

'And I should like to extend my grateful thanks to you all for the wonderful retirement present you have so kindly given to *my wife and I*.'

You've spotted it! The preposition after 'given' cannot introduce a nominative case, so 'I' is wrong and should be replaced by 'me'.

'. . . you have so kindly given to my wife and (to) me.' Here 'to me' is part of an indirect object but 'with me' (accusative) and 'to me' (dative) 'me' looks just the same!

Sometimes speakers and writers who are unsure of themselves in this situation use the word 'myself' in an effort to avoid uncertainty:

'. . . so kindly given to my wife and *myself*.'

This alternative, though very much in use, is not really necessary nor should it be adopted.
   Other errors of this nature include:

Wrong	**Right**
Between you and *I*	Between you and me. (accusative)
The bird returned to *it's* nest	The bird returned to its nest. (possessive)

Positioning of the preposition in the sentence

In advice given to writers earlier this century, it was often stressed that sentences should not end with prepositions. A typical example would be:

Do not write:
   He is the famous artist whom I have heard of.
Rather write:
   He is the famous writer of whom I have heard.

Indeed, the general feeling of the second version seems neater and tighter. However, one of the important factors in such constructions which the grammarians tended to overlook was that there exist in English very many verbs whose meaning is made unique by being fused or combined with a preposition. For example, 'to catch' is very different in meaning from 'to catch out' or 'to catch up with'. Furthermore, down the ages, English speakers have composed or created many hundreds of new verbs by linking simple verbs with various prepositions to form entirely new meanings.
   Sometimes the new verb enters the language as slang:

to come across: After an argument he *came across* with the money.
(meaning he gave it or supplied it)

or it forms a particular meaning when allied to a certain preposition:

to press on: Despite the bitter weather they *pressed on* across the seemingly endless ice.

The result of the use of such verbs which are combined with prepositions is that a particular meaning is applied to verb/preposition combinations like:

to put up with

which has the meaning of managing to remain on reasonably friendly terms with someone or something which is essentially irritating or annoying:

The tired travellers *put up with* the incessant noise from the drunken football fans in the train's corridor.

In a sideswipe at the critics who came down on ending sentences with prepositions, Sir Winston Churchill once wrote:

This is the sort of English up with which I will not put.

In murdering the natural word order of his sentence in this way, Churchill once and for all silenced the narrow pedants who had little feeling for the natural rhythms of English or the need for prepositions which in effect formed parts of verbs to remain in close juxtaposition to them.

In terms of word order, then, you should generally keep a preposition which forms part of a verb group in its natural (usually immediately following) position:

– He *came out of* the situation better than he had expected.
– They decided to use the idea he had *come up with*.

Prepositions as parts of established expressions

From Sir Winston Churchill's quotation it is a short but necessary step to considering those expressions in English which link adjectives or verbs to prepositions to form what are called idiomatic expressions. In this sense, the word and the preposition used with it have become inseparable and form an idiom or set, established expression.

Examples:

Word	Correct preposition
different	*from*
accordance	in accordance *with*
corresponding	corresponding *to*
conjunction	in conjunction *with*
astonished	astonished *at*
consisting	consisting *of*
overtaken	overtaken *by*
see	see *through* (i.e. penetrate a deception)
insist	insist *upon*
desist	desist *from*

Such a list can become very extensive, and it is a matter of learning not only the meaning of the verb or adjective in question but also which preposition correctly precedes or follows it. Fortunately we have already learned very many of these idiomatic expressions at our mother's apron strings, but if in doubt, then a good source of reference is either the *Concise Oxford*

Dictionary or Fowler's *Modern English Usage*, which will provide the correct preposition in current use or explain which alternatives may be acceptable.

No need for confusion!

In examining the role of the preposition, we have noticed how the same word can act as two different parts of speech, depending upon the way it is being used:

– He returned *before* nightfall. (before = preposition)
– He returned *before* the sun had set. (before = conjunction)

The labels 'preposition' and 'conjunction' are not really important other than to identify their respective uses – conjunction: linking word to introduce a subject and finite verb in a clause; preposition: linking word to introduce a single noun (or pronoun) or a phrase. However, knowing this difference can help you to avoid writing sentences such as:

He cut the pattern *like* he had been shown.

Here, 'like' is being used wrongly as a conjunction and should be replaced by 'as'. But in the sentence:

She paints very much *like* Cézanne.

'like' is being correctly used as a preposition.
   In other contexts there are also words which can play the part of more than one part of speech:

– I would prefer one like *his*. (his = possessive pronoun)
– He braked suddenly on *his* motorcycle. (his = possessive adjective)

Again, the importance lies not so much in knowing what technical name has been given to the word 'his' in the context of 'his motorcycle', but in being able to distinguish between the various uses of words which act as different parts of speech and being able to spell them and use them correctly:

whose: possessive case of 'who'
who's: nominative case of who + contracted form of 'is'
     = who is

Thus the essential value of knowing your grammar and the different parts of speech which the same word may act as lies in the confidence you will have in handling such words with assurance – whether in knowing which spelling may be correct or which appropriate sentence construction follows, etc.

HINT!

Tips on using prepositions effectively

- **Remember that they are linking words which can supply very specific meaning, so make sure you choose the most effective:**

  The curfew was imposed *within* a radius of thirty miles of the capital.

- **Remember that there are very many expressions made up in part by prepositions which have, in effect to be learned by heart:**

  to distinguish *between*   to rely *on*/*upon*   *in* accordance *with*   *on* enquiring *into*

  If you become unsure of the appropriate preposition in such expressions then take the trouble to check the current usage accepted in your dictionary.

- Remember that prepositions generally take the accusative case. This is often of no consequence when we cannot tell what case a word is in – like the proper noun 'Peter'. But it does matter with pronouns where the case *does* show:

There was little to choose between the foreign skater and *her* in the finals.

Of course prepositions can sometimes introduce the possessive case:

The cat killed the weakest kitten *of its* litter as food was very scarce.

and sometimes what is in effect a dative case introduced by 'to':

The bridegroom passed the knife *to the bride* for the cake to be cut.

As case shows so little in English nouns, it is, on the whole, just something to be aware of, but be on your guard with pronouns and the adjectives formed from them, where case does show more particularly.

- Remember that there are large numbers of verbs which are made up of several words at times, one or more of which may be prepositions:

to fall *in with*   to look *up to*   to drop *in on*

The best advice here is to leave the prepositions in their customary close position after the 'verb' word of the composite verb:

I never had a father *to look up to.*

sounds and feels much more natural than:

I never had a father *up to whom to look.*
Sometimes, however, the construction of 'to whom' or 'of which' are to be preferred in such constructions:

– She is not a person *to whom* I can relate. (to relate to)
– He is an employee *in whom* I have always placed the greatest trust. (to place . . . in)
– The misery *into which* they had sunk had to be seen to be believed. (to sink into)

In the final analysis, you must be the judge of what sounds and feels most natural and comfortable in terms of the rhythm of the sentence and the natural word order of your English.

Interjections

There is no need to dwell particularly upon the interjection, the eighth and final part of speech for us to consider. The label, 'interjection' derives from Latin and means simply, an exclamation. The sort of words which are interjections often have been made to imitate sounds – of surprise or anger or pain:

Whew! Ouch! Oi! . . . *er*, excuse me, . . .

The novels written earlier this century by Frank Richards about that portly schoolboy, Billy Bunter, were full of interjections which Bunter uttered whenever set upon for his greed or sly ways. The novels' pages were full of 'ouch', 'yarooh' and other similarly expressive interjections. Nowadays interjections are mainly to be found in the speech of characters in comics or cartoon strips and do not normally find a place in prose outside the realms of dialogue and fiction. When they are used – and there are appropriate contexts for interjections – they tend to occur as single word sentences which start with a capital letter and end with an exclamation mark:

– '*Ouch*! That hurt!' cried Jim.
– '*Ouf*! Got you!' cried Paul in triumph at having pulled the bent nail out
of the wooden shelf.

So restrict your use of interjections to those situations – most often fictional
dialogue – when you can use them appropriately.

Assignments

1   How would you define the role of a preposition in a sentence?
2   Identify which words in the following list are able to be used as
prepositions:

over   slow   near   grassy   before   very   at   because   across
from   front   above

3   Compose three phrases each introduced by a preposition by unravel-
ling the following word groups:

a   slippery down hell path the to
b   best my wishes with very
c   my all days in born

4   What case do prepositions generally take? With what part of speech is
it particularly important to know? Why? Explain briefly.
5   What is wrong with the following sentence:

'People like you and I much prefer to be left on our own.'

What is the correction necessary?
6   What advice would you give to a writer wishing to use composite verbs
correctly (i.e. verbs made up in part by prepositions, e.g. to go *along with*)?
7   What is the best approach towards mastering those idiomatic expressions (like 'to distinguish between') where a specific preposition has to be
used – 'between' in the example?
8   What is an interjection? When are interjections normally used?
9   Which of the following could be used as interjections:

hm   whoa   graft   knock   tsk   ugh   pouffe   phew

10   Supply the correct preposition to complete the following:

a   to resort . . . .   The gang resorted . . . . violence in their bid
                               to escape.
b   . . . . due consideration   . . . . due consideration the judge sentenced
                               them to ten years imprisonment.
c   . . . commemoration . . . .   A service was held in the cathedral . . . .
                               commemoration . . . . the drowned seamen.
d   . . . . a regard . . . .   The crowd stood silent for a minute . . . .
                               regard . . . . the passing of the greatest
                               full-back the game has known.
e   . . . . response . . . .   I am writing . . . . response . . . . your letter of
                               21 March 19   .

Chapter 24
Punctuating in English VII: the apostrophe

Of all the punctuation marks, the apostrophe is probably the one we remember as the bane of our schooldays! Seen by itself, dangling in the air like this ' it looks harmless enough and yet many are the exam papers in English language marked every summer where candidates display an artful skill in placing the apostrophe directly above an 's' so that it could be taken to stand either before or after it and an 'each way bet' is hopefully secured!

William the Conqueror fired an arrow which landed in King Harold's eye.

Such artful tactics do not easily fool the examiners, yet they do illustrate the uncertainty in the minds of teenage (and older) writers of English about the rules which govern the correct use of the apostrophe. Part of this uncertainty lies in confusing the role of the apostrophe s when it denotes possession with its other role when it indicates that a letter has been omitted or part of a word left out, called contraction.

This section will examine both roles in detail so that you emerge fully confident about using the apostrophe correctly.

The apostrophe denoting possession

You will recall that in the early pages of this book a little time was spent examining the history of the English language and that the languages of northern Europe, especially Saxon, played an important part in the development of English. Also, you will remember that the notion of inflexion was mentioned, where the endings of words – nouns and verbs – changed according to how they were used and that today we see such changes in pronouns like he, him; she, her; we, us, etc. In much the same way, nouns in the old European languages changed the possessive according to their case (see the section on prepositions). And indeed, case in modern English still reflects the old practice of changing the ending of a noun to show its use and meaning. For example, in modern English we have two ways of showing possession. We can say:

This is the sports car *of John.*

But this sounds rather stilted and peculiar because we would much prefer to say:

This is *John's* sports car.

Both examples convey exactly the same meaning and in the latter, the proper noun John is inflected by adding the apostrophe and then the *s* to show possession. In earlier English, the same change was made but by adding *-es*, and in medieval English, we might have read:

Thisse is Joh*nes* faste steede.

The apostrophe when used in conjunction with an *s*, then, shows that the noun is being used in a possessive sense. Whether we prefer to employ the apostrophe *s* or the construction 'of . . .' very often depends upon the rhythm of the sentence:

– We visited the house of Mr. Jackson.
– The package holiday included a tour of the nightspots of Amsterdam.
– Despite reading it three times, I still could not fathom the meaning of the poem.

In each of the above examples the 'of' construction is used to show possession – of Mr. Jackson etc. Sometimes we prefer to state the same thing more economically – especially in spoken English:

– We visited Mr. Jackso*n's* house.
– The package holiday included a tour of Amsterda*m's* nightspots.
– Despite reading it three times, I still could not fathom the poe*m's* meaning.

In the above examples, the use of the apostrophe to denote possession does not affect the rhythm of the sentences nor produce an ugly effect upon the ear – but it can sometimes, as we shall later discover.

In all of the examples so far, the noun being put into the possessive case has been singular – Mr. Jackson, Amsterdam, poem, – so let us see what happens when the nouns affected are in the plural.

– The gir*ls'* voices rang out beautifully in the high nave of the cathedral.
– The poe*ms'* meaning is easier to understand after several readings.
– Most of all during my trip to Europe, I admired the capital citi*es'* architecture.

In using the apostrophe *s* to indicate possession in the plural, you will have noticed in the above examples that the plural version of the noun (inflexion again with an added *s*!) is employed with the apostrophe this time perched after it right on the end tip of the word:

girls' poems' cities'

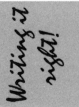

'I could have danced all night!'

Always make sure you write either 'could have' or 'could've' **but never:**

I could *of* danced all night!

You would be surprised how often this little error creeps into print!

Also, in the word 'cities' you will have spotted that where a word ends in *-y* in the singular and changes to *-ies* in the plural, the apostrophe behaves in exactly the same way in that it awaits the changing of the word's suffix from singular to plural and then slips in on the end to denote its possessive case.

Thus with 99 per cent of English words, the change from singular to plural is effected as follows:

Singular		Plural	
girl's	(of one girl)	girls'	(of two or more girls)
poem's	(of one poem)	poems'	(of several poems)
city's	(of one city)	cities'	(of two or more cities)

Notice that in the singular there is *always* a complete break after the word's final letter and the added apostrophe s.

Before moving on, there is one important factor worth drawing your attention to which has been so far overlooked, and that is the change in the word order of a sentence when the apostrophe s is employed. If we speak of the 'nightspots of Amsterdam', then the 'of' construction puts the noun (here Amsterdam) being shown in the possessive case after the noun to which it refers (here nightspots) but when the apostrophe s construction is used, the word being put into the possessive case is inserted in front of the noun to which it refers: '*Amsterdam's* nightspots'. We have become so used to this change in the word order that we scarcely notice it, but it does become important when style and sound are considered and we find ourselves confronted with the ugliness of too many s's grouped next to each other.

The Israelites disobeyed Moses's law.

Here, because of the ugly sound of Moses's, a convention has been agreed upon where the final s denoting the singular possession is left out and the punctuation becomes:

The Israelites disobeyed Moses' law.

Other words can produce the same over-abundance of s's:

St James's Square lies in the heart of London.

Here some writers would prefer to write:

St James' Square lies in the heart of London.

Ultimately it is a matter of personal decision whether to omit the final s in the apostrophized word and it depends on the harshness of the combined sound of the s's. In the latter example above, the St James' part would be pronounced as 'Saint James Square'.

One further point about the use of the apostrophe s in the singular is that when a word ends in double s, then the apostrophe with a further s is added on to it following the customary rule:

– The press's rollers were jammed.
– The bass's top fin was torn.
– The moss's natural green colour had become brown.

Words with an s sound which is spelled with a c also follow the normal rule:

– The lettuce's leaves were brown and slimy.
– The diners praised the spice's subtle flavour.

Where English (or imported) words end in a final s in the singular, then the apostrophe with a further s is added in exactly the same way:

– The demanding conductor praised the chorus's efforts.
– The tutor disagreed with the thesis's main conclusions.

Learn these key words by heart

Remember that an asterisk after a word indicates that it is very commonly misspelled.

accidental, adj.	(accidentally, adv.)
budgeted, v.	(budget, n.; budgetary, adj.)
committee*, n.	(commit, v.; commitment, n.)
desperate, adj.	(despair, v.)
eighth, adj., n.	(eight, n., adj.)
financial*, adj.	(finance, n.; financier, n.)
guardian, n.	
lose, v.	(losing*, adj.)
noticeable*, adj.	(notice, v., n.)
occur*, v.	(occurred, v. occurrence, n.)

Do not forget to enter into your vocabulary book any words with which you are unfamiliar, either in terms of spelling or meaning!

Boost your spelling power

Forming the possessive case by means of the apostrophe in the plural is quite straightforward, as we have seen – an apostrophe is simply added on to the end of the plural form of the word in question. Yet, as by now you will have grown accustomed to expect, there are some exceptions, but this time, very few!

The exceptions stem largely from those few words in English which have a plural formed differently to the normal adding of an s on to the singular:

man/men   woman/women   ox/oxen   child/children   brother/brethren (a plural used seldom nowadays)

Such words, which derive from the old European Saxon languages form the apostrophe possessive thus:

men's clothing   women's shoes   oxen's bellows   children's innocence brethren's prayer meeting

Where words have other ways of forming the plural involving the addition of -es or -ies, the rule remains constant – simply tack an apostrophe upon the very end!

– The fishes' eagerness for the hemp seed made the river water boil and seethe.
– The secretaries' main complaint concerned the delay in the arrival of the word processing system.

Some words in English have optional plural forms:

dwarfs/dwarves   handkerchiefs/handkerchieves

Here there is no problem as the rule is maintained:

dwarfs' caps/dwarves' caps
handkerchiefs' price/handkerchieves' price

One source of exceptions to the rule for the apostrophe in the plural stems from words of foreign origin (both ancient and modern) which have plural forms quite different from the added s:

Singular	Plural	Possessive Plural
formula	formulae	formulae's
basis	bases	bases'
stimulus	stimuli	stimuli's

With the exception of plurals like bases' the rule in general is to add an apostrophe and then an *s* to the plural form of the word in just the same way as for men's, women's, etc.

Lastly, there are a few words which do not change their form in the plural, like sheep and chicken (although there is a plural form chickens). Here the plural in the possessive will look exactly like its singular counterpart:

The sheep's wool was matted and smelly.

In such isolated instances, the number of sheep referred to – whether one or many – must be deduced from the context of the sentence, and most writers would seek another way of expressing the idea:

The ewe's wool was matted and smelly.

RULES

In the singular

Rules for using the apostrophe *s* to denote possession

In the singular, the possessive case employing the apostrophe *s* is created by simply adding '*s* to the singular form of the word, while making sure that both the apostrophe and the *s* are *not* joined on to it:

poem's meaning   book's cover   house's roof

Remember the word order changes to put the apostrophized word immediately in front of the word it relates to:

cat's paw   John's sports car

Remember too that words ending in *s* or double *s* follow the same rule:

press's rollers   chorus's efforts   octopus's tentacles

Keep in mind the option to drop the *s* after the apostrophe in the singular if there are so many *s*'s next to each other that an ugly hissing noise is produced!

Moses' law   St James' Square   the Sissons' house

In the plural

In order to form the possessive case in the plural with an apostrophe *s*, the rule is that, where the plural of the word in question has been formed by the addition of an *s*, an apostrophe should be immediately after it:

girls' voices   cars' exhaust fumes   shops' windows

The only exceptions occur in words which form their plurals in other ways, such as the Saxon derivations:

man's/men's   woman's/women's   child's/children's

where the apostrophe and a final *s* (separated from the plural word) are added on to the plural form.

Where words of one syllable end in *ss* in the singular, and add *es* to form their plural, then the correct plural version of the possessive follows the normal rule:

cross/crosses: crosses' shadows

Words which end in *y* in the singular and add *-ies* to form the plural present no problem since they also follow the normal plural rule:

lady/ladies: ladies' tailor
country/countries: countries' trade agreement

Lastly, remember that some words of foreign origin have inflected plurals which do not end in *s*. By and large these are treated in just the same way as man/men's:

formulae's   stadia's   stimuli's

Further tips

The rule for apostrophizing proper names such as titles is the same as for common nouns:

They took down the Dog and Duck's sign to repaint it.

Where pronouns have no possessive form (like his, hers, its), then they follow the normal rules:

I took someone else's hat by mistake.

If a word is simply in the plural and not conveying the possessive idea, then it does not need any apostrophe:

They drifted into the bar in twos and threes.

Here two's and three's would be wrong.

Remember that if you are using the personal pronoun in its possessive case, it doesn't need a 'belt and braces' job!

Wrong	Right
theirs'	theirs
it's	its
her's	hers

But we do tend to use an apostrophe with an *s* to form the plural of single letters or numbers:

–I was always taught to mind my p's and q's.
–Pass me two 3's and three 4's, please.

Otherwise the normal rules for creating plurals apply.

Final tip: at this stage it is very useful to browse through the entries for plurals and apostrophes in books like Sir Ernest Gowers' *The Complete Plain Words* (Penguin, 1984 edition).

The apostrophe denoting contraction

The second and quite distinct use of the apostrophe as a mark of punctuation is to indicate that a letter or group of letters in a word have been left out and that the word has thus become shortened or contracted:

do not = don't   cannot = can't   will not = won't

Sometimes parts of numbers in years or dates are omitted and this omission is shown by means of the apostrophe:

The Beaujolais wine of '84 (i.e. 1984) was not generally reckoned to be particularly good.

At other times, in popular or slang use a word may be shortened by the omission of a large portion of it:

He gave the prop' (propellor) a desperate heave and the fighter's engine spluttered into life.

Such contractions tend to be used most frequently in spoken English and often occur in print as a part of dialogue. You should always be on your guard when thinking of using such a contracted word in a formal written English context.

When words are shortened extensively in popular usage the inclusion of the apostrophe to denote the contraction or omission tends to fall by the wayside and the shortened version becomes a word in its own right:

perambulator: pram   omnibus: bus

Technically we should write: *p'ram'* and *'bus* but these apostrophes have long since disappeared from general use. Other words which have evolved in English in the same way are:

permanent wave: perm   bicycle: cycle   newspaper: paper

Bear in mind, however, that they are still largely colloquial in their use.

HINT!

Tips on using the apostrophe to denote contraction or omission

- Virtually all words which are contracted display only a single apostrophe. We write *shan't* rather than the more technically accurate *sha'n't*.
- Almost certainly in your daily reading – especially of trading names – you will see apostrophes included where they are not needed. Make sure you don't fall into the same trap!

  Jones & Keen, Newsagent'_s_ (not needed)
  Green & King, Wholesalers_'_ to the Grocery Trade (not needed)

  Or you may see apostrophes creeping into words or word groups where they have no business:

  'It is perfectly al'_right_, I can manage.' (incorrect)

- Avoid using a contracted form of a word unless you are quite sure that the informality or colloquial effect it introduces is appropriate. For example words like *don't* and *can't* etc may be perfectly in order in a handwritten memo to a colleague but out of place in an official letter placing an order.
- Never guess at the correct form of a contracted word or whether to drop the apostrophe altogether – always check it in your dictionary.
- Remember that some words may be being used quite simply in the plural and do not need any apostrophe of any kind:

  on_es_   tw_os_   thr_ees_   three-eight_hs_ etc.

Assignments

1 Punctuate the following sentences correctly using the apostrophe *s* or contraction apostrophe where you think it is needed:

a the three girls handbags were found in the ladies toilet, but their contents had been stolen
b the technicians report indicated that the secretaries typewriters needed servicing and that two full days work would be needed to carry out the repairs
c ive found johns notes but could i borrow yours if its not inconvenient
d to my mind all the e e c countries flags should be flown at tomorrows ceremony
e she forgot to post her brother-in-laws birthday card as she couldnt find a stamp when it was on her mind
f the claret of 63 is infinitely better than its counterpart of 69

2 Rewrite the following sentences by using the apostrophe *s* to show possession.

a *The shoes of the children* in the sale were especially bought in.
b *The ties of the gentlemen* were reduced by twenty-five per cent.
c *The weight of the carcasses* was too heavy for the lorry and five had to be unloaded.
d *The bouquet of the bride* was made of pink carnations and *the posies of the bridesmaids* were beautifully created from pastel shades of sweetpeas.

3 Write down the contracted form of the following:

would not cannot shall not must not would have it is who is they are you are

4 Place the apostrophe in the correct spot according to the explanations given:

a the customers complaints (complaints of several customers)
b the handkerchieves patterns (patterns of two handkerchieves)
c the winepresss handle (the handle of a single winepress)
d the valleys geography (of three valleys)
e the wheats yield (of a ton of wheat)
f yesterdays racing results (the results of yesterday)

Chapter 25

Mastering spelling VII: easily confused pairs of words

One of the major bugbears to overcome in spelling occurs when two (and occasionally three) words sound virtually identical to the ear but are spelled quite differently. Indeed, generations of shorthand writers and audio-typists have had to cope with this problem while acquiring their skills so that they may act as the guardian of their boss's often hazy knowledge of the finer points of spelling! Today's electronic office has resolved the problem to some degree in that dictionaries are now part of the software 'tools' of a word processing system and can interpret a misspelled word and rectify it instantly. But such advanced techniques should not encourage a slothful attitude, since you will surely be in need of your spelling skills often enough when out of the reach of a word processor and its dictionary!

Set out below is a checklist of some of the most frequently confused pairs or triplets of words. Take the trouble to browse through them from time to time while ensuring you know what each word means, and you will soon be able to separate them without difficulty. Also, and most important, do not avoid the use of such a pair of words for it is by incorporating them into your active writing vocabulary that you will overcome any uncertainty lingering in your mind as to their correct spelling.

Another helpful tip is to learn what part of speech each word is (here is yet another good reason for knowing your grammar!) because you will often find that this knowledge alone will solve the problem! For example, once you know that 'affect' can only be part of a verb, then you will never be tempted to use it as a noun!

The ~~affect~~ was to force the product off the market.

Correct noun: *effect*

Easily confused pairs

access	n.	means of entering
excess	n.	too much of
affect	v.	to alter or cause to change in some way
effect	n., v.	n: the resultant change, the result; as a v: to carry out, to bring about

*a*ccept	v.	to allow oneself to be given
*e*xcept	conj.	conjunction: can mean unless
	v.	v: to single out and refuse to include
	prep.	preposition: meaning 'but not'
*a*llude	v.	to refer to
*e*lude	v.	to escape from, not to be able to call to mind
		see also: *allu*sive and *elu*sive
a*ss*ent	n.	n: agreement, permission
	v.	v: to agree to
a*sc*ent	n.	the climbing of
compl*i*ment	n.	a kind of remark on something good or well done
	v.	to praise or speak well of
compl*e*ment	n.	the rest of, or of a ship's crew, all the personnel
	v.	to complete, provide the rest of something
continu*ous*	adj.	meaning not stopping at all
continu*al*	adj.	meaning having the overall effect of not stopping but including the possibility of intermittent stops
		see also: continuou*sly*, continu*ally*
coun*sel*	n.	a barrister in court, prosecuting or defending
coun*cil*	n.	body of people elected to run local government, or a representative body
depend*ent*	adj.	reliant upon
depend*ant*	n.	*person* who is reliant upon
de*s*ert	n.	wasteland
	v.	to leave in the lurch
de*ss*ert	n.	last course of a meal
di*ss*ent	n.	disagreement
	v.	to disagree with
de*sc*ent	n.	climbing down from
	.	(note also d*e*cent with the accent on the first syllable, an adjective meaning pleasant, nice)
ex*a*lt	v.	to praise, to raise up to a high position
ex*h*ort	v.	to urge strongly
ex*u*lt	v.	to cheer or rejoice noisily
economic	adj.	to do with the profitable use of
economic*al*	adj.	thrifty, sparing
fiancé	n.	male betrothed or engaged person
fiancé*e*	n.	female betrothed or engaged person
fr*ie*ze	n.	decorative border (round a room or a cake)
fr*ee*ze	v.	to reduce to a temperature below zero
g*a*ge	n.	a pledge or security
g*au*ge	n.	n: size of, dimensions of
	v.	v: to measure, estimate
		(note also: greeng*a*ge a soft fruit)

*imm*oral	adj.	not moral, bad, of behaviour contrary to accepted conduct
*am*oral	adj.	meaning in a neutral sense, neither moral nor immoral
ingen*uous*	adj.	naive, too ready to accept
ingen*ious*	adj.	cunning, very clever (of an invention)
lose	v.	misplace
loose	adj.	opposite of tight
	v.	unfasten, let go
*o*ral	adj.	spoken, having to do with the mouth
*a*ural	adj.	heard, having to do with the ear
princip*al*	n.	head of a college or private school;
	adj.	main, chief
principle	n.	one of a set of beliefs
qu*iet*	adj.	opposite of noisy
	n.	noiselessness
qu*ite*	adj.	almost, fairly
sensual	adj.	of the senses, but with particular reference to sexual inclinations
sensuous	adj.	of the senses but in a way of transmitting sense of beauty
station*e*ry	n.	papers, envelopes, etc. for writing
station*a*ry	adj.	not moving
wholly	adv.	completely
holy	adj.	revered in a religious sense (note also the plant: holly)

This list should start your collection of the many words in English which sound exactly alike – called homophones – or those which appear to be similar. Take the trouble to jot down any fresh word you meet that sounds very like another you already know. Look it up in the dictionary for its spelling and meaning and then use it in your writing at the first opportunity!

Although not strictly to do with spelling, now is perhaps a good time to remind you of those other pairs of words which are often confused because they either share a common word stem or they look as if they might mean the same thing (but don't!)

uninterested	having no particular interest for a thing
disinterested	impartial, not prejudiced about a matter.

readable	a good read
legible	printed sufficiently clearly for the words to be read without difficulty

Such readily confused pairings should also be collected and distinguished between.

A tip to aid the memory

The brain works often much better than a computer and can think! However, it can also forget what it has carefully learned! Therefore you may find it helpful to settle upon some gimmick or handy means of triggering the memory for a correct spelling. For example, with station*e*ry and station*a*ry, if you think '*e* is for envelopes' then you will seize upon station*e*ry when you want the word for writing materials.

Similarly, you can think that people are *a*nimals, therefore the person who is reliant upon something is a depend*a*nt, the word which ends with *a* for animal! Childish though such memory-joggers may appear, they certainly do work – and who's to know how you arrived at the correct spelling in your mind?

Assignments

1   Write into the following sentences the word which is suited to the context of each sentence. In each case, the appropriate word is to be found in the checklist above.

a   They all .... to his suggestion that production should go ahead and the vote for it was unanimous.

b   There were ten minutes of the game left and the scores were even; the home crowd and the visiting fans all .... their teams to make a final all out effort!

c   The .... decorating the inner temple wall was still beautiful after lying undiscovered for three thousand years!

d   The mechanism which sprang the trap was very ....

e   Having over-indulged during the first two courses, the diner was unable to face a ....

f   The mannequin carried a maroon leather handbag which nicely .... the dark red chiffon dress she was modelling.

g   The inspector put down the arrest of forty nuns for jaywalking to an .... of zeal on the part of the new constable.

h   The .... test consisted of listening to tapes of three conversations in German.

i   You will not get far in retailing if you are the sort who easily .... his temper.

j   'My lord, I speak as .... for the prosecution in this case.'

2   Which of the paired words in the checklist means:

a   having neither good nor bad morals?
b   to raise someone up to a position of power or authority over people?
c   the most important or chief (reason, for example)?
d   without stopping at any time?
e   something given entry to?
f   to do with the mouth?
g   to avoid capture?
h   to cause something to change?
i   to measure, estimate?
j   to be reliant upon?

Write down the word in each case.

Chapter 26
Summary: a respite and review

Having successfully arrived at the end of Part One, we can, like mountain climbers, set up a base camp so as to recuperate from the effects of the climb so far. While we are catching our breath as it were, we can indulge in a look back over the route we have travelled. Indeed, a respite is certainly deserved and a review of the scope of the studies covered will be good for morale!

In reaching this 'halfway house' you have:

- Identified and used the necessary study tools for the job.
- Surveyed the origins of the English language.
- Become proficient in using both a dictionary and an English language thesaurus.
- Examined in depth the nature and roles of the eight parts of speech which make up English sentences:

  the noun   the verb   the adjective   the adverb   the pronoun
  the conjunction   the preposition   the interjection

- Studied the use and effect upon the reader of the eleven punctuation marks:

  the full stop   the comma   inverted commas/quotation marks
  the question mark   the exclamation mark   hyphens   dashes and
  brackets   the semi-colon   the colon   the apostrophe

- Acquired a sound knowledge of sentence structures which occur commonly in correct English and learned how to vary them so as to provide interest and variety.
- Made an extensive study of English spelling rules and guidelines and come to grips with problem words and confusing homophones.
- Considered the effect upon the style of a piece of writing of some good and some bad practices in English composition and – all being well – internalized the good practices and eradicated the bad in your own repertoire of writing skills!
- Collected in your notebook along the way new words which are now incorporated in your active vocabulary, noted good examples of punctuation from newspapers, magazines and books for reference as models

and written down spellings with which you were unfamiliar as a means of memorizing them.
- Most important: worked your way through the assignments methodically so as to gain valuable first-hand practice and to check against the answers that you have grasped the main points of each section.

When surveyed in the detail set out above, the scope and extent of your progress should rightly make you feel good and increase your confidence in your own ability. Now you either have a range of skills in English language writing at your instant command or you know precisely where to go in reference book terms to find out or to check if need be.

Regrettably, very many people – including those for whom expertise in writing is an essential part of their working life – do not attain the skills so far covered. However, an antidote to prevent us becoming too smug is to undertake a personal survey in each of the above ten areas to check what section of Part One may need to be re-read and worked through once more before proceeding further. Also, it will be worth your taking the trouble to revise the sections of Part One from time to time which you found most taxing.

Next steps

Once convinced of your mastery of the syntax, grammar and usage in Part One, and having summoned up your strength for a further onslaught, it is time to tackle the elements of style and effective usage upon which Part Two concentrates. You should keep in mind the fact that, having gained a good understanding of the mechanics of written English, the next step is to acquire a mastery of writing in a range of styles, where each style chosen is most appropriate and effective in the job it is seeking to do.

Lastly, it is now more important than ever that you set aside some time in your working week to read from a range of good publications so that you acquaint yourself with a variety of English styles and see in a series of written contexts new words at work which you may readily acquire for your own store of vocabulary.

Part Two
Style in English

Introduction

In Part One the main thrust of the work you have done has been to develop your knowledge of the rules and procedures of grammar and syntax as well as to improve your ability to spell and punctuate correctly and to avoid the pitfalls of common errors in usage.

In Part Two the aim is to improve your awareness of the overall impact which your writing will inevitably make upon its reader or readers and to develop your ability to create in your writing – quite consciously – a particular style which is most likely to prove effective in a given situation.

For example, the given situation might be having to write a letter of complaint, or to write a letter expressing your condolences to the widow of a friend, or to compose a notice for the office noticeboard offering a first aid course to interested staff.

In each of these contexts or situations a completely different approach is called for, where all that you have learned in Part One – correctness or accepted conventions in the setting down of your words – is not enough! Now you will be needing to give more thought to the selection of the 'best words', to the length and structure of your sentences and to the kind of person you are writing to.

In other words, in Part Two we shall be examining the overall impact of a message expressed in a particular way – the style in which it is expressed. We shall also be developing an ability to create successful styles of writing which ensure that the message is received positively and is therefore effectively written.

Chapter 27
What is style?

Style in writing is much easier to recognize – whether good style or bad style – than to explain!

However, over the years many writers and creative artists have sought to define the main ingredients of style in a short and crisp definition. Three such definitions follow to enable us to think hard about what we understand about style and what it essentially is:

– To me style is just the outside of content, and content the inside of style, like the outside and inside of the human body, both go together, they can't be separated. (Jean-Luc Godard)
– I wish our clever young poets would remember my homely definitions of prose and poetry; that is prose; words in their best order; – poetry; the best words in the best order. (Samuel Taylor Coleridge)
– Have something to say, and say it as clearly as you can. That is the only secret of style. (Matthew Arnold)

Each of these quotations highlight a particularly important feature of what constitutes good style. For Jean-Luc Godard style is virtually inseparable from content – the *what you say* and the *how you say it* form two sides of the same skin and are totally integrated. For Coleridge style is a matter of very careful selection of the best words to perform a particular job and the best structure of sentences or verse in which to compose them. Arnold identifies clarity and having a worthwhile message to communicate as the essence of good style.

So far then, the importance of content, the relationship to it of the words chosen and the structures used as well as clarity and having a worthwhile message have been identified in the make-up of good style.

Our working definition should build on these aspects and may be summarized as follows:

• Style essentially may be regarded as the overall impact that a piece of writing has upon its reader and is made up of:

  • the particular aims and objectives of the piece of writing;
  • the way in which the piece is structured and the sequence into which its ideas are put;
  • the choice of vocabulary employed to express the meaning of the piece;

- the context or situation in which the piece of writing occurs;
- the personality, status and background of the intended reader of the piece of writing;
- the relationship which the writer has or seeks to establish with the reader.

Writing it right!

Beware the double negative!

The trap of the double negative is much more menacing in the spoken word, than in the written:

'I don't know nothing about no robbery, guv!'

Here it is virtually a treble negative. But if you 'don't know nothing', you must know something!

However, be on your guard to avoid:

She did *not* know *nothing* about the burglary.

Either: She did not know anything ...
Or: She knew nothing ...

RULE

Thus the following may be seen for our purposes as the principal ingredients of good style:

- **The aims of the piece.**
- **Its particular structure.**
- **Its chosen vocabulary.**
- **Its context.**
- **The reader's profile.**
- **The relationship of writer and reader.**

Each individual piece of writing will establish a unique mix of style depending on how these ingredients are used and on what particular outcome or effect is intended.

When the style proves effective then the meaning of the piece of writing is communicated immediately and happily. When the style mix proves faulty, then there may well be a resulting breakdown in communication because:

- the message's structure proved too complicated, long and boring, over-simple, etc.;
- the words chosen were too technical and baffled the intended reader;
- for the context, the message was too informal and what, for example, was meant as friendliness was taken as impertinence;
- the writer underestimated the strength of views of people: unemployed, retired, with low incomes, etc. – an inadequate profile of the recipient was taken into account;
- the writer misread his relationship with his reader and thus became condescending, stuffy, cheeky, etc.

And as a result of one or more of these shortcomings, the aims of the piece of writing are not achieved.

Examples of breakdowns in style

Consider these examples of breakdown in style to support the points just made:

Example:

The ambivalent relationship in some writing between the connotative delineation of words and their more ratiocinative and denotative counterparts ...

The writer is trying to say:

Sometimes it is not easy to distinguish between words which have emotional overtones and words which are more neutral and which have only a single, factual meaning ...

The style failure in this example results from inappropriate use of jargon/technical vocabulary if the piece is intended for non-expert readership.

Example:

LETTER

```
Dear Sirs,

I saw your advert in the local paper
and thought I'd have a go for it, because
people round my way have always thought
of yours as being a decent sort of outfit.

Plus the fact that I've had plenty
of experience in handling the sort of
blokes you refer to. . . .
```

The writer is trying to say:

LETTER

```
Dear Sir,

I saw your advertisement for the post
of production supervisor in the local weekly
newspaper yesterday and was prompted to apply
because of the high regard in which your
company is held locally.

Also, I have had extensive experience
of supervising a workforce similar to the
one you refer to . . .
```

Learn these key words by heart

Boost your spelling power

Remember that an asterisk after a word indicates that it is very commonly misspelled.

niece, n.	(nephew, n.)
occasion, n., v.	(occasionally, adv.)
physical, adj.	(physique, n.)
psychology, n.	(psychological, adj.)
quiet*, n., adj.	(do not confuse with quite)
receive, v.	(receipt, n.)
seize, v.	(seizure, n.)
tendency, n.	
weird, adj.	
withhold, v.	(withheld, v.)

Do not forget to enter into your vocabulary book any words with which you are unfamiliar, either in terms of spelling or meaning!

Here the style failure results from the choice of a vocabulary and sentence structure which is too colloquial and which produces a tone which is inappropriate to a formal letter of application – though it might well be acceptable in a conversational context.

Example:

LETTER
```
The Sales Manager
Harry's Hi-Fi Shop Ltd
. . .

Dear Sir,

I am writing to express my disgust at the
really shoddy goods you are selling these days.

Last night the portable hi-fi set you
sold me packed up — after only two days! I
think you will agree that this is a lousy
way to treat a customer who paid cash — but
not for the sort of rubbish I have been conned
into buying.

Please therefore send your maintenance man
round straightaway.

Yours . . .
```

The writer is trying to say:

LETTER
```
The Sales Manager
Harry's Hi-Fi Shop Ltd
. . .

Dear Sir,

I am writing to you to complain about the
breakdown yesterday of the portable hi-fi set
I purchased from you only three days ago. The
model is an Ultrasonic XT, sales invoice number
128734, cost £128.99.

There was no apparent cause for the sound suddenly
dying out. I have tried it on the mains supply and with
fresh batteries, but without success.

As you will know, I am one of your regular customers
and would like one of your maintenance engineers to call
as quickly as possible to rectify the fault or to exchange
the set I have.

Yours . . .
```

Here, style failure results from the writer allowing his anger and frustration to turn his letter into one which is likely to result in the sales manager feeling ill-disposed to act either promptly or sympathetically. The amended version has the aim of getting the hi-fi going again quickly and is more likely to succeed in this aim as a result of its controlled and reasonable tone.

Example:

LETTER
```
While I would be prepared to give sympathetic
consideration to what you are trying to establish
and although the circumstances of the cloud-burst
you describe as having a direct bearing upon the
accident are no doubt — at least in your own mind —
relevant and true, I think you will have to agree
that the arrival of the fire-brigade tender was, to
say the least, coincidental, this will necessarily
depend upon the report of the company's Claims Inspector.
```

The writer is trying to say:

```
I am sympathetic to your argument. Doubtless
the cloud-burst made good vision most difficult.
Clearly you could not have foreseen the arrival
of the fire-brigade tender on the narrow stretch
of road. However, I am obliged to inform you
that no settlement of your insurance claim can
be made until the Claims Inspector has made his
report.
```

The style failure in this example results from the writer attempting to contain all his meaning in a single sentence. As a result, he loses the thread of his argument entirely. His structuring of the main points is faulty.

The above examples serve briefly to illustrate the sort of problems which can occur when the style of a piece of writing is faulty for one or more reasons. In Part Two we shall be considering the impact of style upon meaning in detail and examining the ways of creating and maintaining a good style in various kinds of writing.

Chapter 28
Aims in style

All too often, usually because of pressure of time or ingrained habit, all of us tend to 'leap into print' before having thought sufficiently hard – if at all – about the following:

- What am I seeking to achieve by writing this piece?
- What is the background to the situation I am writing about?
- For whom is the piece being written?
- What is the best written form in which to express the message of the piece?

In one of the examples of the preceding section, we saw how an irate purchaser of a faulty hi-fi set failed to write an effective letter of complaint because he (or she) allowed anger and irritation to take control of the letter's impact so that it became rude and thus almost certainly resulted in 'putting the back up' of the manager reading it. The unsought effect of such a letter is likely to be that the repairs or after sales service etc. are provided grudgingly rather than promptly as was wished. It pays therefore to have crystallized in your mind the intended aims of a piece of writing before setting about the message composing process.

The following sections set out some of the many ways in which a piece of writing may aim to communicate its message to its reader:

Factual writing

- To inform the reader about a set of facts or forthcoming events:

  for example the need of the local water board to shut off the mains supply for three hours in a fortnight's time.

- To set down the results of an experiment, survey, enquiry or review:

  for example the writing up of a scientific experiment, the report of a Traffic Inspector on a public meeting about a proposed bypass, the analysis of a set of questionnaires circulated to obtain information about use of the local public library, etc.

- To provide a set of directions, 'how to use' guidelines or instructions, lists of conditions of warranty, procedures to be followed:

for example instructions on how to build a self-assembly desk, the details of a manufacturer's guarantee for a piece of equipment, a notice displaying local byelaws in a public park.

All such writing has the basic and essential aim of setting down a series of facts or procedures to be adopted in a neutral way. The message aims at being communicated in clear, unambiguous and straightforward manner which may be readily interpreted – usually by a broad range of readers – though sometimes, in the case of the scientific experiment, by fellow-experts. In none of the above types of factual writing is the writer seeking to sway his readership into adopting a series of views which agree with his own, or to ensure that the readers respond favourably to an appeal to the emotions.

Persuasive writing

The same cannot be said for persuasive writing since by its very nature, it is seeking to persuade or cajole the reader to adopt or accept a particular point of view or argument or to carry out a particular action – like buying a certain brand of cornflakes – as quickly as possible. However, this is not to say that persuasive writing is either bad or underhand, simply that its aims are different from those which neutrally set out factual matter.

Persuasive writing may seek:

• To advise prospective purchasers of products and services:

for example, the circular sales letter to shopkeepers and managers about a new lawn-mower, a display advertisement for second-hand cars, a mail-shot offering investment advice.

• To make requests of employees or local inhabitants or experts:

for example, a company may circularize staff about working overtime or accepting a four-day week, volunteers may be sought via the local press to work for 'Meals on Wheels' or old people with a local knowledge may be asked to help the local museum in a project involving school children.

Thus a piece of writing may have as its basic aim either to provide information or to persuade readers to a course of action.

At work or at play?

Another basic aim which will affect a piece of writing is whether it is written for a serious, work-related situation, or simply as a means of providing pleasure or entertainment. For instance, the busy manager may pore intently over a major report affecting his department while on the commuter train going into work but may 'flick and flip' his way through the evening newspaper on his way home later the same day. The writer of the report is aided because he knows that company staff are likely to give it serious attention, whereas the newspaper journalist realizes that a number of stylistic tricks of the trade may be necessary to catch and keep the tired commuter's attention and to maintain an interest which will ensure that the same manager buys a copy of the same paper the following evening.

The background and the readership

Two further factors must be carefully considered when establishing the essential aims of a piece of writing. In addition to examining the basic 'inform or persuade, work or entertainment' aspects the conscientious writer will ensure that the relevant background to the writing situation is taken into account and that the nature and composition of his readership is also considered.

For example, the whole-page advertisement placed in national daily newspapers by the directors of a large enterprise in the throes of a national strike may well take into account in the way in which words are chosen and points made, that employees' feelings are running high and that negotiations with trade union leaders are at a delicate phase. In making its points about the virtues of accepting its latest pay offer, the board of directors will also have ensured that the offer is expressed in extremely conciliatory and 'gentle' terms! By the same token, the writer of a local weekly newspaper's editorial may take very much into account the general exasperation felt by local inhabitants about the time taken at central government level to decide upon the route of a new section of motorway.

In short, very few pieces of writing take place within a vacuum. Even personal letters to friends will reflect the familiarity and warmth of a long-standing friendship and all conscientious writers take into account the effect that events surrounding a piece being written will have upon it.

Also, in terms of clarifying the general aims of a piece of writing, the all-important reader must not be overlooked. In fact the profile of the reader is a topic to be examined at some length later in Part Two. Nevertheless, the reader should be mentioned at this outset stage in terms of the following questions the writer should answer satisfactorily before writing since they will have a direct bearing on the selection of an appropriate style:

- Is my reader an expert or layman?
- Do we share common views and attitudes to the subject I am about to write on?
- Is he or she likely to be sympathetic or hostile to my message?
- What might be the barriers I would need to overcome or take into account in getting this reader (or readership) to accept my message?
- Will the age, education, experience, outlook of my reader influence particularly the ways in which I express myself?

So far, in describing the general aims of a particular piece of writing we have examined two basically different types of writing – informative and persuasive – and have considered the importance of taking into account the background to a writing situation and the effect upon a composition of the type of reader for whom it is intended.

A further basic aim needs to be taken into account:

- How formal/informal should the piece be in order to be acceptable and thence successful?

In an example early in Part Two a letter was included which ran as follows:

LETTER
```
Dear Sirs,

I saw your advert in the local paper
and thought I'd have a go for it, because
people round my way have always thought
of yours as being a decent sort of outfit.
```

```
Plus the fact that I've had plenty of
experience in handling the sort of blokes
you refer to . . .
```

Now the point being made about the style of this letter earlier was that it was not altogether expressed in an appropriate tone of formality – it was too colloquial. The writer was expressing his thoughts in a type or *register* of language which he would, perhaps normally use in his spoken conversations. In other words, his tone was too familiar for the situation of writing a letter applying for a job. He may have been selected nevertheless for an interview on the basis of his experience, but he was not aware of the importance of adopting an appropriate register in a piece of writing, and his letter was likely to be disregarded.

The best format

Lastly, in establishing essential aims, the writer should give attention to the format in which the writing will eventually appear:

Letter?   Memorandum?   Notice on noticeboard?   Advertisement?
Press Release?   Brochure?

As well as deciding which format or medium to transmit the message in, the writer should also decide whether – if sending it to a number of people simultaneously – to despatch individually typed messages or a series of photocopies. With the aid of the word processor this decision is made much simpler by inserting individual names etc. It is, incidentally, worth remembering that messages composed and despatched individually to recipients are given more attention than photocopied circulars, since the use of reprographics to duplicate a message tends to devalue it in the eyes of its receiver.

Summary

Clearly the extent to which the writer pays attention to the above basic aims before setting out to write a draft or to type at the word processor or typewriter will depend upon the degree of importance and complexity of the intended message. Similarly, for the hard-pressed executive, the time available to attend to each of the factors mentioned above will be limited.

Nevertheless, each aspect we have just considered is important! Care about the basic aims one is seeking to achieve will pay ample dividends – the writer is much less likely to fall into the trap of becoming angry or nasty in print, of missing the essential point of his communicating, of patronizing his reader or of failing to take into account the impact of the background to a situation.

So before putting the proverbial pen to paper, make sure you have thought through your answers to:

- What, essentially am I trying to achieve?
- What is the situation, generally and particularly in which I write?
- Who is this for? What difference does it make?
- What is likely to prove the most effective format or medium in which to transmit my message?

and not least important:

- Should I be writing this at all? Would a visit or phone-call prove more effective?

Chapter 29
Register and style

At this stage in examining style in writing it will be useful to understand the idea or concept of register and the impact which it has on any particular piece of composition.

Perhaps the best way of introducing the idea of register is to look at these various ways of expressing a similar idea:

– 'Excuse me, would you mind awfully not smoking in here. It isn't allowed, actually . . .'
– 'Pardon me, but you are not allowed to smoke in here.'
– 'Please put out that cigarette. Smoking is prohibited in here.'
– 'You do know smoking is forbidden in here, I presume?'
– 'Put out that cigarette. This is a no smoking zone.'
– 'You there! Put out that cigarette immediately! No smoking allowed!'

As you see, the above set of requests/commands range from a very meek request at the top to a harsh command at the bottom. In between the ways of making the request strengthen progressively until the imperative ordering form of the verb is employed along with the use of the exclamation mark to denote the strength of the instruction.

What has in fact been constructed around the idea of asking someone not to smoke is a register of the request. In fact the term register is used to denote a range of responses – from, say, formal to informal, or from drily factual to emotionally persuasive, or from cold and distant to warm and friendly. A register may be thought of as a straight line with extremes at either end as in Figure 2.

Formal		Informal
Factual		Emotional
Impersonal		Friendly

Figure 2   The register of an expression.

In between will be various stages or gradations reflecting the strength of the formality or friendliness etc. with a kind of average midway point in the line where the expression is neither particularly formal nor informal:

'Please put out that cigarette. Smoking is prohibited in here.'

As we already know, the English language is extremely rich in synonyms and alternative words and phrases for expressing any particular idea and it is for this reason that it is possible for each and every one of us to construct messages which convey their contents in very wide ranges or shades of meaning. For example, it is possible in English to adopt quite easily a faintly mocking or sneering tone simply by the choice of words:

'I'm sorry, I can't make you an offer for your vase, it's not quite appropriate for the sort of bric-à-brac we normally sell here. You may find one of the newer antique dealers further down the road who would be interested.'

Here, we may be excused for taking 'not quite appropriate' as a sort of euphemism or round-about way of saying 'your vase is nearer to second-hand junk than to the sort of antiques we stock'. Further, the reference to a 'newer antique dealer further down the road' implies someone with not such scrupulous taste or high quality goods for sale. Yet it is difficult to be categoric about such interpretations of what has been actually said, save probably emerging from the antique shop with a feeling of 'having been put down'.

In other ways, the wide range of English available often results in very different registers being used by individuals in different contexts. For example, the manager in his own home will frequently employ a very familiar, colloquial register when conversing with his family:

'Hey, Jane, grab a couple of spuds while you're there!'

And in this particular context, such a register for the request is perfectly normal and appropriate. But bear in mind that the same manager dining in his firm's restaurant is probably more likely to say:

'Jean, would you pass down the potatoes, please.'

Such a register for the request of the potatoes is deemed by the manager to be appropriate and 'in tune' with the way that the staff in his firm talk to one another over the lunch table.

You will certainly be able to recall similar kinds of changes or shifts in register within your own experience. We all move in and around various registers in the course of our working and social days depending upon:

- who we are speaking or writing to;
- the context or situation we are in.

Moreover, we generally use an appropriate register from habit or experience without having to think too hard about it. However, when we *do* use the wrong or inappropriate register the results can be quite dramatic – a customer may take offence at a remark which was innocently intended:

'We don't keep swimming costumes in stock for people your size.'

While this may be the plain and unvarnished truth, a much more tactful register is needed to respond to an enquiry from a very fat lady:

'I'm sorry madam, we don't appear to have anything suitable for you in stock at the moment.'

Similarly, a circular memorandum to staff written in the following register:

MEMORANDUM

```
I am appalled at the slovenly appearance of staff
working in the parts of the store open to our
customers. All such staff are provided with
uniforms and it is amply apparent that these
are being allowed to become dirty and crumpled
and are cleaned far too infrequently.

Unless I see an immediate improvement I shall
take steps to transfer staff as necessary to
other positions within the store.

General Manager
```

Such an aggressively written memorandum would be likely to create an uproar among departmental store sales assistants, even though there might well be justification for the General Manager's concern. If a positive response is sought in such a situation, then the register chosen to express the message must be created in a much more tactful way, while still preserving the urgency of the matter and the need for immediate action.

Summary

The selection of an appropriate register:

Formal–Informal
Official/Correct–Familiar/Friendly
Aggressive–Conciliatory
Blunt–Tactful etc.

is crucial to the success of any communication. Thus the effective writer (or speaker for that matter) will devote careful thought to what is an appropriate level of formality or familiarity in a given context or to what extent – if at all – words or expressions which are colloquial may be included.

It is, incidentally, important to realize and accept that an appropriate register used in *spoken* conversation may not necessarily be transferred unchanged into the written medium. We use much more 'ungrammatical' and colloquial language in the spoken word than we may do acceptably in the written word.

One final point – when we refer to someone as having 'put their foot in it' in terms of a spoken or written remark which is thoughtless, tactless, arrogant or unthinking, much of the problem may be traced back to an inappropriate register having been employed!

Assignments

1 In about two or three sentences write down your own definition for style in writing.

2 List as many as you can recall of the components of style referred to in the section entitled 'What is style?'

3 Give five different reasons why breakdowns in communication may occur as the result of a faulty style having been employed.

4 What factors should a writer take into account when determining the basic aims of a piece of writing?

5 What do you see as the basic differences between writing which is factual and writing which is persuasive?

6 What sort of information is helpful for a writer to possess (as an aid to creating an effective style) about his reader(s)?

7 Write down a brief definition for the idea of 'register' assuming you have to explain it to someone who has never heard of it before. A diagram may prove helpful in your definition.

8 Why is an understanding of the idea of register so important when creating an appropriate and effective style?

9 Devise a register of appropriate remarks in one of the following situations:

● either: from informal to formal.

   Asking someone to vacate a seat in a theatre which is yours. You have the correctly numbered ticket.

● or: from easy and friendly to irritated and authoritative.

   Asking junior office staff to quieten down so a staff meeting you are chairing may begin.

10 Rewrite the circular memorandum on page 167 to departmental store staff about their uniforms in such a way that its register is likely to prove effective and obtain a positive response from the staff who receive it.

11 Assume that your boyfriend/girlfriend or husband/wife has been included in a party to be thanked by the Lord Lieutenant of your county for having collected a large sum of money for a local charity. He/she has been invited to a garden party at the county's administrative centre and may bring a guest along – you! Draft a short letter in what you consider an appropriate register asking your boss at work for permission to attend.

Chapter 30
Structure and style

Well over two thousand years ago a Greek literary critic called Aristotle wrote a treatise on how to write good tragedies. In fact, literary criticism was but one of his many accomplishments. When discussing how a plot should be structured, Aristotle deliberated that it should possess:

- a beginning
- a middle
- an end

This may appear to be so obvious as to be scarcely worth mentioning – even two thousand years ago! But Aristotle was describing a process of structuring a Greek play which was, as you might expect, much more subtle than the above three headings suggest. By having an appropriate beginning, Aristotle meant that the play should start at a point where its audience could readily grasp the situation in which the tragic hero finds himself and where nothing left out at the start becomes crucial later on.

Similarly, by 'middle', Aristotle meant that the events of the play should follow on in a logical and often chronological order – each event leading on naturally to the next. Lastly, by 'end', Aristotle wrote that the play should finish at a point where any further actions or comments were superfluous, where all the actions enacted have led to the inevitable death of the tragic hero.

What Aristotle did was to write down a series of sensible and often sensitive guidelines for aspiring Greek tragedy writers which indicated the importance of a story starting and finishing at points which satisfy its audience's curiosity and sense of having watched a play which is a complete and satisfyingly structured work.

In terms of our own examination of structure and the role it plays in helping create an effective style, the consideration of the way in which sections or sub-structures – beginnings, middles and ends – link together is a good place to start.

A letter of complaint

Let us take for a model or example the following letter of complaint which has been written to an electrical hardware chainstore branch manager to complain about a faulty foodmixer:

LETTER

Dear Sir,

Defective Gourmet Foodmixer: De Luxe model

I am writing to register with you my dissatisfaction with the De Luxe Gourmet foodmixer (model number EPX34992L) which I purchased from your Westchester store last Wednesday, 26 June 19— at a cost of £75.00.

Before settling upon this particular brand of foodmixer, I went to some pains to establish with your sales assistant that it would definitely stand up to mixing dough for home-made bread, since I have made my own bread for some years now. I was assured that the De Luxe model was sufficiently sturdy to do this job on a regular basis, and indeed the mixer came with a dough-hook as one of its accessories.

However, when I came to make bread with the Gourmet for the first time yesterday, all went well until I attempted to mix the dough (carefully following the instruction manual). Almost immediately the machine came to a halt with a series of flashes and a grinding noise from within the motor-casing.

My husband is of the opinion that the machine's motor is not strong enough for the load carried when bread dough is mixed and that it correspondingly blew up. Certainly the Gourmet has not worked at all since in any mode.

As you can imagine I was extremely upset and disappointed at this turn of events, particularly as the journey from my village to Westchester requires at least a morning to undertake if I am to return the mixer to you, and also because I am expecting visitors this week-end.

I should therefore be grateful if you would arrange for me to receive a refund of the £75.00 paid in cash for the Gourmet as a matter of urgency, since I no longer have any confidence in it, and also arrange for the model I have to be collected.

Yours faithfully,

G. Jackson (Mrs)

Before examining the structure of this letter in detail, read it through again so as fully to familiarize yourself with it.

Analysis of the structure of the letter of complaint

Mrs Jackson has given careful thought to the essential aims she wishes to achieve before putting pen to paper. In a nutshell she wants her money back and the defective foodmixer collected from her house as quickly as possible. In order to achieve these aims, she sets out to structure her letter as clearly and straightforwardly as possible so as to provide the store manager with all the information he may require to take instant action.

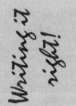

All ready already?

The above words might be said by someone wishing to express:

'Are you all prepared to depart so soon?'

Remember that 'already' (one word) means 'so soon', 'before this time', etc., while 'all ready' refers to all the people who are prepared.

In paragraph terms, the letter's structure goes as follows:

- *Letter's subject heading:* By using the word 'defective', Mrs Jackson makes it quite clear from the very outset what her letter is to be about, and clearly identifies the particular type of foodmixer in question.

- *Opening paragraph:* Here Mrs Jackson starts by registering her dissatisfaction with the mixer and then goes on to supply all the essential information about the time and place of purchase, model type, cost and individual model number. She ensures that her purchase may be quickly checked and confirmed.
- *Second paragraph:* Having set down the transaction details, Mrs Jackson goes on to establish quite firmly that she made clear to the sales assistant one of the principal uses for which the foodmixer was intended. She makes it clear that as far as she was concerned, the mixer should have met her needs and that she sought expert advice before choosing the Gourmet.
- *Third paragraph:* Mrs Jackson now carefully details the nature of the machine's breakdown and points out that she followed the manual's instructions conscientiously. She further emphasizes that it came ostensibly able to mix bread dough as a dough-hook was included in the kit. She also describes the way in which the mixer came to a sudden halt.
- *Fourth paragraph:* Here the point of including her husband's diagnosis of the machine's inadequately powered motor serves to reinforce a sense of disappointment and of having been let down at the point of sale in the store.
- *Fifth paragraph:* Having fully outlined the details of the purchase and the nature of the fault in the foodmixer, Mrs Jackson now proceeds to emphasize the inconvenience caused to her – both in terms of taking the machine back to Westchester and the inconvenience she will experience in being unable to bake bread for her visitors.
- *Closing paragraph:* Mrs Jackson, having made her case, comes to the nub or 'action statement' of her letter of complaint. She makes perfectly clear what action she expects the store manager to take: to arrange for an immediate refund to be paid and for the Gourmet to be collected from her home to save her the time and trouble of taking it back. Also, by employing the phrase 'as a matter of urgency', Mrs Jackson asserts that she does not want the matter drawn out.

In structural terms, then, you can see how Mrs Jackson's letter possesses a distinct 'beginning, middle and end', and that each phase in the letter (marked by the start of a fresh paragraph) serves a particular purpose in making an effective complaint with a view to securing prompt action.

You will also have noticed that in terms of the tone and register of the letter, Mrs Jackson does not allow her annoyance to descend to rudeness or sarcasm. (She realizes she depends upon the manager reacting positively to her letter if much fuss and 'aggravation' is to be avoided.)

Documents and structures

Just as the illustrated letter of complaint has a distinct structure, so also should all good types of writing, no matter what their format. The following examples present some of the ways in which different types of written document may be structured:

- A continuous prose essay entitled 'Are Women Now Liberated?'
  - a Introductory paragraph
    Sets out to define 'women' and what is understood by the term 'liberated'.

b Development paragraphs
Examine in turn various key areas:
– women at work
– women at home
– women at play
– women and finance
– women and families
  etc.
c Closing paragraph
Summarizes points made and reinforces overall conclusions reached –
yes/no women are/are not now liberated.

- An investigatory report
  a Opening section
    – Terms of reference: Sets out to indicate requirements which the
      report should satisfy, e.g. to investigate a problem and offer
      solutions.
  b Middle sections
    – Procedure: Indicates how information was acquired.
    – Findings: A number of sections setting out the information in a logical
      sequence.
    – Conclusions: A brief summary of the major findings.
  c Closing section
    – Recommendations: Very often the report writer is asked to make
      recommendations for resolving the problem.

- Minutes of a formal meeting
  These are structured in an agenda which follows a clear chronological and
  logical sequence.
  a Present: Who actually attended.
  b Apologies for absence: Who advised beforehand that they could not
    attend.
  c Minutes of the last meeting: Verification from members that minutes
    are accurate.
  d Matters arising from the minutes: Brief discussion of some matters or
    updatings given.
  e Series of items for discussion: Here the main items of business
    discussed are reported upon individually.
  f Any other business: Opportunity for members to introduce briefly
    additional items.
  g Date of next meeting: Agreed before members depart.

The above examples serve to illustrate that four quite different types of
writing – a letter, essay, report and minutes of a meeting – all possess a carefully thought-out structure. Such structures or logical organization of
sections and phases both help the writer to clarify his thoughts and to make
his points intelligibly and also aid the reader to understand quickly and
easily the thread of an argument or the process of related events and so on.

It is therefore crucial in developing a readily communicated style in your
writing to structure your major sections or phases of your writing before
proceeding to write. Otherwise your sentences and paragraphs will tend to
ramble and minor details may be inserted before major statements have
been made.

Learn these key words by heart

Remember that an asterisk after a word indicates that it is very commonly misspelled.

aggregate, n., v.
choice*, n.   (choose, v.)
dissatisfied, past part.   (dissatisfaction, n.)
excellent*, adj.   (excellence, n.; excel, v.)
hypocrisy, n.   (hypocritical, adj.)
install, v.   (instalment*, n.)
Mediterranean, n.
penicillin, n.
referred, past part.   (refer, v.; reference*, n.)
separate, v., adj.   (separation, n.; separately*, adv.)
until, conj.
agreeable, adj.   (agreement, n.)
clothes, n.   (clothe, v.; cloth, n.)
distributor, n.   (distribute, v.)
exercise*, v., n.
hypothesis, n.   (hypothesize, v.; hypothetical, adj.)
miniature, n., adj.
permanent, adj.   (permanence, n.)
relieved, past part.   (relief, n.; relieve, v.)
severely, adv.   (severe, adj.)

Do not forget to enter into your vocabulary book any words with which you are unfamiliar, either in terms of spelling or meaning!

Boost your spelling power

Planning a structure for a piece of writing

So far we have studied the ways in which some extended kinds of writing may be structured so that their content is put into a sequence which helps to make it readily understood and its related points clearly grasped as they unfold in a logical pattern.

It is one thing, however, to see how an existing sequence has been constructed, but quite another to create one from a blank sheet of paper yourself! How, then, are sensible structures conceived?

First, it very much depends upon the subject matter. For example, a piece of writing dealing with the history of, say, London or Edinburgh will take on a structure which is both historical and chronological – it would be almost certain to start at the beginning with earliest known settlements and to progress in epochs or ages up to the present day.

Writing a piece about the pros and cons of taking regular vigorous exercise or on whether private schools should be abolished is a very different matter. Here the approach might be to introduce the main argument or issues involved in an opening paragraph and to devote successive paragraphs to dealing with a particular supportive or unsympathetic aspect of the argument, thus proceeding to a concluding paragraph which sums up the main points made and comes down definitely either in favour of vigorous exercise and the maintenance of private schools or against as the case may be.

Yet another approach to structuring a piece of writing might be to deal with the topic in geographical or political terms. For example, an article about how best to deal with criminals might consider in successive paragraphs how different countries treat similar types of criminal. Alternatively, if the subject were unemployment, then the structure of the article might be determined by examining briefly how various countries with different political systems seek to maintain full employment and what then emerges as the best pattern to adopt or recommend.

In the brief review above, you have seen how the structure of a piece of writing might be:

- chronological
- argumentative (for and against points)
- geographical
- ideological (examining different political systems)

Further examples of structures might include the expositional – a rather imposing word which means setting down points in a systematic and logical sequence. Such a structure would be needed in an article explaining how to fit new piston rings into a motorcar engine, or to link together the major components of a home computer.

Another and in many ways more difficult structure to create is the one often used by feature-writing journalists who use their imaginations to write witty or amusing pieces about their weekly experiences or a recent foreign holiday and so on. So to our list of typical kinds of structure we may add:

- expositional
- imaginative

There are of course numerous other ways of setting about the creation of a structure best suited to an author's purpose or a piece of writing's aims. The report writer, for instance, compiling an investigatory report may choose to deal with *major* causes of a particular problem and then to proceed to more *minor* ones.

However, no matter what the structure to be constructed, there needs to be a suitable way of setting the whole process into motion better than just sucking at a pen and staring into space! The following approach is by no means perfect but it is offered to you as a useful way of planning any extended piece of writing so as to ensure that due thought and care are given to devising a suitable and effective structure.

How to devise a plan for a piece of extended writing

For a model or example to serve as a means of seeing the approach to devising a plan in action, let us take the essay title used to provide an example of a structure:

'Are Women Now Liberated?'

Let us also suppose that this is either a homework essay set at school or college, or that we have been asked to write on the topic for a staff magazine at work or for a local voluntary church or social club journal.

The subject has almost certainly been chosen because it is topical and because there are a mass of points both agreeing and disagreeing with the question. In fact the title invites the writer to examine the issues and controversies and to come down eventually on one side of the fence or the other – yes women *are* now liberated or no they *aren't*. The approach is 'argumentative' it would seem – marshalling the arguments for and against.

One of the best ways of tackling such a topic (and indeed many other quite different topics) is to let your brain engage in a 'free flow' of ideas, rather than to attempt to devise a structure as you write.

Starting the plan

In order to employ this approach you should divide a sheet of writing or file paper in half lengthwise and write your ideas or points in any order as they come into your head down the left-hand side in a kind of impromptu list. The following example will illustrate the approach to devising a plan for the liberation of women essay:

Are Women Now Liberated?

1   What is meant by women – teenagers? schoolgirls? working women? housewives? old-age pensioners? mistresses? common law wives?

2   The label 'women' is very wide – cradle to grave?

3   What is meant by liberated? Totally equal with men in every respect?

4   Better off than they have ever been?

5   Liberated from what? Domination by men? Having to bear endless numbers of children? N.B. effect of pill and safe contraception.

6   Liberated from work? Liberated from being tied to kitchen sink and nappy washing?

7   Are there really equal opportunities for girls in schools? N.B. boys more assertive in class: get more of teacher's attention.

8   How many women in top posts in professions? Doctors? Judges? Generals? Govt ministers? Bishops? Stockbrokers?

9   Are we paying lip-service to idea of women now being liberated – are they still really tied to junior posts in firms/local govt?

10   Women still find it much harder to get a mortgage if they are single.

11   Does the woman lose out in getting a full-time job and raising family? Worn out trying to maintain two full-time roles?

12   Can a woman go into a pub on her own today and feel quite at ease?

13   What about increase in offences against women – wife battering, rape? Are things any better today than they were?

14   What about rise in expectations? If women keep raising their expectations about what is theirs by right will they always lag behind?

15   Matter of providing truly equal opportunities – in education, at work, in social life, etc. – for women who must then accept fair competition with men.

16   Does the need to give birth to and bring up children mean that few women will ever be able to take on the men in the career stakes?

17   Should women see themselves rather as already liberated from male obligatory rat-race?

18   As women/men fundamentally different – drives, physique, motivations, etc. can they or should they be striving for exact equality or identical outcomes in all things?

19   Need for fundamental changes in society to allow women total freedom from bearing/rearing children/home-making, etc.?

20   Still need for basic shift in men's attitudes to women – still male chauvinist – women put down so as to limit competition to other men only?

As you can see, these points have been jotted down as they occurred to the author, and are in no particular order. Therefore the next job is to add any secondary points and to see which points would make up a good beginning or introduction, which a series of developmental points in the middle of the article, and which a set of concluding points at its end. This can be done by drawing sets of allied points together in a series of 'strings' or lines of your pen:

Are Women Now Liberated?
'FREE - FLOW' IDEAS

1   What is meant by women – teenagers? schoolgirls? working women? housewives? old-age pensioners? mistresses? common law wives?

2   The label 'women' is very wide – cradle to grave?

Follow-up points + sequence.

①
Use in an opening. para.

3 What is meant by liberated? Totally equal with men in every respect?

Use in an opening para: define what is understood by the terms. N.B. 'liberated' is a relative term.

4 Better off than they have ever been?

5 Liberated from what? Domination by men? Having to bear endless numbers of children? N.B. effect of pill and safe contraception.

6 Liberated from work? Liberated from being tied to kitchen sink and nappy washing?

Include in ①

7 Are there really equal opportunities for girls in schools? N.B. boys more assertive in class: get more of teacher's attention.

② Do a para on women + educational opportunity.

8 How many women in top posts in professions? Doctors? Judges? Generals? Govt ministers? Bishops? Stockbrokers?

② Lead on to career opportunities for women.

9 Are we paying lip-service to idea of women now being liberated – are they still really tied to junior posts in firms/local govt?

10 Women still find it much harder to get a mortgage if they are single.

N.B. also opening bank account + buying on hire purchase etc. Do PARA on women + finance.

11 Does the woman lose out in getting a full-time job and raising family? Worn out trying to maintain two full-time roles?

③ Do PARA on liberation + women in work.

12 Can a woman go into a pub on her own today and feel quite at ease?

④ Do PARA on general attitude of society to women.

13 What about increase in offences against women – wife battering, rape? Are things any better today than they were?

14 What about rise in expectations? If women keep raising their expectations about what is theirs by right will they always lag behind?

Use in concluding para.

15 Matter of providing truly equal opportunities – in education, at work, in social life, etc. – for women who must then accept fair competition with men.

16 Does the need to give birth to and bring up children mean that few women will ever be able to take on the men in the career stakes?

Include in ⑥ closing para.

17 Should women see themselves rather as already liberated from male obligatory rat-race?

Use in 3 work para

18 As women/men fundamentally different – drives, physique, motivations, etc. can they or should they be striving for exact equality or identical outcomes in all things?

19 Need for fundamental changes in society to allow women total freedom from bearing/rearing children/home-making, etc.?

20 Still need for basic shift in men's attitudes to women – still male chauvinist – women put down so as to limit competition to other men only?

⑥ Closing PARA

N.B. No, Women are not yet liberated if that means equal to men in every way or need to provide more equal opportunities + more respect for women's biological role

As the second stage of the devising of the article's plan illustrates, the right-hand side of the note-paper is used to add in any second thoughts and then to indicate by arrows and numbers (each number indicates a paragraph) how the author sees points linking together and how he sees the paragraphs coming together in a sequence which appears logical.

From such rough notes a working plan for a logical structure has emerged. It may be used in such a form as a plan where the author crosses out each point as he makes it but where he elaborates upon his shorthand points in the act of writing them out in sentence form.

If we were to examine the 'skeleton' of the article in paragraph form it would now look like this:

1 Introductory paragraph: defining the terms in the title.

– Term 'women' covers wide range – cradle to grave. Women have different needs at different stages.
– Position better than 100 or 200 years ago – but greater expectations now. N.B. effect of universal education.
– What do we understand by 'liberation'? From being dominated by men? From subservient role? From bearing many children? From role limited to that of housewife and mother?
– Summary: need to examine various contexts in which women function: education, work, finance, social life, family.

2 First developmental paragraph: women and education

– How equal opportunities at school? Are girls 'pushed' into particular career roles via home economics, commercial studies?
– What proportions go on to A-levels?
– Do boys dominate classes and attention of teachers?
– Go on to look at women and professions – how many women doctors, engineers, barristers, etc.?

3 Second developmental paragraph: women and work

– Have equal opportunities laws made a difference? N.B. more awareness of sexual harassment at work etc.
– What sort of jobs done by women? Any truth in view that women make poor managers – too emotional etc.?

– How women cope with young children but economic need to work? N.B. need for more crêches.

– Do men consciously keep women in secondary roles at work?

– Can problem of women as mothers and as full-time career women ever be resolved? Do they lose out in one or other role?

4   Third developmental paragraph: women and finance

– How far are women discriminated against in financial transactions?

– Situation now improving but still more difficult for single woman to get mortgage or business loan from bank etc.

– In some marriages men don't tell wives what they earn.

– But on other hand in others wives do all financial budgeting, purchasing, saving, etc.

– Situation changing fast – plastic credit cards giving more financial freedom to women.

5   Fourth developmental paragraph: women and society

– Large strides made in past 200 years. N.B. wife used to have to give all property to husband on marriage.

– Divorce laws now more equally based – if anything men discriminated against more!

– But still not full liberation – women still unhappy to enter some pubs/bars on own – still liable to unwelcome advances – breweries changing image and clientèle changing – N.B. cocktail bars for young.

– Violence to person of women on increase: wife-battering, assault/rape, etc. Result of poor education/housing/employment or continual attitude of society?

– Women do have more rights in current society but still some way to go to 'full and equal partnership'.

6   Closing paragraph

– Problem of providing precise equality for two very different members of 'homo sapiens'.

– Historically men organized society. Perhaps women wrong in seeking to match men in all things?

– But men complacent about feelings of frustration in women – need to provide more encouragement and opportunity – but not easy in time of recession

– Need for fundamental shift in attitude of society towards nature of marriage and rearing of offspring if women are to engage fully in full-time careers.

– But should they need to? want to?

– Should role of mother/housewife be accorded more respect and status?

– No, in many ways women not yet liberated in sense of having entirely equal access to men's status, opportunities, rewards, etc. But process is evolutionary and much progress has been made.

– Women should maintain their efforts! Society is benefiting from their drive towards more equality, and men becoming less indifferent to women's professional/social needs.

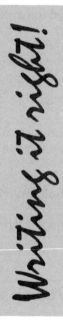

From me to one to you!

A particularly irritating misuse of the person – first, second or third – occurs when a writer forgets which person he is using within a single construction:

Examples:

The older *one* gets, the more *you* value the comforts of home.

Here, the writer uses both 'one' and 'you' in a single sentence which requires the consistency of using the same pronoun for both parts of the construction:

the older *one* gets ... the more *one* values ...
or, the older *you* get ... the more *you* value ...

Similar mistakes can occur in using the first person 'I/me' and 'we/us' in single constructions:

I am pleased to advise you that *we* are able to supply the following information ...

In letters, it is better practice to stick right through to 'I' if you have the authority to write on behalf of an organization. Using 'we' can often appear pompous, especially if 'I' has been used elsewhere within a paragraph.

Summary

In order, then, to devise an appropriate and effective structure for an extended piece of writing, the following steps should be taken:

- Consider the nature of the piece of writing envisaged and whether one of the following approaches would be effective:
  – A historical or chronological approach.
  – An approach of marshalling pro/con arguments.
  – An approach geographical in its treatment.
  – An approach dealing with systems or beliefs.
  – A logical or expositional approach proceeding in steps from A to Z as it were.
  – An imaginative approach.
  – An approach moving from major to minor causes or reasons (i.e. problem-solving in a report).

- Use the 'free flow of ideas' approach on a piece of rough note-paper to ensure that enough ideas and responses to the topic in hand are jotted down.
- Use the right-hand side of the note-paper to add additional and secondary ideas to the jotted points and to organize them into a sequence of paragraphs or sections.
- If necessary produce a skeleton form of the essay, report or article by breaking down each paragraph or section into its component points.
- Elaborate upon the 'free-flow plan' or skeleton draft in the act of writing out the piece in full.

Remember that writers sometimes produce several drafts of an important piece of writing before they consider it to be in its final (most effective) form.

HINT!

It's worth taking the trouble!

You may think that going to so much trouble to achieve an appropriate and effective structure in a piece of writing is 'over the top' or indeed *too* much trouble. The truth is, however, quite the opposite. Remember that, as readers, we are very much accustomed to seeing only the end-product – the finished piece as it appears in our daily newspaper, weekly magazine or paperback novel. What we don't see are the first or rough versions which end up in the waste-paper basket! Very seldom, if indeed ever, does a piece of writing suffer from too much care being taken in arriving at a pleasing and satisfying structure from either the reader's or the writer's standpoint.

Structuring paragraphs

Just as entire articles and essays structures with beginnings, middles and ends, so paragraphs are devised with particular sequences in which their points are made. The following diagram illustrates what points need to be given a structure within the paragraph:

```
        CLUSTER POINTS
         ↘   ↓   ↙
    → KEY POINT ←
         ↗   ↑   ↖
    CLUSTER POINTS
```

And the following section describes three ways of constructing paragraphs.

Three ways of constructing paragraphs

In order to construct effective paragraphs, the first point to keep in mind is that, long or short, each effectively written paragraph will contain a single *key point*. This key point (sometimes referred to as a topic point) conveys the main or most central point of the whole paragraph. It is the pivot around which the whole paragraph revolves. Indeed the other points in the paragraph provide material of a secondary nature which serves to expand upon or to reinforce the information conveyed in the key point.

As you can imagine, the position in which the key point occurs within any paragraph will have a distinct effect upon the way in which the reader absorbs its information. If, say, the key point is saved up until the end of the paragraph, then there will be a sense of suspense or of keeping the reader guessing until the main point of information is released and revealed. If it comes on the other hand right at the beginning, it will have a big initial impact on the reader, but the rest of the paragraph's detail may tend to be glossed over.

The following diagrams illustrate how key points may be situated within a paragraph:

- *The loose paragraph.* Nothing to do with morals, the term 'loose' merely signifies that the key point comes first and that the rest of the paragraph's points are loosely structured after it as in Figure 3 overleaf.
- *The mixed paragraph.* Here the main or key point occurs somewhere in the middle of the paragraph and there is therefore a tendency for interest to mount up and then to decrease before and after the main point (see Figure 4 overleaf).

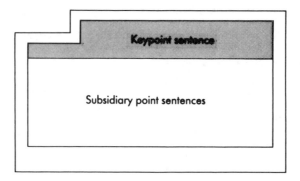

Figure 3   The loose paragraph

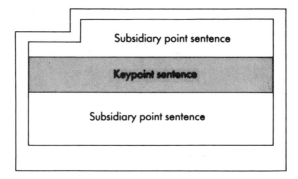

Figure 4   The mixed paragraph.

- *The periodic paragraph.* In this paragraph the key point is saved up until last. By this means a sense of accumulating tension, excitement or suspense may be created by an author who obliges his reader to wade through all the minor or subordinate points to arrive at the all-important key point at the end (see Figure 5).

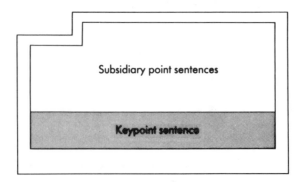

Figure 5   The periodic paragraph.

Perhaps the best way of evaluating this approach to paragraph construction is to examine each of the three paragraph constructions at work.

- *Paragraph 1*
His fingers felt numb and yet his arms ached agonizingly. On the floor in front of his knees dark speckles of his blood coloured the dull grey of the stone floor. Every now and then another dark drop of blood fell from the rivulets which ran from his fingers down the backs of his hands to his elbows and from them on to the floor. He neither noticed nor heeded them. His back glistened with sweat-drops and in his neck the dull ache continued with every chip and scrape his hands made against the unyielding granite of his cell wall. Time passed. He took no rest, save in the steady and ceaseless rhythm of his movements within the hole he had created in the wall of his cell. Indeed, he seemed like a machine whose only function was to dig. Suddenly, his movements ceased. His nostrils had scented fresh air, like a whiff of perfume in his stinking kennel. His head disappeared into the fissure of his own making. There was no doubt. He had penetrated the wall and had found the ventilation shaft that only he had believed in!

- *Paragraph 2*
Idly Kate sifted through the trivia which cluttered her dressing-table. In one corner she found a bottle of toilet water which had made a stained ring upon the envelope of a letter upon which it stood. Carelessly she picked up the letter and screwed the bottle-top more firmly upon her favourite perfume. She recognized the handwriting upon the letter's envelope. It belonged to Charles. At once the letter's contents flooded back into her memory as if insisting upon another appeal, this time in the quietness of her own bedroom and six weeks after Roger's departure for India. Without needing to open the letter, Kate recalled all the loops and curls of Charles' bold and extrovert handwriting. In her mind's eye she re-read his impassioned plea for her to forgive him and to accept his hand in marriage. Perhaps, Kate thought, she had been too hasty in believing Roger's version of the game of cards when she had been won and lost in jest by a group of drunken noblemen, including Charles. At once she made up her mind – she would marry Sir Charles de Livesy. Moreover, the wedding would take place while Roger was out in India! This being settled firmly in her mind, Kate carried on tidying her dressing table. The dust from her face-powder she blew carelessly on to the floor. Her necklaces and rings she scraped up into her jewel-box quite unmindful of their value. She picked up carefully, however, the various patches and imitation black birthmarks with which it was fashionable to adorn a lady's face and in so doing to conceal the scars of the pox. From downstairs came the voice of her maid, Lucy, indicating that a visitor had arrived.

- *Paragraph 3*
She was free! Among the first to emerge from the courtroom, Caroline skipped heedlessly along the corridor and down the stairs into the fresh air of her new world and new beginning. The long months of the divorce proceedings were over at last. No more would she have to endure Clive's endless bouts of drinking and his bullying of both her and the children. No more would she be obliged to argue over personal effects, furniture, photographs and all the other memorabilia of the past ten years! Nor would she need to make those emotional visits to her solicitor. Her elation took her straight in to the King's Head public house across the road, where she ordered her first drink as a divorcee (decree nisi) to celebrate.

Which of the above three examples are which? Can you identify the loose, the mixed and the periodic paragraph from the position of the key point? In case of need, the answers appear at the foot of the page.*

In terms of the impact upon the reader, each paragraph may be seen in the structures expressed in the graphs in Figure 6.

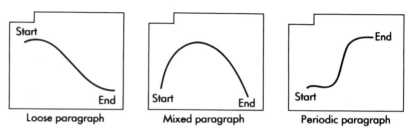

Figure 6   Impact on reader factor.

This being the case, then, there are locations within an article, essay, letter or novel chapter, etc. when each of the three types of paragraph may be used with particular effect. For example, the loose paragraph may be used effectively as the opening paragraph of a piece of writing since its very first sentence is a crucial or key one and should therefore act immediately as an attention getter:

Of the eight hundred and forty-two Allied prisoners of war force-marched to the prisoner-of-war camp only ninety-six were still alive as they were escorted through its main gates.

Such an opening sentence to both a paragraph as well as to a novel or short story is more than likely to arouse the reader's interest and to make him or her want to discover more about the fate of those still alive.

By the same token, a key point in the final paragraph of an extended piece of writing should, like the resounding final bars of a classical symphony leave the reader with a satisfying sense of fullness and completion:

All the hurt and suffering of the past months fell away from her like waves washing off an unyielding rock. She was in his arms again, feeling the warmth of his strong body and his stubbled beard against her cheek. She was home!

In terms of creating variety and effect of a different sort, the mixed paragraph construction also offers many possibilities. For example, in the mixed paragraph illustrated above, the all-important matter of deciding whom to marry is, as far as Kate is concerned, sandwiched between sorting out toilet water and make-up. By creating such a contrast, the author conveys something about Kate's superficial personality and also imparts a sense of irony which, in terms of the paragraph's location in a novel or short story may well be important to both characterization and plot.

One last point to bear in mind when employing such paragraph constructions is that the overall length of the paragraph is most important. Like the short sentence, the short paragraph will have increased impact. Remember also that it is difficult to sustain suspense etc. over too long in a periodic

* Paragraph 1: periodic; paragraph 2: mixed; paragraph 3: loose.

paragraph and that a loose paragraph which goes on for too long will tend to be skipped over by the reader once the main point has been taken in.

Structuring sentences

In Part One we examined the structure of sentences in terms of their grammar and syntax. A brief reminder will help to focus upon this aspect of sentence structure.

- *Definition:* A sentence contains at least one subject and one agreeing finite verb.

- *Sentence types:*
  Simple: Contains a single subject and a single finite verb.
  Compound:
  Double: Contains two co-equal main clauses possessing a subject and a finite verb in each.
  Multiple: Contains three or more co-equal (co-ordinating) main clauses.
  Complex: Contains one or more main clauses governing one or more dependent (subordinate clauses).

  A Phrase: A group of words without a finite verb.
  A Clause: A group of words with both a subject and a finite verb.

- *Examples:*
  Simple sentences:
  – Night fell.
  – She awoke slowly.
  – The manager read the report with a frown of concentration.
  Compound double sentences:
  – She collected the eggs and then packed them in plastic boxes.
  – He took a mixed salad but deliberately left the fried potatoes.
    (N.B. He is understood in the second clause).
  Compound multiple sentences
  – I came, I saw, I conquered.
  – Jim and Sally arrived punctually and they were closely followed by Molly and Tom, but Dick and Carol arrived late, as usual!
  Complex sentences:
  – Jane arrived home late because she had missed the train.
  – Although every precaution had been taken the robbers escaped with the whole payroll.

As we have already discovered, the ability to construct grammatically acceptable sentences is an important skill in its own right. Now it is time to build upon this skill with others which shape and control the ways in which a sentence will have an effect upon the reader. There are two principal factors which act in this regard. One is the length and complexity of the individual words used, and the other is the resulting length and complexity of the sentence formed by them. Consider the following contrasting examples:

- *Example 1*
  He ripped his coat off the hook on the cabin door and tore after her into the cold of the Yukon night. Beneath his feet the ice glinted and he slipped several times without seeming to slow in his headlong pursuit. Once or twice he thought he saw her up ahead among the frozen tents on the edge

of Dawson. He stumbled into town, his breath rising like clouds of steam. From The Golden Nugget came the sound of bawling singing as if to mock his vain efforts. He slumped against the wooden sidewalk cursing angrily at her simple escape!

● *Example 2*
The marketing process commences with several dozen ideas which are evaluated carefully at the drawing-board stage and gradually reduced until a final embryonic product is created. The next phase is to develop in the research and development department a number of prototypes aimed at evaluating the product's capabilities and applications as well as finalizing design and appearance factors. During this process test marketing will have been undertaken to assess the acceptability of the product by the public and this may result in modifications being made to the prototype in the pre-production phase. Eventually the product will go into production to be launched in a fanfare of pre-planned advertising.

Given that the subject-matter of the two examples is quite different and that the second example employs a specialist vocabulary, it is nevertheless interesting to compare their respective word and sentence structures.

	Example 1	*Example 2*
Number of words	100	109
Number of sentences	6	4
Average number of words per sentence	16.66	27.5
Number of syllables in first 100 words	131	184
Total number of syllables	131	201

When paragraphs are analysed in this way it quickly becomes clear why one should be that much more easily absorbed and comprehended than another. Moreover, the factor referred to above of whether the vocabulary employed is of a general or specialist nature is of additional significance when considering the reading difficulty produced in a given set of words and sentences.

Professor Fry in the late 1960s produced the graph in Figure 7 for estimating readability in any piece of writing.

Directions: Randomly select three 100-word passages from a book or an article. Plot average number of syllables and average number of sentences per 100 words on graph to determine the grade level of the material. Choose more passages per book if great variability is observed and conclude that the book has uneven readability. Few books will fall in grey area but when they do grade level scores are invalid.

Example:		*Syllables*	*Sentences*
	1st 100 words	124	6.6
	2nd 100 words	141	5.5
	3rd 100 words	158	6.8
	Average	141	6.3

Readability: 12.8 years (see dot plotted on graph)

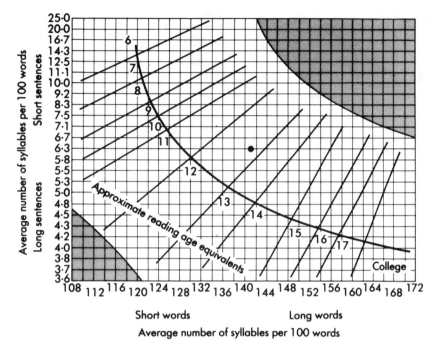

Figure 7   Professor Fry's graph for estimating readability.

For further information and validity data see the April 1968 *Journal of Reading* and the March 1969 *Reading Teacher*.

Additional directions for working readability graph

1   Randomly select three sample passages and count out exactly 100 words beginning with a beginning of a sentence. Don't count numbers. Do count proper nouns.
2   Count the number of sentences in the 100 words estimating length of the fraction of the last sentence to the nearest tenth.
3   Count the total number of syllables in the 100-word passage. If you don't have a hand counter available, an easy way is to simply put a mark above every syllable over one in each word, then when you get to the end of the passage, count the number of marks and add 100.
4   Enter graph with average sentence length and number of syllables; plot dot where the two lines intersect. Area where dot is plotted will give you the approximate Reading Age.
5   If a great deal of variability is found, putting more sample counts into the average is desirable.

By employing the test of the Readability Graph, we can establish that the first paragraph about the Yukon would require a reader to have a reading age of approximately 11–12 years, while the second paragraph about product research would require a reading age of about 18-plus and an attainment level of college standard. While such readability tests may not be a hundred per cent precise, they do provide a very useful rule of thumb about the comprehension demands being placed upon a reader. In this context, recent research in the United States indicates that sentences of more than

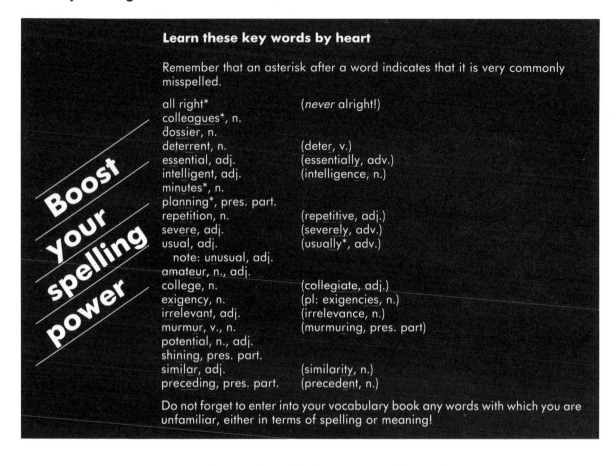

Learn these key words by heart

Remember that an asterisk after a word indicates that it is very commonly misspelled.

Boost your spelling power

all right*	(*never* alright!)
colleagues*, n.	
dossier, n.	
deterrent, n.	(deter, v.)
essential, adj.	(essentially, adv.)
intelligent, adj.	(intelligence, n.)
minutes*, n.	
planning*, pres. part.	
repetition, n.	(repetitive, adj.)
severe, adj.	(severely, adv.)
usual, adj.	(usually*, adv.)
note: unusual, adj.	
amateur, n., adj.	
college, n.	(collegiate, adj.)
exigency, n.	(pl: exigencies, n.)
irrelevant, adj.	(irrelevance, n.)
murmur, v., n.	(murmuring, pres. part)
potential, n., adj.	
shining, pres. part.	
similar, adj.	(similarity, n.)
preceding, pres. part.	(precedent, n.)

Do not forget to enter into your vocabulary book any words with which you are unfamiliar, either in terms of spelling or meaning!

twenty-five words are likely to cause problems of comprehension among an average readership. Again, this view should be treated with caution because much longer well-punctuated sentences may still remain crystal clear. However the following guidelines do emerge:

HINT!

Guidelines in constructing sentences

- Follow the maxim of the Fowler brothers and use the short word in preference to the long one, and the word of Saxon origin rather than the Latin.*
- Beware of constructing sentences which (especially if containing subordinate clauses) sail on into thirty or forty words apiece.
- Always be ready to stop and start again. In other words to construct shorter rather than longer sentences.
- Check that your punctuation is providing a help to readability rather than a hindrance.

* Anyone who wishes to become a good writer should endeavour, before he allows himself to be tempted by the more showy qualities, to be direct, simple, brief, vigorous and lucid.

This general principle may be translated into practical rules in the domain of vocabulary as follows:

- Prefer the familiar word to the far-fetched.
- Prefer the concrete word to the abstract.

- Prefer the single word to the circumlocution.
- Prefer the short word to the long.
- Prefer the Saxon word to the Romance. [Romance standing for the European languages closely derived from the Latin.] (H. W. and F. G. Fowler, *The King's English*, Oxford Paperbacks).

Useful sentence starters

In Part One some attention was given to words which start clauses and the following list (to which you can add other words or phrases you meet) will provide you with some alternative ways of starting sentences. The list is divided into two halves, those starters which reinforce or add to what has been written in the previous sentence, and those starters which introduce a contrasting or modifying statement:

- Reinforcers

  Moreover,
  Furthermore,
  Indeed,
  This being the case,
  In addition,
  If further evidence were needed . . .
  Certainly,

- Contrasters

  However,
  On the other hand,
  Even so,
  Notwithstanding,
  Nevertheless,
  Yet
  Granted that . . . . nevertheless.

- Moving on to the next stage

  Having . . .
  After having . . .
  Once the . . . has been . . .
  Next,
  Turning to . . .
  Now . . .

- Useful pairs in sentence constructions

  Not only . . . but also . . .
  Both . . . and . . .
  Either . . . or . . .
  Neither . . . nor . . .
  The more . . . the more . . .

- Starting the sentence with a subordinate/dependent clause
  Remember that to create suspense and to keep the reader waiting for the information in the main clause, it is often useful to start the sentence with the subordinating conjunction:

Although,
Though
If,
Whether,
Because
In order that . . .
So that . . .
Since,
When . . .
After,
etc.

- Phrases for openers

In the event,
As it turned out,
Despite the difficulties,
Even allowing for . . .
No matter what . . .
In short,
To summarize,
First to consider is . . .
A careful analysis of the facts reveals . . .

- A caution about clichés!
What makes any sentence opener boring and irritating is that it has become a tired cliché – a phrase so commonly used as to have lost all its original zip and impact. Here are some to avoid:

With reference to . . .
With regard to . . .
In connection with . . .
As a result of . . .
In response to . . .
I acknowledge your . . . of . . .
In confirmation of . . .
By and large . . .
This being the case . . .
All things being considered . . .
At this point in time . . .

All writers get stuck for a beginning sometimes, but you should try to write freshly at the outset of your sentences to catch and keep your reader's interest:

– Your complaint in your letter of . . . has caused me great concern and I have spent much time in our factory finding out what went wrong.
– I can reassure you that your urgent order of . . . is being processed and will reach you by . . .

Assignments

1 In your own words explain what you think constructing an appropriate beginning, middle and end means in terms of the structure of a piece of writing.

2   Produce a 'free-flow of ideas' plan on the lines of the example shown on page 176 for *one* of the following topics to be composed as a magazine article:

a   There is no longer room for the amateur in sport.
b   Far from educating the masses, television is sending them to sleep nightly, from 6 p.m. until bedtime!
c   Good neighbours.
d   I could solve the unemployment problem but they won't give me the chance!

3   Write down against each of the following a brief explanation of what sort of structure they stand for in a piece of extended writing:

chronological   argumentative   expositional   imaginative

4   As a follow-up to the rough plan you drew up in assignment 2, take it a stage further by producing it as a series of skeleton paragraphs. Refer to the example on pages 178–79 to refresh your mind.
5   And now – you've guessed it! – write out the full version of the article you have been planning in assignments 2 and 4 in about 750 words.
6   What do you understand by the terms loose, mixed and periodic with regard to structuring paragraphs? Write down a brief explanation for each using a diagram if you wish.
7   Construct three short paragraphs in which the key point in each occurs where it should according to whether the paragraph is loose, mixed or periodic. If you are stuck for ideas, here are a few to write a paragraph upon:

falling asleep   getting arrested   winning the prize   feeling ashamed losing your wage-packet

Make sure you compose an example of a loose, mixed and a periodic paragraph and not just three of the same type!
8   Using the graph for estimating readability on page 187 work out the approximate reading ages for each of the paragraphs you constructed in assignment 7.
9   Imagine that your boss has just been taken into hospital with appendicitis and is now recovering from his or her operation. Compose an appropriate letter aimed at cheering him or her up.
10   Assume that you have been asked at work to produce a list of guidelines to help junior office staff in composing messages, memoranda, letters and so on. Produce that part of your list which refers to structuring a piece of writing, listing 7–10 helpful main points in sentence form.

Chapter 31
Choosing the right words

So far in our study of style we have concentrated upon the aims of a piece of writing and approaches to structuring it. It is now time to examine in some detail the effects upon the creation of a particular style of the individual words and phrases chosen.

A number of different factors influence the overall impact of words and phrases in any given piece of writing:

- How long the word/phrase has been in use.
- Its usual tone or register – formal or slang, official or familiar, etc.
- The extent or limitation of the meaning – or meanings – given to it.
- The context or situation it is being used in within the piece of writing.
- The degree of familiarity it enjoys – whether it is in common, everyday use or whether it is a specialist word known only to some people.
- The level of difficulty it has in being understood.
- Whether its effect is mainly upon the reader's emotions or his reason, or on a little of each.

Two basic categories of words

With the above factors in mind, it is helpful to divide words into two basic and contrasting categories. Though the titles may seem daunting, the differences are readily understood:

- **Connotative:** Words which we may label connotative have generally been in the English language a long time (or are new slang rich in meaning) and may be said to possess many layers or shades of meaning.
- **Denotative**: Words which are called denotative generally have a precise and single meaning which is universally accepted. Such words tend to be devoid of emotional appeal.

There are other, additional ways in which we may define the two types of vocabulary:

Connotative words
- Subjective in their impact. That is they have their effect on the heart rather than mind.

Denotative words
- Objective in their impact and affect the reader's logical and rational thought processes.

- Have a tendency to stem from the Saxon and Norse roots of English.

- Commonly found in poetry, expressive writing in novels, advertising copy propaganda, copies of political speeches and so on.

- Tend to be short: single or double syllabled

- Tend to derive from the the Latin and Greek roots of English.

- Usually found in factual kinds of writing like scientific reports, sets of instructions, textbooks on subjects like medicine or chemistry or in serious reporting in some newspaper articles, etc.

- Tend to be long and multi-syllabled

Some examples of connotative and denotative words

Perhaps the most useful way of explaining the two categories is to set down some typical examples:

Connotative counterparts	Denotative words
on the dole	unemployed
revenge	retaliation
home	residence
choke, stifle	asphyxiate
live with	cohabit
land	acreage
a rip-off	excessively priced
attacker, mugger	assailant
lingerie	underwear
helpmate	ancillary worker
wrong	erroneous
lying	mendacious
bastard	illegitmate

Examples of connotative words at work:

The curfew tolls the knell of parting day,
　　The lowing herd wind slowly o'er the lea,
The ploughman homeward plods his weary way,
　　And leaves the world to darkness and to me.
　　　　　　　　　　　　　　(Thomas Gray)

This opening stanza of Thomas Gray's 'Elegy in a Country Churchyard' perfectly captures the quiet stillness of a country evening with night falling. Given that the word 'curfew' was more widely used in the eighteenth century to mean the bell ringing a 'closing down' of the day, and that to 'toll the knell' means to ring a bell dolefully on someone's death, then even today we can appreciate the beauty of the visual and sound picture which Gray paints in words which are almost all connotative and rich in the meanings they conjure up from our memories. Most of us have seen a herd of cows slowly 'winding' or ambling towards the farmyard at tea-time – sometimes bellowing in impatience to be milked. Similarly, we can conjure up the picture, long before the days of farm mechanization, of the ploughman leading the plough-horse on his solitary way back to the farm and village. As the cows and the ploughman disappear, we can imagine Gray alone and motionless in the churchyard watching the skies darken as night falls. And indeed, as anticipated in the above checklist, virtually all of Gray's vocabulary is Saxon rather than Latinate.

Another example, this time from our century, is taken from a speech of Sir Winston Churchill's during the dark days of World War II, when the German army was expected to invade the south coast of England at any moment:

We shall go on to the end, we shall fight in France, we shall fight on the seas and oceans, we shall fight with growing confidence and growing strength in the air, we shall defend our island, whatever the cost may be, we shall fight on the beaches, we shall fight on the landing grounds, we shall fight in the fields and in the streets, we shall fight in the hills; we shall never surrender. (Sir Winston Churchill, 4 June 1940)

In this magnificent rallying cry to a people nervously expecting to be overwhelmed, Churchill displays his mastery of expressing his message in what is virtually poetic language masquerading as prose! Consider for example his key words:

We shall   fight   seas   oceans   growing confidence   strength
air   defend   island   cost   beaches   landing grounds   fields   streets
hills   never surrender

Again the origins of almost all the words are Saxon/Norse and the words themselves are predominantly single syllabled. The repetition of the refrain 'we shall fight' serves to give the passage a solemn rhythm and the effect of the punctuation to slow down the pace reflects the grave situation in which Churchill spoke to the British people. In effect, Churchill in his most careful use of the English language chose those words which were calculated to pluck at the nation's heart-strings and to encourage the blood to rise in the act of summoning up the resolve to fight it out with the Nazis to the death so as to save the homeland.

In total contrast to the above two illustrations, here are two examples in which the aims are quite different and therefore the words selected denotative, rather than connotative:

Broken bones

Keep the patient warm and immobile and treat for shock if necessary. Apply a cold compress to the painful area and support it as comfortably as possible. If a broken bone protrudes through the skin and there is severe bleeding, stop the bleeding, but do not attempt to push the bone back in place. Make no attempt to clean the wound. Call an ambulance, or get the patient to a doctor.

If it is essential to move the victim to prevent further injury, immobilize the affected limb with splints to prevent further damage. For emergency splints, use anything that will keep the broken bones from moving – newspapers or magazines or broomsticks or boards for arms or legs. Make sure the splints are long enough to reach beyond the joint both above and below the break. Apply them over the clothing, pad them with cotton wool or clean rags and tie them snugly, not too tightly, in place.

When an accident victim must be moved from a car, immobilize a fractured leg first, if possible. Using bandages, belts, ties, or strips of

Learn these key words by heart

Remember that an asterisk after a word indicates that it is very commonly misspelled.

Antarctic proper n.
anxiety, n.   (anxious, adj.)
corroborate, v.   (corroboration, n.)
convenience, n.   (convenient, adj.)
consistent, adj.
connoisseur, n.
perseverence, n.   (to persevere, v.)
pleasant, adj.
preliminary, adj.
prestige, n.   (prestigious, adj.)
professor, n.
pronounce, v.   (pronunciation, n.)
synonym, n.   (synonymous, adj.)
sonic, adj.
statutory, adj.   (statute, n.)
proprietory, adj.
courteous, adj.   (courtesy, n.)
criticize, v.   (criticism, n.)
cursory, adj.
apparent, adj.
appropriate, adj.
Arctic, proper n.
argument, n.   (to argue, v.)
ascend, v.   (ascent, n.)
athletic, adj.   (athlete, n.)
audio, adj.
automation, n.   (automatic, adj.)
awful, adj.   (awe, n.)
coming*, n., pres. part.   (to come, v.)
compatible, adj.

Do not forget to enter into your vocabulary book any words with which you are unfamiliar, either in terms of spelling or meaning!

Boost your spelling power

clothing, tie the injured leg to the uninjured leg above and below the fracture site and immobilize it as much as possible with an improvised short splint. (*Reader's Digest Handbook of First Aid*)

Notice the use of the specialist vocabulary needed:

immobile   protrudes   severe   affected   fractured   injured
improvised

and that this vocabulary is Latinate in its origin and tends to provide a single and precise meaning devoid of emotional overtones. But notice also that a significant amount of the vocabulary is simple and mostly monosyllabic:

keep warm treat shock cold push back clean wound
move limbs boards pad rags belts ties etc.

Remember that in a manual of first aid, the writer will want to communicate with readers spanning a wide reading age and will therefore want to
express his instructions as simply as possible, bearing in mind the need from
time to time to include specialist vocabulary such as 'sterile' and 'antiseptic'.

Assembly instructions

Remove all parts from the carton and check that they are complete and
undamaged. Parts consist of: fire-bowl, frame leg assembly, perforated steel
grate, cooking grill, windshield, spit, forks, motor.

NB. Any shortages etc. *must* be reported within 14 days of purchase.

1 Lay fire-bowl, bottom side up, on non-marking surface and assemble
   four straight leg rods into frame. Insert leg assembly into brackets on
   fire-bowl. Stand unit upright.
2 Windshield simply clips onto rear tongue(s) of fire-bowl first, then press
   into front left and right clips. If clips are initially too tight, slightly pry
   open to facilitate later removal for storage etc.
3 Lay charcoal grate in fire-bowl.
4 Grill fits windshield to give four working heights.
5 Rotisserie fits windshield slots.

Notice that the writer here is seeking to provide a clear and logically
sequenced set of instructions. The instructions are expressed either by using
the imperative of the verb: remove, check, lay, assemble, etc. or the present
tense: consist, clips, fits, etc. In each case the sentence structures are kept
short. Again the vocabulary is denotative in its effect upon the reader:

remove parts complete undamaged consist of frame leg
assembly non-marking surface to facilitate later removal see lighting
instructions overleaf etc.

The intention is to provide as straightforward and unambiguous a set of
assembly instructions as possible to a distant third party who cannot ask
questions directly if baffled. Also notice that the tone is impersonal and
factual without being cold or remote. The context calls for such a factual
tone. Notice too, that the vocabulary has been selected to provide a single
and specific meaning:

- The verbs: remove check lay assemble insert stand clip
              press fit etc.
- The nouns: parts carton firebowl assembly grate grill
              windshield spit forks motor brackets etc.

Lastly it is interesting in the context of our studies on structure and style to
note how short the sentences are to aid comprehension, and that as one
might expect, the instructions are set down in a numbered sequence.

As a further insight into how different kinds of writing require different
types of vocabulary, consider the following checklists taken from very
different working situations:

- The world of advertising

  new instant whiter fresh simply mild soft tangy improved sparkle gleam mature strong sharp fast-acting bigger more extra real totally great prefer silky dreamy fast resistant take home family younger lovelier

- The world of the law courts

  allege apparently circumstantial corroborate inadmissible defendant plea mitigation evidence statement proof witness factual contradictory claims summary verdict acquittal re-trial exhibit objection submission

- The world of finance

  account debtor creditor overdue double-entry auditor statement invoice assets liabilities bankrupt cash-flow days of credit banker's draft withdrawal facilities depreciation stock plant fixed costs

- The world of the theatre

  first-night dress rehearsal follow-spot downstage backdrop 'break a leg!' (meaning 'good luck') to fold (meaning a show flops soon after its first night) understudy to dry (meaning to forget one's lines) angel (one who provides financial backing for a show) set in-the-round one-night-stand (single evening production usually as part of a tour)

As each of these contrasting checklists indicates, there are many different kinds of vocabulary which are in particular use within a given world or environment. The world of advertising seeks to win our hearts over with emotive words, the world of the law courts seeks to be precise and devoid of emotions, the world of finance employs precise language which is highly specialized, while the world of the theatre, which employs the spoken word a great deal contains much colloquial vocabulary which is a specialist vocabulary of a different sort and tends to be picturesque and expressive.

The following checklist provides you with some helpful guidelines on what to adopt and what to avoid when selecting a particular vocabulary for a piece of writing. However, the best piece of advice at this stage is to collect different words and expressions within the various contexts or worlds of advertising, finance, law, theatre, sport, etc. as avidly as the collector of stamps or autographs! Why? Simply because *your* access to various words of which one may be absolutely ideal for your purpose depends entirely upon those at your disposal in *your* brain's word-bank! (Although the English language thesaurus is on hand to help.) But only *you* can develop a feeling for how words are used and how readers will react to them. So keep that vocabulary notebook handy, and develop good reading habits – the quality daily and Sunday newspaper, the library book always in process of being read, the trade magazine in your own field and so on!

HINT!

Do's and don'ts of effective choice of words

Do aim for	Do avoid
●Simple, clear and direct writing	● Obscure, complex and jargon words

- Brief, short and straightforward vocabulary
- Vocabulary appropriate to the situation:
  helpful   polite
  sincere   solicitous
  clarifying etc.

- Longwinded, rambling expressions and constructions
- Vocabulary which is pompous over-familiar, cold and unfriendly, officious remote, according to the situation

- Words or expressions which are: fresh   natural   honest

- Using words or expressions which are: stable   clichéd   hypocritical consisting of stock responses

This approach will make your writing easily read, accepted and acted upon as you would wish.

This approach will alienate your reader or obstruct the communication of your message and lead to delay, inaction or indifference.

Keep a constant check that your vocabulary:

- is conveying the precise meaning you wish;
- is pitched at the appropriate level, for your readership. i.e. not obscure but not over-simple;
- is not a collection of stale clichés devoid of real meaning; and
- is not unconsciously curt, rude, condescending, sarcastic, impatient, etc.

Assignments

1   Write down a checklist of the characteristics of words which will affect their reader – for example, whether they are slang or not.
2   Write down a brief explanation of these two descriptions of the meaning of certain words:

a   connotative
b   denotative

3   What do we mean when we say a piece of writing is objectively written?
4   In what types of writing would you expect to meet:

a   a connotative vocabulary?
b   a denotative vocabulary?

Make a checklist of the types of writing for *a* and *b*.
5   Imagine you are working in the training department of a large organization. You have been given the task of writing the page in a staff training manual for new staff on guidelines for selecting an effective vocabulary in a given piece of writing. Compose about 200–300 words in a layout of your own choosing which you think would be appropriate to your briefing.
6   What criticisms can you make of the vocabulary and arising tone of the following extracts?

a   I have to inform you that your enquiry will be dealt with in due course.

b   I must apologise for the delay in your receiving your vehicle after service.
    As you will readily appreciate, motor-vehicle wheels need to be balanced dynamically as well as statically to avoid the transmission of vibration through the steering linkage.
    Moreover, the diagnosis of mis-alignment in the nearside front wheel revealed that feathering and premature wear had been caused to the tyre, which as you realise, being asymmetrical in tread design is incompatible with tyres of another make.
    I trust this explanation will satisfactorily account for the delay.

c   The reason I am writing to you on a plain piece of notepaper is because of the incompetence of your firm in supplying my order for company stationery, which you may just recall you received last December.

d   'Mr Johnson said to tell you we seem to have dropped a bit of a clanger over the grinding machine. The drive belt's come adrift and we're up the creek for a spare. He says we're due for a drop next Monday and he'll give you a tinkle, OK?'

e   It has come to my attention that departmental staff are in breach of their conditions of service as a result of unpunctuality.
    Unless a substantial improvement is discerned in the immediate future, disciplinary measures will be taken.

f   'Thank you for your enquiry, but my company only deals in genuine antiques.'

g   Our current inability to meet the requirements of your recently remitted order is occasioned by an unanticipated shortage of the spare parts specified.

h   Due to circumstances beyond our control, there has been a temporary delay in effecting repairs to your lawn-mower, which we hope to rectify as soon as the situation eases.
    Assuring you of our best attention at all times.

i   Further to your memorandum of 14 June 19—.
    Of course, in normal circumstances my department would be only too pleased to be of assistance with the provision of advertising material for your display on 21st August.
    Regretfully, however, only reference copies of such material are kept centrally. You may care to try Sales.
    Do let me know if I may be of any assistance in any other sphere.

j   Recommendations
    Any future improvement in company turnover is entirely dependent upon either lowering or raising the price or the quality of our current product range.
    If the latter option is adopted, the prospect of increased competition or a reduction in gross profits must be faced.
    In such a clear-cut situation, the action needed to resolve the problem is self-explanatory.

k Much as I sympathize with your predicament, I do feel that, I am not in a position to grant you further leave of absence to nurse your sick parent. I am sure you will see the difficult position in which I feel myself to be placed in that I do not consider myself to be entirely unfeeling in such matters, having experienced a similar situation myself. Perhaps if you call in to see me a solution will readily suggest itself, which will prove acceptable to you yourself.
(D. W. Evans, *People and Communication*, Pitman)

7   Choose one of the following situations and compose a suitable leaflet to advertise the event. Take particular care in selecting what you think are the best words for the context:

a   A forthcoming fête your church or club is mounting.
b   The opportunity for company staff to learn an EEC foreign language one evening a week with all fees paid for by your firm.
c   A residential week-end your school or college is mounting to encourage a variety of sports such as: rock-climbing, canoeing, horse-riding, orienteering, etc. to be held in Snowdonia.

Chapter 32
Style and context

Already in our study of style it has been necessary on numerous occasions to refer to the 'context or situation' in which a piece of writing is being composed.

Indeed, the importance of meeting the needs of context in achieving an effective style cannot be over-emphasized. We all recall the careful way in which we pick and choose our words when seeking to patch up a row we have had with someone close. Similarly, we are usually quite conscious of the words we choose and the tone of voice we adopt when asking a favour of someone.

In other words, we are constantly in the process of selecting certain words put into particular constructions – and if spoken – uttered in a special tone of voice to suit the circumstances in which they are to be used.

The following examples will serve to reinforce the point:

Examples of a style of writing to suit a particular context

The first example is that of a final letter to secure overdue payment before taking legal action:

LETTER

Dear Sir,

OVERDUE ACCOUNT: £1492.43

In spite of the copy statement and reminders sent to you on 3 April 19—, 21 April 19— and 7 May 19—, your account for February 19— still remains outstanding; enclosed please find a final statement.

As previously stated, the period of credit extended to your company was agreed as one calendar month from receipt of statement.

Unless the above overdue account is settled in full within seven days, I shall be compelled to instruct my company's solicitors to undertake the necessary legal action to recover the debt.

Yours faithfully,

Notice here that, though not becoming rude or aggressive, the tone of the letter is deliberately terse and formal. The accounts manager has given up hope of securing payment of the debt while keeping the customer's good-will, and has settled for recovering the money and cancelling the customer's credit arrangement.

Notice the following constructions which help to create the tone:

In spite of . . . still remains outstanding; . . . the period of credit extended to your company . . . Unless the overdue account is settled in full within seven days . . . compelled to instruct . . . to undertake the necessary legal action to recover the debt.

The writer deliberately distances himself from the reader in such formal language and the terse 'either . . . or' construction of the final paragraph.

Compare the tone of this letter with the sort of letter the accounts manager is likely to send when the account first becomes overdue and only a polite reminder is felt appropriate:

LETTER

Dear Sir,

OVERDUE ACCOUNT: £1492.43

I should like to draw to your attention that the statement of account rendered to you at the end of March 19— for goods purchased in February 19— does not appear to have been paid according to our accounts records.

I should therefore be grateful if you would kindly confirm that the goods delivered (delivery notes XB 45367, XC65434 and XG54786) proved satisfactory and that there is no reason why you should be deferring payment.

Please advise me as soon as possible if you are experiencing any problem in this regard, otherwise I shall look forward to receiving your cheque for £1492.43, which is now overdue according to the credit arrangements between us.

Yours faithfully,

Contrastingly, the writer takes pains not to cause offence – the account may have been paid and an error occurred on the accounts computer, or payment may be being withheld because of a query which has not been communicated to the accounts department. Thus the tone and language employed are much more tentative. The accounts manager does not want to lose a good customer by upsetting him – certainly not at this stage:

I should like to draw your attention to . . .

Writing it right!

Alltogether or altogether or all together?

Let's dispense straight away with the first one. There is **no such word as** 'alltogether'!

However the other two versions do exist and mean something quite different:

– all together = everyone doing something at the same time
– altogether (one *l*!) = completely or totally

Examples:

– They jumped into the swimming pool all together.
– The damaged radio was altogether useless.

---

statement of account rendered does not appear to have been paid. . . . if you would kindly confirm . . . that there is no reason why you should be deferring payment. Please advise me . . . if you are experiencing any problems in this regard . . .

Notice that the constructions are much less terse and more politely structured and that words like kindly and please emphasize the writer's feeling of reluctantly having to remind the customer of the overdue account.

An example of a style of writing in quite a different context is found in this extract of a direct mail sales letter to house-owners seeking to sell them a full insulation service to double-glaze and insulate their homes:

LETTER

```
Dear Householder,

A SURE WAY YOU CAN SAVE MONEY THIS WINTER!

Will your bank-balance get blown away by an 'overdraught'
of cold air again this winter?

Our research has proved that up to 30 per cent of all money spent
on home heating virtually goes up in smoke each year!

The guilty culprits are ill-fitting, single-glazed windows
and doors, poor insulation in lofts and attics and exposed
cavity walls.

Can you afford to let yet another year go by with your
heating bills far larger than they need be? . . .
```

In this introductory part of the letter the tone is much more easy and friendly – the firm of insulators is trying to establish a rapport or bond with the prospective customer, who is thus addressed not as Dear Sir or Dear Madam, but as Dear Householder, which appears less formal. Notice the attention-getting subject-heading of the letter. Who of us doesn't wish to save money? Also, the opening sentence poses a direct question which reinforces this subject-heading in a cheery, cheeky way by the studied use of the pun of 'draught of cold air' and bank 'overdraft'.

This friendly approach continues in the second paragraph with the deliberate use of the colloquialism 'goes up in smoke'. The use of persuasive language is also evident in the third paragraph, where single glazed doors and windows become 'ill-fitting', implying that only double-glazed doors and windows will fit snugly! Lastly, the letter's author introduces a rhetorical question from his repertoire of stylistic devices in the fourth paragraph which invites the reader's response:

'No, I can't go on for another year letting my heating bills be far larger than they need be!'

From this brief survey of three letters written in different contexts, it becomes clear that the circumstances in which a piece of writing is produced will have a significant impact upon the creation of a particular style.

What guidelines, then, should the writer adhere to in taking this particular factor into account?

RULES

Guidelines on managing context in writing

- **Before writing, it is important to review mentally, or by means of retrieving a customer file or similar available details any background information or record of correspondence. Such preparation will serve to remind the writer of the circumstances of a particular situation. For example, an important customer of your firm may have been involved in making a complaint two months ago, and might still therefore be 'prickly' or sensitive in his relationship to the company.**

Being forewarned or reminded of this fact may make all the difference in how a letter is worded or a telephone call made.
• Consider carefully the relationship between you the writer and your recipient. There is a world of difference in the following illustrations:

−boyfriend and girlfriend (relationship tentative)
−brother and sister (n.b. ties of blood)
−husband and wife (ditto)
−retailer and customer (n.b. paying relationship)
−doctor and patient (n.b. ethical code)
−sales representative and firm's general manager (n.b. position of each in company's hierarchy)

Inevitably, the tone of what we write takes into account the relationship between us and our recipient. We are bound to be more cautious and more formal in writing to the senior boss at work than to, say, a close personal friend or relative.
• Consider carefully what register the context requires − whether an easy, friendly one such as that in the mail-shot sales letter above, or the terse formal one of the final reminder of an overdue account.
In this particular area, consider also whether colloquial language would be appropriate to the context or not.
• Again, before writing or activating an audio-dictation machine, give careful thought to what format would best suit the context of the message to be written.
Would a personal memorandum to staff individually best get an urgent message read, or would that be too time-consuming and costly? Would a single notice on the staff noticeboard do the trick?
Again, should invitations to a social event be personalized in the shape of individual letter invitations, or would a 'top and tailed' photocopy letter be satisfactory? Up to 25 per cent of a message's impact depends on how it is 'packaged' and in terms of context, this fact is most relevant, if a new customer is to be won or a senior official 'wooed'!
• Lastly, keep firmly in mind that, once a written message has been printed and despatched − whether via internal mail or the postal service − you have lost control of it for ever! Therefore, before releasing any written message, make sure that its tone and overall language fit its context.
For example, if you were angry or 'up-tight' when you composed the message − especially if you dictated it − wait several hours or until the next day and read it again after having cooled off. It is surprising how many such stinging missives thereby end up rightly 'posted' in the waste-paper basket! Finally in the context of work, never allow something you have dictated to be typed and despatched without your having seen the message in its final form in print. It is surprising how different the written word can appear as opposed to its dictated counterpart!

Chapter 33
Style and the reader

You will have already noticed in Part Two how difficult it is to consider the various components of style in individual compartments. Aims, structure, vocabulary and context inevitably overlap, and are better regarded as strands of an interwoven thread which makes up style.

The same is true of the way in which the anticipated needs and expectations of the reader will influence the style of a given piece of writing.

Of course, some kinds of writing are aimed at a very large and many-faceted readership, such as articles and reports in national newspapers, where the journalist can only have a broad notion of the type of person who will read the piece, based on market research on who buys the newspaper.

Other kinds of writing – like the local club magazine – enjoy a much smaller and more narrowly based readership. For instance, a local wine club may attract members from similar backgrounds, and the local secretary may know most of them personally.

Whatever the kind of writing and destined or intended readership, it pays to know as much about the reader and his general attitudes, views and outlooks as possible – not merely to pander to them, but to be aware of how your points are likely to be received and thus how to present them so they may gain acceptance.

The manager applying for a new job, for example, will often take the trouble to research the background of the advertising firm's directors so as to avoid 'putting his foot in it' unconsciously in letter or interview. By checking up in *Who's Who*, the manager may avoid being highly critical of the foreign country of which the managing director is a citizen, or of the educational system of which the personnel manager is a product, or of the sport in which the sales director has an abiding interest!

Similar care or forethought is always worthwhile before producing any writing intended for a readership the writer does not already know well.

The following table provides some useful guidelines in this respect:

Guidelines on the aspects of a reader's profile which will influence the style created

- *Age*
  The age of a reader or group of readers will have a significant effect upon views and outlooks. What may seem to be exciting and stimulating music

for one group may be dismissed as an unholy cacophony by another! The deeply etched personal memories of one group of a world war may be reduced to the impact of a history book for another.

- *Background*
  The way we are brought up, the localities in which we live, the sets of people we live among, all influence deeply the way we view life and the issues arising from living through it. The person brought up in a larger city will absorb different experiences from those of country villagers. The person from an affluent background will have a different experience of life from that of the person who always had to scrape a living.

- *Education*
  While education may be universal (and available free in some state systems), the ways in which it is delivered vary enormously. For example, the regime followed in a private girls-only boarding school may be very different from that of a large mixed state comprehensive – not better, necessarily, but different. Similarly, the person who went to a university and studied for an arts degree will have received a very different type of education from the person who followed a vocational sandwich degree course at a polytechnic. Moreover, the person who did neither, but studied part-time in the evening over a number of years at the local 'tech' will have had yet another kind of educational experience and the person who has been educated in the 'university of life' yet another.

- *Interests and outlooks*
  While people at work may only use their particular expertise and professional skills while doing their jobs, they carry their hobby or sports enthusiasms with them wherever they go! It is a brave man, for example, who runs down the game of rugby in front of a Welshman, or who makes light of golf in front of a week-end (or any time a game can be fitted in) golfing enthusiast!
  A knowledge, therefore, of a reader's likely interests will help the writer to establish common ground and a rapport and to avoid insensitively trampling over someone's pet hobby or interest.

- *Specialisms and responsibilities*
  It is vital to be aware of the reader's particular area of specialism or expertise if at all possible. Nothing is more tedious to an expert reader than to be given by the writer an over-simple and lengthy explanation or description of what is already intimately known. By the same token, the use of specialist words (only 'jargon' when they are not shared) will enable the writer to communicate concepts and ideas in a mutually shared kind of shorthand with the expert reader. Thus awareness of this kind enables the writer to pitch the writing at the correct level.

- *Relationship of reader to writer*
  The relationship of the reader to the writer will also influence the style of writing created. Easy familiarity and leg-pulling in one relationship will appear much too presumptuous in another.
  In another context, for example, the public service clerical officer would need to think carefully about appropriate style, vocabulary and structure when writing to an infirm, elderly resident so as to avoid using technical language familiar to a local government officer but baffling to the old person.
  Alternatively, the ongoing relationship between retailer and customer

where the former owes his livelihood to the latter will always colour and influence the style of the retailer's writing to the customer.

Summary

In a nutshell, the writer will successfully write for his readership as long as he maintains a caring approach, for it is largely indifference and selfishness which takes the attitude:

– 'Let my readers make what they can of my vocabulary. If they can't follow it that's their bad luck!'
– 'If people are going to take offence at what they read that's their problem! I write the way I feel!'
– 'Look, you can't go around worrying about what some retired old buffer from Cheltenham thinks about rock music. You know who's going to like your kind of writing and who isn't.'

Writers displaying attitudes like those above may get read and may get their readers to accept and even enjoy their writing, but the chances are that their potential readership will dislike either the arrogant attitude that comes through in their writing or will simply shy away from a kind of writing which makes no concession either to their ability, outlook or limitations.

Thus the conscientious writer should always consider his reader's particular needs and expectations. In a sense, it is 'selfish' on the writer's part so to do, because it is precisely in this way that what he or she has to say will gain the widest circle of readers and achieve the desired aims and outcomes the writer has in mind.

Keep this checklist in front of you when you write and you won't go far wrong!

RULE	**Meeting the reader's needs**
	Research the reader's background carefully before starting to write.
	Ensure you have considered what is the appropriate register for your writing.
	Adopt an appropriate vocabulary to suit the reader's needs.
	Do not over-estimate or under-estimate the reader's ability or knowledge.
	Expect your reader on occasion to hold views different from yours and allow for the fact.
	Remember that effective communication is usually couched in a language and style which the reader finds easiest to absorb and accept!

Assignments

1   Write a passage in about 150 of your own words explaining how you think the context in which a piece of writing occurs affects its overall style.
2   Why should differences in the status of the writer and the reader either at work or socially affect the style a writer adopts?
3   What advice can you give someone about to become involved in composing frequent written communications about meeting the needs of his readers and creating a style in each piece of writing which will help to achieve this? Write a paragraph of about 150 words setting down your advice.

4   Make a list of those characteristics of a reader which were referred to in the Profile of a Reader on pages 205–206 which the writer should always take into account. Can you think of any which have been omitted?

5   What unwished-for outcomes do you think are likely to occur in a reader's reactions to a piece of writing which falls short of keeping the reader's needs firmly in mind?

6   Take a 'straw-poll' either at school, college or work among your colleagues of the sort of things which irritate, frustrate or annoy them in the ways in which various people write material which they either have to read, or read for pleasure. Ask yourself then why should such and such a colleague be annoyed and add the particular fault to those you mean to avoid in your own writing!

Chapter 34
Conclusion

The title of this closing section of the book is in some ways inappropriate, for although it aims to provide a few closing words to summarize what you have achieved, it ought perhaps to be entitled, 'Beginning'. Why? Simply because that is what you now have made available to yourself through your hard work and 'stickability' – the opportunity to make a new beginning in your writing and use of English!

In reality, though, I am sure your new beginning began some time ago, imperceptibly, as you conquered one grammar, spelling and punctuation peak after another, and started to give more conscious thought to the style of what you were writing.

Now you have attained the goals set you by this text, it is worthwhile to look back, like the traveller after a hard day's journey, to review what it is that you have achieved.

At an early stage you learned how to use effectively both an English language dictionary and thesaurus and these two reference books should remain your constant companions always within reach by your writing desk. You also studied some of the origins of the English language and, all being well, developed an interest in this absorbing area. Then you got down in Part One to mastering the grammar and syntax surrounding the parts of speech in English and the construction of phrases, clauses and sentences with a practical approach. Interspersed with this field of study, you surveyed some of the guidelines to aid your spelling and examined all the eleven punctuation marks.

In Part Two you surveyed the ways in which an effective style is created by having particular thought for the aims of a piece of writing, an appropriate structure for it, selecting the best vocabulary, fitting the style to the context and taking the needs and expectations of the reader into account.

In order to assess your mastery of all these areas of study, you undertook assignments at every stage and checked your answers against models and specimens provided. All being well, you carried over your studies into other areas, such as widening the range of what you read, or looking in a new way at what people at work or study centre wrote to you, or discussing various points at issue with relatives, friends or colleagues.

Reviewed in this way, that's a lot of ground to cover! And provided that you have worked through this text conscientiously, you should now feel rightly proud – especially if you have undertaken the study largely on your own. Moreover, you should feel much more confident about your powers of expression and your ability to compose prose which is not only grammatically correct and written according to current convention, but which is also effective in terms of achieving your predetermined aims.

In this case, why think of yourself as making a fresh beginning? The answer which you should carry with you into your next project or study undertaking is that education and self-improvement is never a 'one-off' phase that ends with compulsory schooling, apprenticeship course or higher education. It goes on for as long as we allow our minds to remain open and curious, and for as long as we have the motivation to improve. If you accept and adopt this outlook in your working and social life, then your English will continue to develop and improve (along with other skills and specialisms) well beyond the scope which this single text could offer you!

On this note of optimism I take the opportunity of wishing you all success in your coming writing and speaking of English. And offer you a last piece of well-meant advice: provided you continue to make an effort, you will continue to improve and make progress. In the words of a master writer and critic, Dr Samuel Johnson:

A man may write at any time, if he will set himself doggedly to it

and:

What is written without effort is in general read without pleasure.

Good luck!

Desmond Evans

Answers to assignments

Chapter 2 Where the English language came from

1 *kayak*: from Eskimo *carpet-bagger*: from American, a derogatory term for a profiteering businessman taking advantage of the poverty caused by the American Civil War *guitar*: from Spanish and French *pork*: from Norman French *friar*: from Middle English/Old French/Latin *sword*: from Old English/Old High German/Old Norse *ambidextrous*: from Latin *hermit*: from Middle English/Old French *photograph*: from Greek *kindergarten*: from Modern German *mackintosh*: from the name of its Scottish inventor, C. Mackintosh.

It is interesting to note that the trade names of companies or the names of the inventors of products sometimes become English words in their own right:

hoover biro cardigan wellington boot ovaltine

With such words, be on your guard since sometimes they are only to be used colloquially:

He carefully *hoovered* the carpet.

2 Plural forms:

ox: oxen *scarf*: scarfs or scarves *handkerchief*: handkerchiefs or handker- chieves *aquarium*: acquaria or acquariums (the *-ia* ending is the Latin-based one, and the *-iums* the English, more popular one.) The same is true for stadia or stadiums. Nowadays, modern usage is tending to opt for the 's' plural rather than for its Latinate counterpart. *monsieur*: messieurs (from the French). Remember also, the plural for madame is mesdames. *basis*: bases – another word which, coming from the Latin does not have an English 'add s' plural *tobacco*: tobaccos *louse*: lice – another tricky plural version to remember like, mouse, mice *hero*: heroes

Note: The spelling of plurals is dealt with in more detail on page 46.

3 There are too many alternative versions of each cliché to illustrate here, but the following may be compared with your own versions:

sort of funny: I began to feel faint/dizzy/sick/nauseated
nice drive, very nice pub, really nice lunch: leisurely/enjoyable/exhilarating/ relaxing drive; picturesque/homely/cheerful pub; tasty/appetizing/

ample lunch. Any one of these alternatives is likely to help the listener to conjure up a more accurate and informative picture of the outing to the pub.

OK, nothing out of the ordinary: acceptable/satisfactory/reasonable/of some interest but in no way remarkable/memorable/exciting

felt really awful: felt particularly embarrassed/self-conscious

awful bloke: a chap/fellow/boy/young man whom I took an instant dislike to/found immediately distasteful/irritating

terrible haircut: outrageous/ridiculous haircut

queer sort of accent: unfamiliar accent/dialect or pretentious accent – meaning putting on a false accent/ugly accent

you don't half talk funny: you really do overdo your accent don't you/I think your accent is very affected

I felt a bit funny myself afterwards: afterwards I felt ashamed at my rude behaviour/felt I spoke too brusquely to him/was too short with him

Clearly some of the options shown above would not easily fit into a 'chatty' kind of conversation, but they do illustrate some of the very many ways in which such conversations could communicate much more interesting meaning to the listener. So here the tip is – take the trouble to find and use interesting and even arresting expressions for certainly people will then take more notice of what you have to say.

4 What you had probably guessed about most of the words set out for you to check in your dictionary is that they stem from Latin.

A further tip about the use of long words of Latin origin is that while they often describe the meaning of an idea very accurately, they are also much more difficult for the reader to absorb and understand. Consequently, you should always take care to ensure that the type of word or expression you wish to employ is suited to the background of your reader and the nature – formal/informal etc. – of your message. This aspect of tone and style is dealt with in more detail in Part Two on page 205.

Chapter 3 How to use your dictionary effectively

1 You may find that your dictionary gives you a different way of representing the pronunciation of words, so the words in question are given with the *Concise Oxford Dictionary* (*COD*) pronunciation symbols and a simple 'home-made' phonetic spelling:

raison d'être: razawn da'tre, -e'- (*COD*) [rayzon dettruh]
charabanc: sharabang (*COD*)
lingerie: la'nzhere (*COD*) [lonsherry]
vol-au-vent: vol-o-vahn (*COD*) [vol-o-von]

Do make the effort to pronounce foreign words as they should be in English – that is, either in their foreign pronunciation or in their accepted anglicized form. There is nothing more grating on the ear of someone who has studied a foreign language than to hear some of its words mangled by an uninformed English speaker!

2

AAA	Amateur Athletic Association or American Automobile Association
cl.	classical

do.	ditto
exc.	except
HRH	His/Her Royal Highness
Mme	Madame
NALGO	National and Local Government Officers Association
prop.	properly (also proprietor)
WHO	World Health Organisation
UNESCO	United Nations Educational Scientific and Cultural Organisation
E&OE	Errors and Omissions Excepted
prov.	proverb (or provincial or provisional)
pp.	pages

You will have noticed that the abbreviations above have not been separated by full stops (NALGO, UNESCO). The trend nowadays is to run abbreviations shown in capital letters together – largely as a result of the saving in typewriter or keyboard strokes or depressions. Either with or without is acceptable but it is good style to stick to the same one within a single piece of writing. By the same token the full stops separating abbreviations like i.e. or e.g. are often omitted today (ie, eg) as is the final full stop after abbreviations like etc., which used to indicate that the word was abbreviated. Again, the best advice is to be consistent. Also, if you are studying for a typewriting or word processing examination, make sure you abide by the conventions accepted by your examinations board!

3 How many meanings did you find?

peer	noble, lord (noun)
	stare hard at (verb)
	the same as, equal (as in peer-group, noun)
rig	ropes or tackle of a sailing ship (noun)
	to assemble or set up (verb)
	tower or structure (as in oil-rig noun)
	type of small horse-drawn carriage (noun)
	to set out to cheat (verb) as in 'to rig a deck of cards'
grave	site of a buried person (noun)
	serious (adjective)
	grave, pronounced *grahve*, accent over French words
fair	amusement park, sideshows, etc. (noun)
	just, equitable (adjective)
	fine (adjective) as in 'the wind is set fair'
	of complexion, the opposite of dark (adjective)
	beautiful, handsome (adjective)
	of average quality, reasonable (adjective)
catch	to clutch in hands, as of cricket ball (verb)
	a trick or trap (noun)
	locking mechanism (noun)
	an amount of fish landed (noun)
	to entrap (verb)
	to overtake, to catch up with (verb)
bind	to bandage or tie up (verb) as of a wound
	to stick together (verb) as in dough
	a chore or nuisance (noun, slang)

Note that when a word is used as a verb or action-word with words like *up*, *across*, *with*, *to*, etc. (called prepositions) its meaning may change totally:

to catch out   to catch up with   to catch on etc.

Remember: You must check in your dictionary if you are not sure whether you are using a word correctly, or if you are uncertain of the accepted meaning of the word or expression you want to use.

Otherwise, you will just play safe, use an old tired but familiar expression and will have lost the chance to extend your active vocabulary!

4   Prefixes and suffixes

pre-	before, in front of: predestined premonition
bi-	of two, appertaining to two: bicycle biped
hyper-	extremely or very: hyperactive
contra-	against: contradict contraceptive

-ist	one who is: atheist communist
-ism	the subject or idea, concept of: paganism
-ious	used to form an adjective or describing word: infection/infectious
-graph	from the Greek word for writing: photograph, literally 'writing with light'

You will see prefixes and suffixes dealt with in much more detail on pages 101–114. Meanwhile, collect in your notebook those you come across and make a note of the ones whose meaning is unfamiliar.

By the way, did you notice that all the prefixes and suffixes illustrated originated from either Latin or Greek? By making sure you know what they mean, you will often have a good clue to the meaning of a newly encountered word.

5   Proverbial expressions

pride: a pride of lions   pride comes before a fall
blue: until blue in the face   feeling blue
die: as straight as a die   I could have died of shame!
fine: fine words butter no parsnips
fool: a fool and his money are soon parted   fool's gold   You can fool some of the people all of the time, but you can't fool all of the people all of the time

Proverbial expressions are most likely to be met in the spoken word, but, carefully used, may often enliven a piece of descriptive writing.

6   One word, hyphenated or two words? The horrors of English!

race-track   racehorse   postcard   sea-breeze *or* sea breeze (but each has a different meaning, the first blowing from the sea, and the second, any sea breeze!) ladies'-tailor   stomach-ache   underground = under the ground Underground = London subterranean transport system   all right (Note there is no such word as alright)

English being the lovable but unpredictable language it is, we all have to look up words which are joined together – either as one word or by means of a hyphen – if we are not sure of the spelling. There is, unfortunately, no simple rule to rely upon – hence *race-track* but *racehorse*! Moreover, in the matter of hyphens, English is constantly changing according to popular usage.

By now you should have become much more familiar with your dictionary and if you have scored over 70 per cent in finding correct answers, you can give yourself a deserved pat on the back.

Now see what you can find out about the English language thesaurus!

Chapter 4 How to use an English language thesaurus profitably

1 In *a* the challenge is to find an alternative to the word 'growth', in the sense of an increase in the business which makes up a national economy. By referring to 'growth' in the index of *Roget's Thesaurus*, we are referred to: increase (noun) head 36. Head 36 reveals a range of potentially suitable alternatives:

Increase − N: *increase*, augmentation, crescendo, growth, growth area, build-up, boom town, development, etc.

Of the above group of nouns – all suitable alternatives for 'growth' – but not all suitable for our needs – the most likely synonym or alternative would be:

increase or development.

We might use the word 'productivity' in head 36 to arrive at:

additional productivity.

With *b* the problem is to find an alternative for the verb 'to acquire'. Again, the first step is to consult the index. Under 'acquire', we are directed to head 771 vb for the meaning of 'acquire' as opposed to 'receive'.

The verb entry under 771 starts with *VB acquire* and lists:

get come by earn gain obtain procure find come across pick up light upon etc.

In the sense we need, the most likely alternatives would be:

obtain find come by get

2 The clues were listed underneath the passage, and the alternatives suggested are:

1 *pleasure:* delight enjoyment
2 *improving:* enhancing developing upgrading furthering
3 *route:* way path road
4 *communicate:* transmit information inform others pass on information
5 *patiently:* steadfastly doggedly determinedly persistently
6 *practice:* exercise regular process of regular work of repeated attempt at

All being well, you will have discovered for yourself with your thesaurus some of the alternatives shown above, and you may have found yet others which would fit equally well, for English is – as we have already established – an extremely rich language for alternative expressions – otherwise known as synonyms.

3   The answers to the words set in italics are:

agitated: nervous   anxious   worried   apprehensive
extremely lively: animated   high-spirited   enthusiastic   full of energy
in a sociable frame of mind: approachable   friendly   responsive to others
   receptive   to the approaches of others   companionable
dictatorial: authoritarian   tyrannical   dominating   autocratic
   bossy (slang)
havoc: destruction   chaos   confusion   devastation
had resented: had taken exception to   was offended by   objected to
   took umbrage at

4   The answers to the definitions provided are:

youngster: urchin   waif
mistake: negligent act   gross error or misjudgement
evil: diabolic   satanic   devilish
to be cheeky: to be insolent   rude   impertinent   offensive
to voice: to utter   to articulate   to enunciate   to pronounce carefully

By now you should have gained sufficient practice in using your thesaurus to have realized what a great help it can be whenever you are really lost for either the right word or another to replace one already used. Make sure you keep up the habit of using it to help you extend your active and working vocabulary.

Chapter 5 Improve your written English

Nouns

1

a   All the nouns in this sentence are common – they are everyday objects – except Mrs Jones!:

hilltop	common
boy	common
bicycle	common
basket	common
wheel	common
packet	common
groceries	common
Mrs Jones	proper

b   Irritation and news are the nouns which lie outside of the world and are thus abstract. Note also 'peal of bells', peal being collective:

irritation	abstract
news	abstract
church	common
peal	collective
bells	common

c   As pointed out in this section, all the proper nouns have initial capital letters:

Beethoven	proper
'Fifth Symphony'	proper

work   abstract
Promenade Concert   proper
The Royal Albert Hall   proper

d Here each noun describes either a mental processs or an activity requiring thought and analysis:

problem   abstract
planning abstract
thought   abstract

e series   collective
plays   abstract
Independent Television   proper
December   proper
number   here collective: *number* of viewers
viewers   common

f tourists   common
Tower of London proper
repairs   abstract

g The Cutty Sark proper
tea-clipper   common
run   abstract
India   proper
England   proper
century   abstract

h Henry   proper
duke   common (believe it or not!)
Thomas   proper
earl   common
rules   abstract
precedence   abstract
procession   abstract

2

a The indefinite article – the word 'a' – is used to introduce words where 'no particular one' is being identified, just a single one of its kind:

a bat   a ball   a boat etc.

Notice that whenever we are asked to compose a definition, it is helpful to introduce some examples as illustration.

b Of course! Each proper noun begins with a capital letter.

c There are others, but we explored: *-ness, -ism, -ion, -ment*.

d Collective nouns are words which are used to label either groups, sets, collections of (hence 'collective') things or people sharing something in common, such as membership of a team or the fact that all are lions!

the *team* of hockey players   the *pride* of lions

e Here you must decide whether you have assembled the examples, but if you have studied this section carefully, you will almost certainly have made the right choices.

At this point, with the exception of the need to know a proper noun when you see one because of the capital letter punctuation convention, it may be stated without much fear of contradiction that your future writing is unlikely to be affected too much by your ability or otherwise to distinguish an abstract or collective noun from a common one.

However, it *is* important to be able to identify nouns, as we shall see when it comes to deciding whether what you have written is a sentence or not. Furthermore, when we come to consider style in writing, you will want to be able to detect rapidly whether what you have written comes across to your reader in an abstract and remote way, or in a realistic and immediate way, and the kind of nouns you choose will have a great bearing on this, so the basic effort you have put into this section will by no means have been limited to learning labels to no particular end.

Verbs

1   The single words or 'verb clusters' acting as finite verbs are:

a   had been concluded   walked   had changed   sank   had been run
Notice that single sentences can be written which include five finite verbs. This type of sentence is considered in more detail on page 89 onwards.

b   shall be returning   will have left
c   should arrive   has been posted
d   shall be getting   am surprised   observed
e   was falling   stared   caught   was walking
f   glanced   would (not)*   have finished
*Not part of the finite verb: Notice that sometimes parts of the verb are separated from each other by the insertion of words which are other parts of speech:

returned   shall have (to persuade)   thought   would save

As a double check on the working of the rules governing finite verbs, go back to each of the above sentences and write down the word or words acting as the subject of each of the finite verbs identified above. (Answers at the end of this section.)

2   A verb which is being used actively in a sentence expresses directly the action of the doer word or subject.

3   The old church was visited only occasionally by the relatives of the departed.

4

a   I <u>would</u> go to the disco if I had the entrance fee.
b   The dance team <u>would have been</u> entered for the competition by their instructor if she had felt they stood any chance of winning.

5   The specialist phrase we have adopted is: Agent of the Action.

6   The answer is passively – one of the clues, apart from the words making up the past simple passive tense of the verb is the inclusion of the agent of the action: 'by him'.

7

a The number of a verb can be either singular or plural – the verb is expressing the action of a single subject (singular) or a subject comprising more than one thing or person (plural).

b The person of a verb consists of the first, second or third, singular or plural – the word 'person' embraces the words *I, you, he, she, it* in the singular and *we, you, they* in the plural, where *I* and *we* are first person, both *you*'s second person, and *he, she, it* and *they* third person.

8 To qualify as a finite verb in a sentence, a verb must possess a tense, a number and a person (and must also agree in number and person with its subject).

9 The job of a subject in a sentence is to act as the doer word which governs the action of the verb.

10 The following are grammatically acceptable sentences:

c d h i

All the others fail to meet the criteria we have learned. In *a* there is no subject and part of the finite verb is missing. It would be all right if re-written as:

<u>The children were</u> running down the road before the storm broke.

The same fault is true of *b* – who is doing the referring? The idea would be much better expressed as:

I refer to your letter of 30th June 19––.

In *e* the problem is one of a lack of agreement between subject and verb – did you spot it? The subject is *coach* – singular – and its finite verb therefore should be *was held up* not *were held up*. Remember to watch out for such constructions as 'a number of passengers' where number is the ruling singular noun, or 'a set of books', 'a cluster of grapes', etc.'

The sets of words in *f* and *g* are simply groups of words formed around the present participles of verbs (see pages 26–27). Neither *dashing* nor *broken* nor *smashed* has a subject.

The set of words in *j* represents a classic example of where the writer of a series of ideas becomes tangled up in them and loses all control of the structure of the sentence. Nowhere to be found is a finite verb nor the appearance of a subject controlling the meaning of a finite verb!

Thus the three key questions to answer in checking whether what you have written can stand on its own as a complete sentence are:

● Where is the subject (or subjects) controlling the finite verb (or verbs)?
● Where is the finite verb – or verbs if more than one?
● Do both the subject and the finite verb meet the criteria set down?

11

a The *roar* of the racing cars *could be heard* over a mile away.
b In order to qualify as a sentence, a *group of words must include* both a subject and a finite verb.
c The ancient *building* with the broken fence *was creaking* in the wind.
d *Mr Jenkins will be engaged* with a customer until 2.30 p.m.

    e   *The city of Liverpool has acquired* a world-wide reputation for the wit of its inhabitants.

    f   Although delayed by fog, *the match will take place* under floodlights.

    g   The *mannequin modelled* the costume expertly.

The most natural word order in English is for the subject of the sentence to come first, immediately followed by the finite verb, as in examples *d*, *e* and *g* but notice in the other examples, how groups of words are employed to begin a sentence before the subject is introduced:

– In order to qualify as a sentence . . .
– Although delayed by fog . . .

in order to vary a word order for the sake of interest and to avoid the boredom of having constructed each sentence of a passage in an identical way (see page 117 onwards for further details).

12   It *is* important that you *learn* to recognize nouns easily whether as single words or in word groups because nouns *form* the subjects of sentences. As you already *know*, all sentences *must possess* at the very least a subject and a finite verb. And you *are aware* that, sooner or later, someone you *work* for *will be expecting* you to be able to write grammatically correct sentences or perhaps to correct draft letters which *may* not *be* grammatically correct. So it pays to know. *Check* how much you know by working through the above assignments again in case you have made some unspotted errors.

Subjects	Finite verbs
a the match	had been concluded
both teams	walked
they	had changed
(they) understood	sank
the baths (which)	had been run
b I	shall be returning
the last tube	will have left
c The parcel	should arrive
it	has been posted
d We	shall be getting
I	am (not) surprised
the Yorkshire farmer	observed
e the rain	was falling
she	stared
A figure in a sodden overcoat	caught
who	was walking
f The secretary	glanced
she	would not have finished
Mr Jackson	returned
I	shall have to persuade
she	thought
That	would save

Here it's worth remembering that the person whose grammar knowledge is confident and who can write grammatically correct and acceptable sentences and proof-read accurately is a person with skills which are always in demand in the world of work.

Chapter 6 Punctuating in English I

1 One principal use of the full stop in punctuating English writing is to mark the end of a sentence. Sentences invariably start with a capital letter as the first letter of the sentence's first word:

*B*eneath the trees a breathtakingly beautiful carpet of bluebells stretched away into the distance.

Another use of the full stop is to indicate at the end of a word that it is, in fact, an abbreviation of a longer one:

a.m. ante meridiem (before noon)   Bart. Baronet   Dipl. Diploma

A further use of the full stop is, when employed in a set of three thus . . ., to inform a reader that a phrase or sentence has been omitted from a quoted passage:

Interested readers may wish to refer to the entry in the Appendix on page 259. . . . However, the main conclusion to be drawn is that determination has a great deal to do with success, irrespective of a person's innate intelligence.

2 After a busy day at the office, Jenny reached home. Closing the door behind her, she struggled to remove her soaking mackintosh. As usual, her cat, Snowball, started to rub against her legs, letting Jenny know someone else was hungry. In the kitchen the remains of breakfast, cereal bowl, plate, cup and saucer and marmalade pot were just as Jenny had left them in her usual morning rush. Following her customary evening routine Jenny filled the kettle with water and plugged it in. Next she turned on the radio and said as usual to Snowball, 'Who's for his dinner, then?'

Did you get them all right? Notice that in devising interesting sentences it is helpful to start with a descriptive phrase:

After a busy day at the office . . .   In the kitchen . . .   As usual . . . Following her customary evening routine . . .

before introducing the subject word. Also, did you remember a capital letter each time for Jenny and Snowball? And the capital *w* for *Who's* because it started the direct speech sentence?

3

a The small boy shouted for the ball to be given to Frank. He was the team's centre-forward and idol of the small band of supporters at the Gasworks End.
    'Frank' and 'Gasworks End' are both proper nouns here, since we are writing about a particular person and a particular place, just like Manchester United's Stretford End.
    As a new idea begins with 'He was the team's centre-forward', a new sentence must be started. Now check that each has a subject and a finite verb in agreement with it – just to check the system and your mastery of it. Answers at the end of this section.
b After a few minutes of careful thought, the young child looked straight into its mother's eyes and asked, 'Is it true that babies are found under gooseberry bushes?'
    Remember that whenever direct speech (within the quotation marks)

is introduced inside a sentence, it starts with a capital letter – here 'Is'. Also, since a direct question is being asked the direct speech ends with a question mark.

Direct speech is dealt with in detail on page 78, and the question mark on page 96.

4 etc. P.S. et seq. p.m. m.p.h. Ph.D.

Remember that with the abbreviation for Doctor of Philosophy the 'Ph' comes first because of a Latin word order not found in English, since originally the abbreviation stood for the Latin form of Doctor of Philosophy.

Also, where Latin phrases like ad libitum (according to pleasure) and et sequitur (and what follows) are abbreviated into ad lib. and et seq. the full stop is only used after the word being abbreviated.

Additional answers to 3

a 1 Subject: The small boy
       Finite verb: shouted
   2 Subject: He
       Finite Verb: was

Chapter 7 Mastering spelling I

1 *adversary:* adversaries   *miss:* misses   *abbess:* abbesses   *soprano:* sopranos   *wharf:* wharfs or wharves   *cutlass:* cutlasses   *belly:* bellies *chief:* chiefs *tumulus:* tumuli *fungus:* fungi *dynamo:* dynamos *hoof:* hoofs or hooves *opus:* opera *axis:* axes *virtuoso:* virtuosi *turkey:* turkeys *batch:* batches *menu:* menus *negro:* negroes *valley:* valleys *sheaf:* sheaves

2 hero dwarf bureau brother basis (or base) formula fuzz monsieur anthology cupola corps

If you spelled twenty-five or more of the above correctly, then you did very well!

Check through the correct spellings again, making sure you learn the ones you misspelled.

Chapter 8 Improve your written English II

1
a rushed double-decker slow winding Swiss

Notice here that 'holiday-makers' is a noun, while 'double-decker' is describing 'bus' and is therefore an adjective. Also, note that though the word Swiss has a capital letter to denote its derivation from the word 'Switzerland', it is being used here as an adjective to describe 'alps'.
b icy broken dust-covered abandoned Dutch

Here 'abandoned', though derived from the verb 'to abandon' is being used adjectively to describe the dresser. Like the adjective 'winding' above, 'abandoned' is a participle, and participles can be used as adjectives.

2

Describing	Pointing out	Questioning	Possessing	Showing quantity
straight	those	which	our	every
sharp	that	what	its	some
shining		whose	their	two
huge				most
mended				few
				all

3   The two parts of the verb which may be used adjectively are: the present participle, which ends in *-ing*, and the past participle, which usually ends in *-ed*, unless the verb is irregular like 'to break': broken etc.

4   The adjective in this sentence is 'enormous'. Most frequently, adjectives come before the nouns they modify, but sometimes, as in this sentence, they are part of an additional group of words – in this instance the word 'which' is a repeat word for 'crowd':

The crowd (the crowd was enormous) was assembled to see the match.

   It would of course be much more economical of words to write:

The enormous crowd was assembled to see the match.

but sometimes writers change their constructions to add variety to a passage of prose. Also, though long-winded, the expression in the sentence 'which was enormous' does give greater emphasis to the idea of 'enormous' than if it were placed immediately in front of the word 'crowd'.

5   The adjectives modifying other adjectives are:

bright (blue)   dark (brown)

6   Perhaps the best advice would be to use adjectives sparingly. Avoid piling them up in twos and threes in front of the nouns they modify. Vary their position in the sentence for effect. Use an English language thesaurus to find the most suitable adjectives rather than 'trotting out' worn clichés time and again.

Chapter 9 Punctuating in English II

One version of the passage aimed at removing unwanted commas and overuse of adjectives might be:

The old man stooped to pick up the box of matches, half full of charred match-sticks. With arthritic fingers he struggled to extract an unused match, his shrivelled hands white with cold in the damp basement. His cat, its fur fluffed out against the cold, watched his every move.

   By making some careful omissions from the text, we may lose a little of the meaning, but the impact of the old man struggling in the cold remains. Changing to the adjective 'arthritic' has the effect of communicating 'with shaking, gnarled fingers', and reconstructing the idea of his white and shrivelled hands in the damp cold basement air conveys the same idea but more economically. Lastly, this version has made three sentences out of the single one of the original which enables the reader to absorb the meaning much more easily.

1

a   Before pulling away, look behind for pedestrians or oncoming vehicles, signal your intention, check your rear-view mirror and avoid causing other vehicles to slow down as you move off.

   We can either punctuate the above sentence as a list of commands, as shown above, or break the sentence into two, by starting a fresh sentence with the word 'signal'.

b   The charges he faced included impersonating a gas board official, breaking and entering, resisting arrest and forty-two other offences he had asked to be taken into consideration.

   Here the sense and drive of the sentence's structure requires it to be punctuated as shown above. Notice the rhythm of the grouping of each set of words between the commas.

c   The defence counsel insisted that, despite the case against him, he was basically a man of good character.

   Here the normal sentence structure has been interrupted by the insertion of 'despite the case against him' which therefore needs to be separated by commas.

d   'The trouble with you,' he said angrily, 'is that that you never think before you speak!'

   Take careful notice here of the precise locations of the commas, inverted commas and the exclamation mark.

e   There is good reason to believe, however, that she may have been able to pass on the message before she was captured.

f   Even so, by following the instructions carefully you will be able to set up the equipment yourself.

g   Though they had been duly warned of the inevitable consequences of their actions, they still went ahead with their plan to kidnap the chief constable as part of the university's rag week.

   Here, if we were thinking of a particular chief constable and particular rag week, we might correctly use capital letters to indicate them as proper nouns.

   Also, the length of the two halves of this sentence warrant the use of the comma acting as a pivot.

h   If you go she will want to go too.
   If you go, she will want to go too.
   A case could be made for either punctuation.

i   The chairman's office, which was situated on the top floor, was reached by a private lift.

   Here the sense is probably that the relative clause 'which was situated on the top floor' is non-defining, so commas are appropriate. You may, however, wish to urge that your answer saw it as defining and that is why you omitted them! Without more detail of the context of the sentence either would be allowable!

Chapter 10 Mastering spelling II

1 No single correct answers here for the thousands of alternative answers, but your list should include words like these:

a Long *a* made   blame
b *ai* pain   await
c *ei* weigh   sleigh   feint
d *ay* stray   flayed

2

plead
procedure
exceed
formulae
frieze
seize

Note that when 'procedure' is used in its verb form it is spelled 'to proceed' and retains the double *e* spelling in all its tenses.

Don't confuse 'frieze' with its colder pairing 'to freeze'.

Remember the singular of 'formulae' is 'formula'.

3 The words which I have chosen to illustrate the long *o* sound are:

as *ow* mown   tow   follow
as *oa* coastal   floating
as *oe* toe   sloe   floe
as *ough* furlough
as *eau* Beau Gest   eau de cologne*   bureau*

*Most *ow* sounds spelled *eau* come from the French language as do my examples.

4

isle: aisle   I'll
bore: boar
bale: bail
beer: bier
earn: urn
dew: due
pair: pare   pear
fate: fête
faint: feint
review: revue
vale: veil
vain: vane   vein
new: knew
taught: taut (tort, an expression used in law)
wine: whine
liar: lyre
straight: strait
slight: sleight
sole: soul

The above represent just some of the many homophone pairs or triplets which abound in English. It is good spelling practice to collect them in your notebook whenever you meet a new word which will make up a pair or a triple set. How many of the above three and four letter words are you unsure of the meaning of? Yes – you've guessed! Now check them up in your dictionary!

5 The seven famous *-ough* words which I have chosen as illustrations are:

cough   rough   through   thorough   plough   fought   dough
off   *uff*   *oo*   *uh*   *ow*   *aw*   long *o*

Of course there are many more and it helps to collect them as you meet them.

6 Four words illustrating the *aw* sound:

as *aw* awful
as *augh* daughter
as *ough* fought
as *au* pause

Make sure your words list these four different vowel spellings.

7 slaughter   bought   haul   awning   gnaw

8

a one who inherits is an h*ei*r
b a row of seats or levels on a cake is a t*ie*r
c a bill for goods is a rec*ei*pt
d the word of French origin is, of course, bur*eau*

9 Cluster groups
Two typical cluster groups might look like this:

Anchor word: rein
feint   reindeer   sleigh   feign   reign   deign   weigh   weight
freight etc.
Anchor word: fought
words rhyming with 'fought': bought   ought   sought   brought
nought (but be careful about the *au* variants like   caught   taught
daughter etc.)

10 The false friends:

  a   persuade
but *b*   pursue
  c   council
but *d*   counsel
  e   stationary
but *f*   stationery

A good way of remembering the differences between such words is to make up little personal rules. For example when stationery means letter-paper etc. it has an *e* in it for 'envelopes'. A counsel is one who "*e*lps' you in court. Silly they may be, but they do work! Try some such 'rules' for yourself.

Chapter 11 Improve your written English III

1 The types of adverb so far learned are:

- of time: *When*
- of place: *Where*
- of manner: *How*

- of reason: *Why*
- of degree: *To what extent*

2   True. Adverbs can occur as single words, most often ending in *-ly* or they can be conveyed via groups of words – in adverbial phrases or clauses. For example:

Single word adverbs: quickly   contentedly   high   fast
Adverbial phrases: by the end of the month   in a slow rhythm
Adverbial clauses: When I felt like it   because I was hungry

3   The word or words being used adverbially in the passage are:

Slowly   very (modifying 'detailed' – here an adjective)   cautiously
in a friendly way   then   here by tomorrow   high   cheap
because of their low price

4   Here are some words commonly used in an adverbial sense which do not end in *-ly*:

quite   very   almost   high   low   fast   slow   too

5   Adverbs can also extend the meaning of adjectives or other adverbs.

6   Like adjectives, adverbs should be chosen with particular care and used sparingly – like an expensive perfume! It is best to avoid adding two or more adverbs on to a verb in order to wring out more meaning. Much better to choose in the first place a graphic verb. This means that extending one's active vocabulary has an important part to play in developing good writing – and in choosing the best adverbs!

Chapter 12 Punctuating in English III

The party was proving to be as boring as Laura had anticipated. In the corner by the hi-fi silenced two hours previously by a spilt Harvey Wallbanger, Arthur Spiggott and Marcia Ferndrop were indulging in their annual duel of name dropping and literary insults.

'What did you think of Sinclair's new novel *Wind Across the Saltflats?'* asked Arthur as an opening move.

'I thought it overrated and a considerable disappointment compared with his earlier work *Cruise Along the Wind,'* replied Marcia, disposing of a seven hundred and forty-three page novel in seventeen crisply delivered words of dismissal.

'Really!' responded Arthur. 'Surely you must have missed its delicate similarities to Grimthorpe's *March of the Walrus*. Now there's a masterful attack on modern-day values if you like!'

'Humph!' grunted Marcia, admitting no such thing. 'Actually I'm off the modern novel nowadays,' she observed with a sniff. 'They seem to attract too many intellectual snobs!'

'I say!' spluttered Arthur, digesting the insult with a mouthful of sour Spanish white wine. 'You're surely not including me in that remark are you? I mean to say, I've always believed that the modern novel should communicate with the working class.'

'You wouldn't recognize a member of the working class in the middle of the Crown and Anchor public bar on a Saturday night!' concluded Marcia as she moved across the room with the confidence of one who has achieved a second round knockout.

Talking points

- Make sure you understand why each proper noun introduced with initial capital letters is a proper noun. Here they are either names of people or titles of books, except for Harvey Wallbanger which is the name of a cocktail popular in the 1980s.
- Notice that this answer avoids commas as far as possible, such as:

In the corner, by the hi-fi . . .

It is interesting to notice how the absence of such commas hurries the passage along, so that the dialogue remains crisp and spikey – at least on Marcia's part.
- The passage illustrates well the setting out of fresh direct speech on a fresh line, as well as the convention of indenting.
- Some of the exclamation marks in the direct speech may be regarded as optional. Do you think they have been overdone? Or would the passage lose something without them? What may be lost is the sense of Arthur's indignation and the tartness of Marcia's observations.
- No single quotation marks have been put around Crown and Anchor as the convention nowadays is to leave the names of pubs, hotels and the like simply in initial capitals.

Chapter 13 Mastering spelling III

1 The four prefixes are:

il- im- in- ir-

Two words for each you may have chosen are:

illicit illegitimate   immoral immodest   innocent innate
irreplaceable   irresistible

2 The general rule is that the addition of a prefix or a suffix to a base word does not affect the spelling of the base word:

navigate/circumnavigate national/international hope/hopeful
art/artist human/humanism

There are some exceptions, particularly affecting final *e*'s, as we have already discovered.

3 Generally, words ending in a *y* drop the *y* and add *i* before an *-ly* suffix:

hasty/hastily   thirsty/thirstily

4 The general rule is that with words of one syllable ending in a single consonant preceded by a vowel the final consonant is doubled when a suffix is added:

e.g. pit/pitted   fat/fatter etc.

5 No, the rule does not work:

happen/happening   open/opener

But, bear in mind: begin/beginning.

6

The *ssss* sound:	as a single *s*
	a double *s* (*ss*)
	c followed by a vowel
	sc
The *sh* sound:	as *sh*
	a single *s* (often followed by a *u*)
	a *t* followed by a vowel (*-tion -tious*)
	sch
	c followed by a vowel
	part of the *x* sound as in noxious
	ch in French words such as chateau
The *ch* sound:	as *ch*
	a *t* followed by a vowel, especially a *u*
	tch
The *kuh* sound:	as a *k*
	ck
	q (always followed by a *u*)
	ch
	hard *c*
	cq (always followed by *u*)
The *juh* sound:	as a *j*
	a soft *g* followed by an *e* or *y*
	dj
	du
	dge
The *eff* sound:	either as a single or double *f*
	as *ph*
	-ough- or *-augh-*
The *jzuh* sound:	as a single *s* or a single *z* followed by a vowel
	soft *g* followed by an *e*

7 plaque   acquaintance   accommodation   referred   illegible unnecessary   occurred   professor   dessert   omitted

If you scored 10 out of 10, you are well on your way to spelling success!

8 An *e* usually follows a soft *g* as in:

mirage   garage   barrage   montage   ménage (à trois).

Notice that the spelling is the same for all those English words which we pronounce with the *-idge-* ending since they originally stemmed from Norman French – words like:

passage   carriage   wastage   bandage etc.

9 The spelling rules affecting *q* are:

a   it is always followed by a *u* in words of English origin;
b   it never ends a word in English which is not slang.

There is no word of English that ends in *j*. (Raj is of Indian origin.)

10 *ascent:* assent   *baron:* barren   *council:* counsel   *decent:* descent (accent is on last syllable; note also dissent, meaning to disagree)   *cord:* chord *guerilla:* gorilla   *lightening:* lightning (note: the version with the *e* means making less heavy, and without the *e*, the electrical discharge in the thunder-storm) *need:* knead *palate:* palette (check you know the difference! Actually there is a slight difference in pronunciation) *shake:* sheikh *weather:* whether (and, archaic, wether, sheep) *holy:* wholly *practice:* practise (remember that the noun is always with the *c* and the finite verb version with an *s*. Make up your own catch-phrase to remember this, like: a noun names or *c*alls, so practice with a *c* is the noun.) *draught:* draft (Which is the spelling for the one which makes you shiver?) *arc:* ark *nave:* knave

11 The guideline has to do with the pronunciation of the vowel preceding the consonant which may have a single or double identical letter. If the preceding vowel is long, then the following consonant sound may be a single letter spelling; if short, then a double:

spīney/spĭnning tāmer/hămmer fīler/fĭlling

12

Anchor word: leisure
Cluster words: pleasure measure closure disclosure seizure azure vision lesion fusion rediffusion allusion illusion

13

a acquire acquisitive acquisition acquaint acquaintance acquit acquittal acquittance
b gracious spacious specious audacious fallacious mendacious precocious
c science scientific scientist scientology sciatica prescience nescience conscience miscellany miscellaneous scent ascent descent condescending descend

Chapter 14 Improve your written English IV

Quick revision

1 The basic and indeed essential components needed to make a sentence grammatically acceptable are:

a a subject and
b a finite verb agreeing in number and person with the subject and expressed in an active or passive tense:

John worked. Caroline lazed.

are both perfectly acceptable sentences, whereas the following are most certainly not!

– Referring to your letter of 10 June. (No subject or finite verb.)
– Your order of 14 May to hand. (No finite verb.)
– Going down the road on his first bicycle. (No subject or finite verb.)
– Around the corner and through the trees. (No subject or finite verb.)
– Mrs Brown's shopping-bag hanging down almost to the pavement. (No finite verb.)

2   Essentially a phrase is a group of words which does not include a finite verb. Very often phrases are introduced by prepositions like:

in   from   under   to   upon etc.
down the road   after the lovely open-air lunch

A clause, on the other hand does include both a subject and a finite verb (sometimes, if it is a main clause, it could act as a sentence by itself). However, it usually forms part of a compound or complex sentence which is made up of two or more clauses.

3   As we have so far discovered, the 'rest of the sentence' can be made up of:

a   an object:

– She inserted *the notepaper*.

b   an adverbial word or phrase:

– The sales representative talked *persuasively*.
– The sales representative talked *in a most persuasive manner*.

c   an adjectival word or phrase:

– The company's sales performance grew *worse*.
– The company's sales performance was *slow and patchy*.

4   A simple sentence is one which includes only one subject and a single finite verb.

5   In straightforward terms, an object in a sentence is a person or thing having something done to him, her or it. An object 'receives' upon itself the action of the 'doer' or the subject through the action of the verb (words in italics are the object):

Julia carefully typed out *the circular letter*.

Here the letter 'receives' the action of Julia and is the object. Further examples:

– The angry farmer threw *the protest placard* into the duck pond.
– 'Please be so kind as to give *this file* to Mr Johnson as quickly as possible.'
– After several quiet minutes, Sir Charles had *a brainwave*!

Sentences and style

6   Generally speaking, the effect of introducing a sentence with a phrase before the mention of the subject plus finite verb is to create some suspense as a result of the delay the reader experiences before learning the main point of the sentence:

At eleven forty-five p.m. last Thursday evening, Mr James Gilroy was found brutally murdered.

As you can see in the above example, the reader is kept waiting for the actual outcome of the sentence until the very last word!

7 Contrastingly, if such additional information included by a phrase is put after the subject and finite verb, the effect is a tailing off of the impact of the phrase:

Sussex won the County Championship *after a very closely run contest with their near neighbours Kent.*

The 'busy reader' takes in the first important piece of news – in effect the nub of the sentence – and tends to skim-read the rest of it.

8 Briefly, a compound sentence is one which incorporates two or more clauses in the following kind of ways:

Main clause + main clause + etc.

while a complex sentence structure is:

Main clause + dependent clause etc.

We shall be looking at the structure and effects upon style of longer, complex sentences in a later section.

9 The part of speech which links clauses is termed a conjunction. See page 117 onwards for a detailed examination.

10 The passage might be re-written as follows:

Developed during the late 1960s, the microprocessor or silicon chip revolutionized the office equipment business. First manufactured commercially in 1971 by the USA company Intel, the silicon chip looked about as big as a postage stamp and as thick as cardboard. Equipment manufacturers soon realized the potential of this tiny chip with its powerful memory, which was able to control the production and distribution of large amounts of information via microcomputers and word processors. Soon small enough to sit atop office desks, such equipment was networked by larger companies in the early 1980s. Networking enables such equipment to intercommunicate where, for example, a word processor provides copy for a photocopier which is able to make multiple copies after a process of optical reading. Again, a facsimile transmitter could send computer-designed plans to a building site thousands of miles distant. In such ways the microprocessor is transforming the working lives and indeed leisure habits of millions of people.

This version has been produced to provide you with some illustrations of the ways in which phrases can add information more economically than separate sentences and to show how sentences can express more than one idea clearly. Also, as a matter of interest, the above version is over fifty words shorter than the original. Only one or two words have been changed to make the second version more interesting to read.

Check the above version for phrases which have been constructed with the help of past participles:

– Developed during the late 1960s, . . .
– First manufactured . . .

Notice also how clauses can be introduced by the word which (here used as a conjunction) in order to express an additional idea in one sentence:

– which was able to control . . .
– which is able to make multiple copies . . .

and lastly, how the word 'computer-designed' expresses the meaning of what was a whole sentence.

Such techniques help to make a piece of writing much more interesting than the boring repetition of largely simple sentences which always start with subject plus finite verb.

RULE	**Memory note**

But keep firmly in mind:

● **Longer, complex sentences are much more demanding and difficult for the reader to absorb and extract the meaning from.**
● **Short sentences have their own important place in the communication process.**
● **Often varying the mix of long with short sentences achieves the writer's desired aim.**

Chapter 15 Punctuating in English IV

1 Bear in mind before checking through the following answers that, while some punctuation marks are clearly seen to be needed without argument, some – like the exclamation mark – may be regarded as 'optional extras' and it is a matter of personal choice in some writing instances whether to use them or not.

a 'How do you like your steak cooked, sir?' enquired the waiter.
  Note the straightforward use of the question mark in direct speech, which stands by itself at the end of the direct question apart from the closing inverted commas.

b 'Just show it the frying pan briefly!' answered the American with a grin.
  Similarly, the exclamation mark within direct speech follows same rules. Don't forget a capital letter for the *A* of American – following the proper noun rule. A comma after American seems unnecessary here.

c 'Get your lovely tights and stockings here! They're guaranteed! They're a bargain! They're going fast!' shouted the street trader to the passing Christmas shoppers.
  Since all the direct speech is made up of four slogans the street trader is shouting to gain attention, then it is appropriate to indicate this with an exclamation mark after each one. Did you remember to include the contraction punctuation comma each time in 'they're'?

d I asked the price of a return ticket to Edinburgh.
  I hope you did not fall into the trap of putting a question mark at the end of this sentence. Be on your guard for sentences which convey statements even though the verb used to do so is 'asked' or 'enquired' or 'wondered' etc.

e What are the consequences of acid rain? Foresters all over Europe can show you the cost in dead and dying precious trees!

The use of direct speech inverted commas has not been made here, since the assumption is that this is a piece of journalism where the writer is employing the rhetorical question technique. However, you may have considered it, justifiably, as direct speech and so inverted commas are allowed!

The inclusion of the exclamation mark at the end of the second sentence is justified because of the feeling of anger or frustration or because of the emphasis the writer wishes to communicate to the reader.

f 'Get out!' shrieked Juliet in a fit of rage. 'And don't come back!'

Apart from perhaps a comma after Juliet, there is not much here for anything other than the punctuation of the above.

g She posed the question of what should be done about the unsold copies of 'Your Garden in Winter' by Jack Green.

The above is a statement and so no question mark is required – the writer is simply stating the nature of the question which 'she' asked. Did you remember the initial capitals for the proper noun title of the gardening book? And also for its author, Jack Green? Lastly, the single comma quotation marks around the book's title might nowadays be regarded as optional.

h Going away this Easter? Here are some tips to make your visit more fun for you and more bearable for your host!

The question mark is needed to show that a direct (rhetorical) question is being asked in the first sentence. The exclamation mark is used here to show that both reader and writer are aware that making visits to relatives or friends can be boring for the visitor and stressful for the host and so the writer is conveying via the exclamation mark a shared confidence indicated by this exclamation mark.

HINT!

Morale Booster!

By now the punctuation of direct speech should hold few fears for you and you are almost certainly now taking in the use in the text of labels like 'proper noun' and 'verb' as used in the above comments on answers because you now know precisely what they stand for. So an important further value in acquiring a knowledge of English grammar is that you are now building up a working vocabulary which is essential if writers like me are to be able to communicate clearly and immediately with you!
'Keep up the good work', as they say!

Chapter 16 Mastering spelling IV

1 This time you can check all your own answers on your own by using your dictionary!

2 It is surprising how many words there are using the prefixes listed, I think you will agree. As a result of their Latin/Greek origin, a great many of them tend to occur in specialized contexts, such as science, law, government, administration, economics, business, etc., and tend not to be so common in everyday popular or conversational use.

3 Answers to definitions:

a a collector of matchboxes is a *phill*umenist

   b   to leave a country for good is to *e*migrate
   c   speaking only in single, short words is to be *mono*syllabic
   d   many-sided shape – a *poly*gon
   e   someone who photographs well is *photo*genic
   f   a hater of women is a *miso*gynist
   g   able to use either hand equally well is to be *ambi*dextrous
   h   an instrument for 'listening at a distance' is, of course, a *tele*phone
   i   to break away from a country or an organization is to *se*cede

If you scored seven or more before losing friends or alienating relatives or throwing your dictionary at the wall, you did well!

Chapter 17 Improve your written English V

1

   a   I   personal
       her   personal
       she   personal
       me   personal
   b   it   personal
       mine   personal (possessive)
       yours personal (possessive)
   c   who   interrogative
   d   you   personal
       us   personal (acting as the indirect object – see below)
       more   indefinite (acting as object – i.e. what you owe)
       you   personal (subject)
       them   personal (acting as indirect object – see below)

This is perhaps a good point at which to make mention of indirect objects as an extension of direct objects. Consider the following sentences:

– John gave the ball to Jackie.
– John gave the ball to her.
– John gave her the ball.

In each of them, 'the ball' is the direct object – what John gave. The person to whom the ball was given – Jackie or 'her' – is called the indirect object. As the above examples also illustrate, sometimes the word 'to' is left out, being considered to be 'understood'. It is in this category that it is difficult to separate the direct from the indirect object. In the examples of the assignment, 'more' is the direct object – what 'you' owe and the indirect object is '(to) us', and (to) them.

   e   she   personal
       herself reflexive
       she   personal
   f   whom   interrogative
       you   personal
   g   I   personal
       this   demonstrative
       which   interrogative
       you   personal
   h   many   indefinite
       few   indefinite

> *i*   which   relative
>   he   personal
> *j*   that   demonstrative
>   that   relative
>   I   personal
> Notice here the difference in use between the two 'thats'.

RULE	**Memory note 1**
	People are always 'who' or 'whom' or 'whose', things are 'which' or 'that' or 'whose'.

RULE	**Memory note 2**
	Always use the 'object' version of the personal pronoun to form the first part of the reflexive pronoun:
	*them*selves not *their*selves *him*self not *his*self

Chapter 18 Punctuating in English V

1

a   The children had a wonderful time at the fairground. They had goes on the big dipper, the merry-go-round, the roller-coaster and the helter-skelter.

Two complete ideas are expressed, therefore two sentences are needed. Notice that the names of the rides at the fairground are almost all hyphenated, since the words which go to make them up are virtually now accepted as a single word – except for big dipper, which the dictionary separates so that 'big' is seen as an adjective simple describing the size of the 'dipper'. 'Fairground' on the other hand has become completely fused into a single word. This example clearly illustrates the need to check potentially hyphenated words in your dictionary to be sure since there is no rationale or logic to depend upon other than 'this is the way we have agreed to punctuate the word'.

b   She sat in the waiting-room of the antenatal clinic. As usual she felt the nausea of morning-sickness and hoped the check-up would not take too long.

Perhaps a comma may be inserted after 'As usual'. Notice the hyphen in 'check-up'. Many words which link prepositions (here 'up') to verbs are hyphenated:

lock-up   sit-in   push-over etc.

c   The learner-driver took the roundabout too fast and only just managed to stop at the traffic-lights. The instructor made him do a three-point turn in a cul-de-sac and then asked him to reverse into a narrow side-street.

d   'I say, is the stage-manager there?' asked the playwright (knowing full well that he was off the set having his lunch). 'I want to make some changes to the furniture in front of the backdrop – the plaster of Paris statue is too near the front of the stage.'

Instead of the brackets the writer might have used commas. Notice the

use of the dash to add on the playwright's afterthought. Also, no
hyphens to link 'plaster of Paris', believe it or not!

e The china display – in effect the whole display area – needs to be dism-
antled and given an out and out cleaning.

The use of dashes best punctuates the way in which the speaker
changes his mind while talking by deciding that it is the 'whole display
area' which needs cleaning. No hyphens to link 'out and out'.

f Seeing how thoroughly the customs officials were examining the
suitcases of every returning holiday-maker, Albert began to worry
about his five hundred cigarettes (not to mention the camera wrapped
up in his dressing-gown), his two bottles of brandy and the brand new
wrist-watch which seemed to be burning a ring around his wrist.

Dashes might have been used instead of the brackets, and if so the
comma after the second dash:

. . . in his dressing-gown –,

would still be needed as it is behind the second bracket since the writer
is providing us with a list of Albert's worries which is punctuated in the
normal way, with commas preceding a final 'and' as you have already
learned. Although wrist-watch is currently hyphenated, it is almost
certainly one of those words which will shortly become fused into
'wristwatch' following the trend to discard hyphens in favour of run-
together words.

g Having bottled your elderberry wine, leave it for at least three months –
longer if you can avoid the temptation to try it – and you will have a
wine well worth the effort spent in its making.

Of the available punctuation (brackets or dashes), here the dashes
best punctuate the additional comment inserted in the instructions.

If you have needed to make constant reference to your dictionary in
order to complete the assignment, then you have no reason at all either to
feel guilty or downcast! The punctuation decisions relating either to leaving
two words as two, hyphenating them or running them together are
extremely difficult, especially where words or expressions are concerned
which you have not encountered frequently before. A major consolation
for all of us is that most writers make frequent mistakes in this area unless
they keep to the discipline of checking the dictionary whenever in the
slightest doubt!

Chapter 19 Mastering spelling V

1

-graph	generally means to do with writing, e.g. telegraph
-logue	means to do with talking, e.g. monologue – a speech or dramatic rendition spoken alone; see also: dialogue duologue etc.
-ology	usually means 'the study of', e.g. biology geology theology etc. 'logos' in Ancient Greek meant 'word'
-oid	literally, 'having the kind of shape of', e.g. humanoid rhomboid planetoid etc.
-ics	the *ics* suffix usually conveys the sense of the concept or study/subject of, e.g. physics mechanics linguistics etc.
-arch	chief, or foremost, most senior, e.g. monarch patriarch

HINT!

Turn to the section on suffixes from time to time to refresh your mind on those which are not often met. A knowledge of the meaning of suffixes will be of much help in broadening your active, working vocabulary

2

(to) deceive	deceiver deceived deceiving deceit deception deceptive
(to) tolerate	tolerated tolerating tolerable toleration
(to) help	helper helped helping helpful helpless helpmate
(to) examine	examiner examined examining examinee examination

3 This time you must check your own answers in your dictionary for correct spelling and to make sure they mean what you think they mean!

4

leg . . . legible	meaning able to be read (i.e. not indecipherable)
read . . . readable	meaning able to be read with interest and enjoyment
depend . . . dependant	is the *noun* meaning one (i.e. person) who relies upon someone or something else
depend . . . dependent	is the *adjective* meaning relying upon someone or something else
dia . . . dialogue	is the conversation between people
conduct . . . conductor	is the person who controls the orchestra's music or takes the fares on a bus, and it could also mean the wire through which electricity passes easily
less . . . lessee	person who buys the lease of a property

Note that today, as a result of the movement towards acknowledging the equality of women alongside men in jobs, certain words with feminine suffixes are not used in certain contexts any longer:

manageress	For posts which could be held by either a man or a woman, the term manager (e.g. personnel manager) would today be correct for either sex.
directrice	This word for a female director is nowadays virtually archaic.

As a consequence of constant changes in popular usage and the preferred version of words, it pays to keep your eyes open in your daily reading for examples and confirmations of accepted current usage.

Chapter 20 Improve your written English VI

1 Briefly, a conjunction is one of eight parts of speech which is used to link together two groups of words known as clauses. These clauses each contain a subject and finite verb in their own right.

Conjunctions may be used to link together clauses which are co-equal in value, which are called main clauses. They may also link to a main clause a subordinate clause which is dependent upon the main clause for its meaning.

2 There are two kinds of conjunctions:

1 conjunctions called 'co-ordinating' which link together main clauses and

2 conjunctions which are called 'subordinating' which link a subordinate clause to a main clause.

Checklist of commonly occurring conjunctions:

Linking main clauses (Co-ordinating)	Linking subordinate clauses to main ones (Subordinating)
and	when before after until
	where
	how
but	why because as since
next	though although even though
then	however whatever
yet	if unless whether
or	so so that in order that
	with the result that
(n) either . . . (n) or	who which that
both . . . and	that what

3 A simple sentence is one that contains a subject, a single verb and sometimes additional words expressing further information.

A complex sentence is made up of two or more clauses, both of which will contain a subject and finite verb, where one dependent clause (or more) is dependent upon the main clause for its meaning.

As a result of their shorter length and simpler construction, 'simple sentences' convey their meaning quickly and straightforwardly. However, when set down in a sequence, a succession of simple sentences may give an impression of immaturity and dullness simply because of their unsophisticated structure, especially if they all follow the pattern of:

Subject + finite verb + rest of sentence extensions

By linking two distinct ideas (as clauses) into a single sentence, the complex sentence provides a more mature and adult impact since more meaning is being presented within a single sentence structure. Also, there is a flexibility available in writing complex sentences where the main clause or the dependent clause may open the sentence. This helps to provide variety and open up opportunities for stylistic devices such as the creation of tension, suspense or drama.

4 The following is one way of rewriting the passage. Do not, however, think that your variations are necessarily wrong or not as good. A helpful approach would be to get some of your friends to rewrite the passage as well and then for you all to compare notes.

It was hot *but* the heat was dry, unlike the dripping humidity of the swamps they had climbed up from *after* they had managed to escape from the furious tribesmen. They reached a shady plateau *where* they sank down exhausted from their climb. They had no rations or blankets *but* this had not seemed important in the rush to escape from the brandished assegais of the Zulus. *Yet* they had forgotten the first rule of survival, *which* was always to carry on your person the basic tools of survival. Hopelessly they looked around for some sticks to rub together to make fire. *That* they were unsuccessful and tired led to angry words. A sudden roar in the dusk brought them instantly back to their need to survive – if only until morning.

Did you spot that 'Yet' opens a separate sentence while acting as a link to the previous one? Clearly not all writers obey our rules!

In the passage the conjunctions introduced have been italicized to help you to spot how the sentences have been linked and their meaning conveyed in a more varied and interesting way. Now turn back and compare your version and the one above with the original to see the effect of using compound and complex sentence structures.

5   *Although* (*though, even though*) he was under age, he strode confidently up to the bar *where* he ordered a double whisky *which* the barman poured without any concern at all!

Notice that where several clauses are connected by conjunctions into a single sentence, the pace of the sentence often moves briskly since full stops are avoided. This technique helps to impart in the example above a sense of quickness and audacity which reinforces the meaning of the four clauses.

As a matter of interest, the main clause around which all the dependent clauses are built is:

... he strode confidently up to the bar ...

Now that you feel quite confident about clauses and sentence structures take the trouble to look more closely and in a consciously analytical way at the manner in which journalists construct their sentences in good quality newspapers. Take an interest in the effect of sentence structure upon a writer's topic and how the structure may affect the tone and impact of a piece of writing – for better or worse!

By now you should rightly feel pleased with the way you can look at any piece of writing critically instead of perhaps simply accepting whatever piece of writing your eye alights upon!

Chapter 21 Punctuating in English VI

1

a   Laugh and the world laughs with you; weep, and you weep alone.

In actual fact, the above example is part of a poem by Ella Wheeler Wilcox (1855–1919) called 'Solitude' with more lines following a comma after 'alone'.

b   The time had passed for second thoughts; he shot his right arm up in the air and volunteered to join the mission.

c   The following is standard procedure to be observed on hearing the fire alarm sound: close all windows; shut all doors without locking them; leave all your belongings behind and walk without rushing to the nearest fire exit.

It is a matter of preference whether commas are used instead of semi-colons to punctuate the list.

d   Have you ever come across that old but true saying: 'Don't kill the goose that lays the golden egg.'?

Notice here that 'Don't' starts with a capital letter in the middle of the sentence because it is the beginning of a quotation which is a sentence in its own right, and that the question mark comes last as it is punctuating the question of the entire sentence.

e   Jenkins screwed up the letter into a ball; he threw it over the parapet into the murky river; that was definitely the end of the whole wretched business.

The use of semi-colons instead of full stops is to be preferred in this example since they create less definite pauses and help to convey better the sense of three distinct phases which are separate but very closely connected.

f 'You have a simple choice: either you own up of your own accord, or I report you!'

Here the more significant pause of the colon may best introduce the stark options and help to convey a grim, slow pace to the utterance.

HINT!

Remember

Keep your eye out for examples of the semi-colon and colon in use during your reading of magazines, books or newspapers and jot down in your notebook good examples which you may imitate.

Also, do try out your own constructions involving semi-colons and colons now that they have been 'demystified' for you! You will certainly find they are very helpful in extending your punctuating repertoire and thus the various ways in which you can convey your ideas.

Chapter 22 Mastering spelling VI

1

a *k*nead
b acquitted (notice also the double *t* ending)
c acquaintance
d inde*b*ted
e *p*neumonia
f scimitar
g *g*narled
h ex*h*ume (literally the Latin source means 'from the earth')
i w*h*isk
j signor (note also signora (Mrs) signorina (Miss)
k The two most common:

– the *pneu-* grouping: pneumatic
– the *psycho*-grouping psychology

Note also the *eff* sound grouping: ne*ph*ew *ph*oto etc.

l Here the following groupings are common:

– *h* following *g*: g*h*erkin g*h*etto
– *h* following the prefix *ex-*: ex*h*ort ex*h*ibition
– *h* following *w*: w*h*ale w*h*opper

m The most likely spot for a silent *k* or *g* is at the very beginning of a word:

*k*new *k*not *g*nome *g*nu

n Most frequently found after a silent *w* is *r*:
w*r*ench w*r*estle w*r*ist etc.

A tip on absorbing the spelling of these irritating words is to form groupings in your mind, such as all the jobs a 'wright' can do:

playwright wheelwright shipwright etc.

Or to create little rhymes or jingles to act as memory joggers:

Ghouls and ghosts are ghastly in ghettos eating gherkins!

Another helpful way of approaching the task of memorizing such silent letter spellings is to remember the various forms of the base word where a silent letter occurs:

acquaint   acquainted   acquaintance
acquire   acquired   acquisition   acquisitive

Perhaps the most painless way of learning such spellings is by extending the time each day and week you spend reading, for the more times you encounter particular words in print, the more likely you are to 'photograph' them in your mind's eye for later recall and reference.

Chapter 23 Improve your written English VII

1   A preposition is a part of speech which either introduces a noun or a pronoun as a single word, or which introduces a phrase. Prepositions act as linking words to show relationships of one sense group of words to another:

- Place in relation to people or other places: He stood *in* the foyer *in front of* the display case.
- Time in relation to events: They finished the work *after* three days frantic effort.
- Manner in relation to action: She crept *on* tip-toe past her parents' bedroom door.

In fact prepositions may introduce all types of adverbial phrases.

2   The words in the list which may be used as prepositions are:

over   near   before   at   across   from   above

3   The three phrases introduced each time by a preposition are:

a   *down* the slippery path to hell
b   *with* my very best wishes
c   *in* all my born days

4   Generally prepositions take the accusative case. Whatever case they may take does not always seem to matter because it is not possible to see it in the form or ending of most nouns. The accusative case can be seen, however, in personal pronouns:

	Singular			Plural	
Accusative	me	him	her	us	them

It matters therefore that the accusative case of pronouns is used after prepositions:

like *him*   between *you* and *me*   over *us*   through *them* etc.

Prepositions like 'of' can introduce words which are in effect in a possessive case though it is not always readily apparent:

The dealer played the last of *his cards*.

Or, in the same way (except that it can be identified by the word 'to' introducing it) the dative case of the indirect object:

The waiter passed the bill *to the host*.

5   The mistake lies in the word 'I', which is in the nominative case. It should be 'me' in the accusative case. We often talk in ways which do not accord with correct grammatical use, but we should be particularly careful to adopt accepted grammatical usage in our writing.

6 Briefly, to keep the prepositional part of the composite verb closely following the 'verb' part of it. This avoids the natural rhythm of the sentence becoming strained.

I confirmed that the second alternative was the one I was prepared to go *along with*.

rather than:

. . . the one *with* which I was prepared to go *along*.

7 The only sure way of mastering idiomatic expressions involving prepositions is to learn the expression off by heart, and to check in the dictionary if you are unsure.

One important aspect to bear in mind in terms of the style of such idiomatic expressions is that many of them have become tired clichés:

– *with* due care and attention
– *in* all sincerity
– *in* respect *of*
– *with* regard *to*

We all tend to clutch for a cliché when we are tired and cannot be bothered to find a fresher phrase or expression, yet when such clichéd phrases are closely connected, the effect can be very depressing!

I write *with regard to* your letter of 13 May *in respect of* the consignment you say you have not yet received. I should like to assure you that the consignment was packed *with due care and attention* and despatched *in all sincerity* to your Bradford depôt. It was only after despatch that your recent removal to new premises came to our attention. I am therefore arranging for your consignment to be re-routed . . .

How much better is the revised version:

I was sorry to learn in your letter of 13 May that you have not yet received your order of three dozen gross of paper cups. The consignment was most carefully packed here and despatched to your Bradford address as we believed you were still there. Only later did we learn that you had moved to new premises. I am therefore arranging for the order to be re-routed . . .

7 An interjection is a word often made up to sound like a particular human sound of emotion –

Examples:
– *Phew!* might be used to signal a sense of relief after a moment of tension.
– *Er* . . . is often used to denote uncertainty.
– *Hm!* may be used to seek someone's attention politely.

Interjections are normally used in direct speech dialogue in novels, stories, comics, cartoon strips, etc.

9 The words which could be used as interjections are:

Hm! Whoa! Tsk! Ugh! Phew!

10
a   *to* resort *to* violence . . .
b   *After* due consideration . . .

c   *in* commemoration *of* the drowned seamen
d   *out of* a regard *for* the passing of the greatest full-back . . .
e   I am writing *in* response *to*

Chapter 24 Punctuating in English VII

1

a   The three girls' handbags were found in the ladies' toilet, but their contents had been stolen.

Two straightforward plural forms needing the apostrophe to show possession are shown in this example.

b   The technician's report indicated that the secretaries' typewriters needed servicing and that two full days work would be needed to carry out the repairs.

If the report had been submitted by several technicans, then we might

properly have written: technicians' report. Notice particularly in this example the punctuation of 'two full days work'. If we meant the work of two full days, then we would need to punctuate it as:

two full days' work

If, however, we see 'two full days' as adjectives describing 'work', then we can leave it as it is.

c   'I've found John's notes but could I borrow yours if it's not inconvenient?'

Here there are two contractions: I've = I have and it's = it is.

'Yours' is here the possessive case of the personal pronoun and needs no apostrophe of course!

d   To my mind all the EEC countries' flags should be flown at tomorrow's ceremony.

That is, the flags (plural) of all the EEC countries (also plural).

e   She forgot to post her brother-in-law's birthday card as she couldn't find a stamp when it was on her mind.

Notice the difference between the plural: brothers-in-law (sisters-in-law) and the possessive singular: brother-in-law's.

f   The claret of '63 is infinitely better than its counterpart of '69.

Firstly, an exclamation mark would be quite justified here from the words used. Notice 'its' when it means 'of it'.

2   The rewriting of the sentences to show the apostrophe s in use:

a   The children's shoes in the sale . . .
b   The gentlemen's ties were reduced . . .
c   The carcasses' weight was too heavy . . .
d   The bride's bouquet . . . the bridesmaids' posies . . .

3   Contracted forms:
would not: wouldn't   cannot: can't   shall not: shan't   must not: mustn't   would have: would've   it is: it's   who is: who's   they are: they're   you are: you're

4   Apostrophe placements:

a   the customers' complaints (plural form)
b   the handkerchieves' patterns (plural form)

    c the winepress's handle (singular form)
    d the valleys' geography (plural form)
    e the wheat's yield (i.e. the yield of the wheat singular, when we understand a bulk and think of it as a single unit)
    f yesterday's racing results (singular form)

HINT!

If you know it – use it! Or, if you've got it, flaunt it!
By now you will have become proficient in using the apostrophe in both its roles – to denote possession or to indicate contraction or omission. Last word: now you have conquered the apostrophe, always be on your guard to spot when it is needed. To ignore it is to become careless and indifferent to what is an essential part of the way written English is correctly communicated!

Chapter 25 Mastering spelling VII

1
    a They all *assented* to his suggestion that production should go ahead . . .
    b . . . the home crowd and the visiting fans all *exhorted* their teams to make a final all out effort!
    c The *frieze* decorating the inner temple . . .
    d The mechanism which sprang the trap was very *ingenious*.
    e The diner was unable to face his *dessert*. Think of the two s's in 'sweets'.
    f The mannequin's maroon handbag nicely *complemented* the dark red chiffon dress she was modelling.
    g The constable's *excess* of zeal led to the nuns' arrest.
    h The test involving listening to tapes was an *aural* test.
    i The sort who easily *loses* his temper will not get far in retailing. (Remember: to lose = misplace – one *o*; to loosen = make less tight – two *o*'s.)
    j 'My lord I speak as *counsel* for the prosecution in this case.'

2 Words from the checklist:
    a neither moral nor immoral: amoral (note *one* m)
    b raising someone up to a position of power: to exalt
    c most important or chief: principal
    d without stopping at all: continuous
    e something giving entry to: an access
    f to do with the mouth: oral (think of the mouth as an *O*)
    g to avoid capture: to elude (remember the adjective – 'elusive')
    h to cause something to change: to affect
    i to measure, estimate: gauge (note spelling tip – *a* comes before *u* in alphabet).
    j to be reliant upon: dependent upon

Chapters 27, 28, 29 What is style, aims, register

1 Check your own definition against the one on page 156. Essentially you should have included these aspects:

    a Style may be thought of as the 'how we say it', while content may be thought of as 'what we say'. These two aspects of a piece of writing are very closely related and interconnected.
    b The creation of a particular style is influenced by: the words chosen, the structures used (sentences, paragraphs, clauses within sentences, etc.)

the context in which the piece is written and the nature of the intended reader, together with his/her relationship with the writer.

2   The components referred to are:

- the aims of the piece of writing;
- its particular structure;
- its chosen vocabulary;
- its context;
- the reader's profile;
- the relationship of reader and writer.

3   There are many reasons for communication breakdowns as a result of faulty style, and those mentioned in the text were:

- the message's structure becomes too complicated or long or boring and the reader loses interest;
- the words chosen are too technical and baffle the layman or non-expert reader (but remember that much writing is intended for experts and includes jargon or technical language as a way of expressing shared ideas in a kind of shorthand);
- the writer has not pitched his writing at a level appropriate to his readers who thus feel patronized or talked down to, etc.;
- the writer misread the likely reactions of his readership by overlooking their profile/background etc.;
- the selected register of the piece proved inappropriate and what was meant as friendly familiarity is taken for cheeky impertinence, and so on.

You will be able to recall many other such breakdowns which result from a faulty style having been created, which may include readers taking offence at tactless remarks, or resenting officiousness, and so on.

4   Essentially, and before starting to write, the writer should consider:

- What is he or she basically wishing to achieve in writing the piece.
- What is the background to the situation about which the piece is to be written.
- For what type of recipient is the piece intended and what are his/her likely reactions to receiving it.
- In what format should the piece be written – letter, memorandum, hand-written note, etc.

5   Basically, factual writing seeks to impart or transmit information which is not a series of assertions – it is simply true or may be proved or demonstrated. Moreover, the writer is not seeking to sway the reader or influence his response to the writing. Persuasive writing on the other hand seeks to promote a point of view or argument so that the reader will readily agree with it and accept it. Often persuasive writing makes an appeal to the reader's emotions or inbred attitudes while factual writing seeks to appeal to the reader's rational and logical thought processes.

6   Though it is not always possible to possess such information to any great extent, it is helpful for the writer to know about his readers':

age range   educational background   qualifications and work experience
social/income group   outlooks   views and attitudes

Such knowledge helps the writer to avoid talking down to his readers or bemusing them with vocabulary and expressions they can hardly be expected to follow. To keep firmly in mind during the act of writing the profile of one's readership is excellent advice to the aspiring writer.

7   Briefly the meaning of the term 'register' in the context of style in writing is the level at which a piece of writing may be measured against a kind of range or scale. This scale may be thought of as a straight line with extremes at either end. For example, a register may be constructed of remarks, requests or instructions. The register may range from very formal to very informal, or a scale may be constructed of language ranging from very official and depersonalized to very colloquial and friendly.

The following diagram illustrates a scale of register seeking to attract someone's attention, from very polite to rudely aggressive:

Very polite ⟵————————————————⟶ **Rudely aggressive**
'Excuse me, please!'
        'Pardon me!'
                'Hello there!'
                        'I say . . .!'
                                'You over there!'
                                        'Oi you! Yes, you!'

8   An understanding of the concept of register is important in devising an effective style in a piece of writing because it will make the piece appropriate in its given context and therefore likely to be readily interpreted and accepted by its intended readership.

9   Check the spread of your register against those already provided as illustrations in the text.

Here is one such for the request to someone to vacate the theatre seat:

Informal
↑ I'm sorry to trouble you, but I'm afraid you're sitting in my seat. Look, here's my ticket.'

'I'm afraid you're sitting in my seat. Would you mind giving it up please.'

'Excuse me, you're occupying my seat. I'm sorry, but you'll have to find another.'

'This is my seat, actually. I have the ticket to prove it. I should be glad if you would allow me to take it.'

'Madam, you are in fact occupying the seat I have purchased. Kindly
↓ check the number on my ticket and allow me to take my seat.'

Formal

The most important point to keep in mind about register is the need to select the words and structures most appropriate to the situation and most likely to achieve the desired effect. Which of the above requests do you think most likely to result in the seat being promptly vacated without fuss?

10   A more acceptable version of the memorandum might be:

MEMORANDUM

```
I wish to advise you all of my serious concern about
the appearance of some staff recently working in
parts of the store open to our customers. Though
our sales staff are provided with two sets of uniforms,
a number are failing to maintain the level of smartness
and crisp turnout expected at all times.
As you will know an allocation is made to all sales staff
as part of their salary to meet the expenses of maintaining
uniforms.
I appreciate that the store has been enjoying a busy period
in the run-up to Christmas but must emphasize that I cannot
accept a fall in our customary high standards of turnout.
I am therefore expecting an immediate improvement where
it is needed and shall be paying particular regard to
this important matter in my regular visits to all our departments.
```

If you analyse this memorandum carefully you will uncover the following points:

- Not all the staff are included in the criticisms. Those staff who are always well turned out would resent being included with those who are not.
- The sales staff are reminded of the fair and reasonable conditions they accepted – two sets of uniform being provided together with money to cover washing or dry cleaning and replacement.
- The General Manager concedes that the store has been going through a particularly busy period but does not see this sufficient reason to accept a fall in standards.
- He does not threaten staff with banishment to the despatch department or stockrooms but rather indicates that he may tackle individuals personally, which is probably a more effective approach.

Notice that the language employed is neither bullying nor over-assertive or aggressive. Yet it does not baulk at conveying the sense of serious shortcomings which are to be rectified directly. The writer is careful to treat his staff with due respect allied to justifiable criticism. Which words or phrases in the above version do you think prove particularly effective? Are there any you would amend? Why?

11   The following letter seeks to create the tone or register which the writer hopes will result in his being given the time off:

LETTER

```
Dear Mrs Brown,
As you will know, my wife, Julie, has been particularly
active over the past year on the Committee of the Lord Lieutenant's
Charity Appeal for funds to build a hostel for paraplegic young
men and women who work locally. As a result of local generosity
the target of £200,000 has been exceeded.
As a way of thanking the Committee and their associates,
the Lord Lieutenant is giving a Garden Party next Wednesday at
County Hall from 3.30p.m. to 5.30p.m. and I have received an
invitation to accompany my wife.
I should be grateful for your permission to attend, and
should, of course, take care to clear all urgent matters prior
to my departure.
Julie and I have been asked to reply to the invitation
by Thursday of this week.
I look forward to hearing from you.
Sincerely,
Jack Harris
```

Of course such a request would be dealt with in many organizations by word of mouth in the boss's office, yet some firms do require leave of absence requests to be made in writing.

Consider your own version and the one above and check on the following.

- Is the boss given sufficient detail so as to understand the background of the request and the status of the inviter?
- Does Jack take it for granted he will be given permission?
- How does Jack make it easier for his boss to approve his request?
- How does Jack tactfully ask for a prompt response from his boss?

The answers to the above questions bear on the creation of an appropriate tone and register in which the request is presented. Jack makes sure the boss is aware that the invitation comes from one of the most senior officials in the county. Indeed it might be good public relations for Jack to attend and mix with customers, associates, etc. Jack's request is made in such a way that the letter does not take the approval as read, but he does emphasize that he will dutifully attend to urgent work matters before going off. Lastly, he tactfully informs his boss of the deadline for the reply to the Lord Lieutenant's office and therefore of the need for a prior response from his boss.

Notice that the tone of Jack's letter is by no means colloquial or informal. In real life the selection of an appropriate register for such a request will also depend in part on the ongoing degree of formality/informality which exists when departmental colleagues correspond.

Chapter 30 Structure and style

1   Your explanation of what a beginning, middle and end should convey in a piece of writing will almost certainly include the following points:

A beginning

- Should make clear to the reader what the piece is to be about – what its main theme is.
- At the same time, the beginning should set the tone for the whole piece: serious   informal   official   entertaining etc.
- By way of acting as an introduction to the main theme, a beginning should provide the reader with brief details of the main people involved, any relevant details of dates, time or places and any background information it is important to know at the outset.
- In some kinds of writing – especially that which argues and discusses – the beginning will convey what the main issues are, or what the major bone of contention is.

A middle

- The middle of an extended piece is often made up of several sections or paragraphs and these will each develop a principal part of the main theme, one major point per section as a key topic reinforced by supplementary topics or points.

- The good writer will also take pains to ensure that there is a thread or logical sequence which connects the developmental points of the middle section.

- The approach to structuring the middle section could be chronological, moving from major to minor, and so on.

An end

- On reaching the final part of the end, the reader should feel that he has been given all the necessary information to make sense of the piece, and that no major factor has been ignored or overlooked.
- Many 'ends' provide summaries of the main points which have been set out at length in the 'middle', or re-state briefly the main arguments stated.
- Another main function of an end is to come down off the fence in favour – with reasons – of advocating one particular viewpoint or argument in a discussion.
- Lastly, an end should not suddenly go off at a tangent or suddenly introduce new main points. It should tie up the ends of the discussion of the middle or make a final justifiable statement based on the material of the middle and relating back to the points or issues raised initially in the beginning.

2   As your 'free-flow of ideas' plan will be unique to you, it is not possible to provide you here with a 'correct' version of it to compare with your own. Also, you have the model to guide you on pages 176–178.

Instead, here is another 'free-flow' plan for you to study to see how another mind has tackled a particular topic. Bear in mind as a rule of thumb that some 15–20 main points usually indicate that enough material has been assembled in its first form:

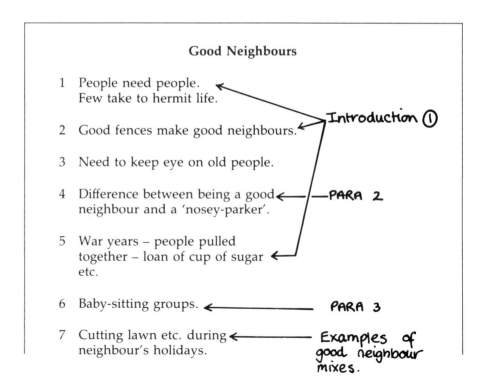

Good Neighbours

1   People need people.
    Few take to hermit life.

2   Good fences make good neighbours.   →*Introduction ①*

3   Need to keep eye on old people.

4   Difference between being a good ←——*PARA 2*
    neighbour and a 'nosey-parker'.

5   War years – people pulled
    together – loan of cup of sugar ←
    etc.

6   Baby-sitting groups. ←————— *PARA 3*

7   Cutting lawn etc. during ←————— *Examples of
    neighbour's holidays.   good neighbour
                                       mixes.*

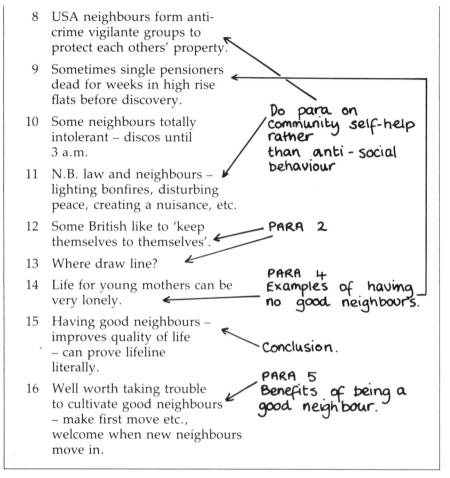

8 USA neighbours form anti-crime vigilante groups to protect each others' property.

9 Sometimes single pensioners dead for weeks in high rise flats before discovery.

10 Some neighbours totally intolerant – discos until 3 a.m.

11 N.B. law and neighbours – lighting bonfires, disturbing peace, creating a nuisance, etc.

12 Some British like to 'keep themselves to themselves'.

13 Where draw line?

14 Life for young mothers can be very lonely.

15 Having good neighbours –
– improves quality of life
– can prove lifeline literally.

16 Well worth taking trouble to cultivate good neighbours – make first move etc., welcome when new neighbours move in.

Do para on community self-help rather than anti-social behaviour

PARA 2

PARA 4 Examples of having no good neighbours.

Conclusion.

PARA 5 Benefits of being a good neighbour.

3

Chronological: proceeds through extended piece of writing from earlier time to later or current time in a logical progression.

Argumentative: takes reader through both sides of an argument but eventually shows preference for one side.

Expositional: usually a factual account set out in a logical sequence.

Imaginative: no set pattern of structure – depends on how writer approaches the subject.

4 Show your skeleton plan to a friend or someone who could give an informed and objective opinion and let him or her tell you whether the scheme makes sense and whether a structure is there to be seen.

5 If you are at school or college, ask a teacher to read your article and give you an opinion of its structure and overall effect. If you are at work, ask a suitable colleague to do the same. You may well find members of your personnel department receptive to your work on improving your English who would be more than prepared to act as a critic and sounding board.

6

The loose paragraph: in this sort of paragraph, the key sentence containing the major point comes first.

The mixed paragraph: here the main point occurs approximately in the middle of the paragraph.

The periodic paragraph: here the main or key sentence comes last.

7 In order to obtain some objective feedback for your efforts here, you should either follow the advice given for assignment 5, or alternatively construct an example of a loose, mixed and periodic paragraph at the earliest opportunity in your next school or college classwork/homework assignment, or in, say, a memorandum at work and see what feedback you receive.

Another way of evaluating the impact of paragraph structures is to check through a magazine or newspaper article to identify where the journalist has located the key sentence for each paragraph and the consequent effect of the locations.

8 Bear in mind that when a piece of writing has a reading age of, say, fourteen this doesn't mean that its content or value is limited to a set of fourteen-year-olds! It means that younger readers would find it difficult (by and large) and that adults – that is those with reading ages of 17–18 plus would absorb it easily. We all read pieces of varying reading age demands every day.

9 Here is one version of the letter to the boss:

LETTER

Dear Mrs Greenfield,

We were all sorry to learn at work today that you were rushed into hospital last night for an emergency appendicitis operation, but very pleased and relieved to be told by Mr Pearson this morning that all has gone well and that you are well on the road to recovery.

I imagine it must be both funny and in a sense frustrating for you to find yourself in a hospital ward this morning when only yesterday afternoon we were discussing how we would re-organize this afternoon the arrangements for next week's conference. Well, let me reassure you on this subject. Mandy and I are going to do the job as planned this afternoon and you can look at our ideas as soon as the doctors say you may!

So the message from the office is: don't worry about a thing and simply concentrate on getting well. By the way, we are all intending to come and eat up your grapes for you as soon as Mr Greenfield thinks you are well enough to put up with our visit!

Meanwhile, take good care.

Sincerely,

Penny

Notice that the tone or register Penny has chosen is friendly and chatty without being over-familiar. Also, she takes pains to reassure her boss that matters are being well taken care of so that she will not fret. She also tactfully indicates that the office staff will wait upon medical/family approval before visiting. Overall, the letter is short – it does not tax the reader, the tone is light and good humoured and the intended aim is by and large achieved – to show a genuine concern and to reassure and to cheer up. To this particular end a conversational vocabulary proves quite appropriate.

10 The points aimed at providing guidelines for junior office staff on how to structure a piece of writing may include:

- Do not rush immediately into the act of writing or keyboarding. If you are composing anything other that a short or simple message, you will first need to assemble your main points in rough.

- Follow this approach to devising a plan:
  - Jot down your ideas/points in no particular order but just as they occur down the left-hand side of a piece of notepaper.
  - Then check for any major ones you have missed out.
  - Next add any additional points next to those already listed.
  - Finally by connecting lines or by alloting numbers to points pull together on the page those points which closely connect and which may form a section or paragraph and then decide upon the sequence you consider most appropriate for each section.
- Remember that an effective piece of writing will possess:
  - A beginning which introduces the main topic, relevant introductory details and sets the tone.
  - A middle which develops the main points clearly and logically.
  - An ending which makes a justifiable conclusion, which sometimes summarizes the main points made and which leaves no major aspect untreated or overlooked.

Chapter 31 Choosing the right words

1　These are some of the major characteristics of words which will influence their reader:
- Whether the word is rich in meaning or whether it conveys only a single, precise meaning.
- Whether it is used as slang or colloquially or whether it is part of a formal type of vocabulary.
- Whether it is a commonly used word or whether it is technical and specialized.
- In what sort of register it appears: friendly, familiar, easy-going or serious, formal and disciplinary, etc.
- Whether it appeals to the emotions or to reason and logic.

2　The two words may be briefly defined as follows:

Connotative: Describes a word or expression which possesses many layers or shades of meaning, which can spark off the reader's imagination and conjure up memories and recollections. Words rich in connotative meaning tend to have an emotional effect upon the reader and are often used in persuasive kinds of writing like poetry and advertising copy.
Denotative: This term is used to describe those words which express a precise and single meaning, and which appeal to rational and logical thought processes. Thus they tend to occur in factual types of writing such as some textbooks, scientific reports, instruction manuals, and so on.

3　The word 'objective' is used to describe a style in writing which is impersonal – that is, the feelings and attitudes of the author are not allowed to affect a style which is basically factual and rational.

The opposite of objective in this context is 'subjective', where the writer does give his opinions and views and where the writing does persuade as well as inform, or does affect the emotions.

4 The following is a checklist, by no means exhaustive, of the sort of communications which might be expected to be written in mainly connotative or denotative language:

Connotative	Denotative
poems	business reports
novels	scientific papers
advertisements	encyclopaedias
sales circulars	dictionaries
direct mail leaflets	reference books
personal letters	instructional manuals
get well cards	press releases
leisure magazine articles	trade magazine articles
estate agents' particulars of houses for sale	insurance policies

At this juncture it is interesting to note that bodies such as the Advertising Standards Association exist to ensure that advertising copywriters do not get so carried away in using persuasive and connotative expressions that truth gets lost along the way!

5 Your page in the training manual on guidelines for selecting an effective vocabulary should include some if not all of the following points:

- The history of the English language, stemming from a number of Saxon languages as well as from Latin and Norman French, means that a very wide range of vocabulary exists to choose from in most situations.

- Vocabulary may be divided basically into two kinds:
  words which convey a single meaning in a rational and unemotional way, and words which appeal to emotions or prejudices via many shades or layers of meaning.
- All forms of writing create a particular register or overall tone, depending upon the situation in which they are used – ranging from formal to familiar, warm and friendly to cold and distant, and so on. This register is largely created by the choice of words made and the way they interconnect.
- Care should always be taken in choosing particular words to follow these guidelines:

  - Use a short word in preference to a long one.
  - Use fewer rather than more words if possible.
  - Avoid slang and colloquial expressions except in certain personal and informal contexts.
  - Always consider the reader's needs – do not use specialist, jargon words if he or she is a layman.
  - Alternatively, do not 'talk down' to an expert by using over-simple vocabulary.
  - Care should always be taken to read through written work to check for mistakes and slips of the pen before despatching it.

6 Criticisms of 'Extracts for Analysis'. Compare your criticisms with the ones provided below:

a The use of the word 'have' in 'I have to inform you' implies a reluctance on the part of the writer in 'having' to take the trouble and the overall

overall tone of the sentence is cold and unfriendly – the 'in due course' conveys a sense of 'when we decide to get round to it'.

b   The use of the word 'must' in 'I must apologize' may give the impression of not really wanting to!

Notice also the use of the jargon words and expressions to do with balancing motor-car wheels which the layman will scarcely understand: balancing 'dynamically' and 'statically' and also technical phrases like:

– transmission of vibration through the steering linkage
– diagnosis of misalignment
– asymmetrical tread design

It is most unlikely that the use of such technical vocabulary is likely to do any thing other than to 'satisfactorily' baffle the letter's recipient!

c   The whole tone of extract c is of bitter sarcasm based on the idea of writing on a 'plain piece of notepaper'; also, the writer uses harsh words like 'incompetence' and note the sarcastic tone of 'you may just recall'.

Such a tone – the result of a bad oversight on the stationery supplier's part – will only antagonize and is unlikely to have any positive response other than having got the matter off the writer's chest.

d   The appropriateness of d very much depends on the circumstances it is being said in. If it is to a customer over the telephone, then he or she may well resent the extensive use of colloquialisms and slang, especially since the caller is conveying bad news. Such easy, familiar language is best restricted for use among close workmates within an organization rather than to contacts outside it.

e   The first sentence here is a very pompous way of saying:

Staff are arriving late for work and are failing to honour their conditions of service.

Notice that the passive voice is used in sentence two:

Unless an improvement is discerned . . .

which makes the meaning very impersonal and aloof.

Overall, the tone is cold, distant and pompous. It may well be that a formal, disciplinary tone is required to remind staff of their obligations, but it is doubtful whether this approach would obtain a positive response.

f   The use of the word 'genuine' in this sentence implies that whatever the prospective seller is holding is probably a fraudulent copy and that he is taking up an expert dealer's valuable time.

The tone is altogether what the Americans would term a 'put down'.

g   This extract shows how easy it is to use five words where one would do!

I am sorry the spare parts you ordered are out of stock at present. (They are on order and I will let you know as soon as they arrive within the next few days.)

h   Here the criticism validly levelled also concerns the longwindedness of the extract. Phrases like 'due to circumstances beyond our control' are usually a cover for something the writer does not wish to reveal. Often it would be better to reveal a truth such as oversight of the job, or having taken on too much work, etc. rather than to fob the customer off with expressions such as 'as soon as the situation eases'. What situation? Of course, the one beyond the writer's control!

i The language of this extract conveys a distinctly off-hand attitude:

... in normal circumstances' ... Regretfully ... reference copies ... are kept centrally. ... You may care to try Sales.

The whole of the last sentence just seems a stock response which isn't really meant and acts as a cover-up in case of complaint by the recipient!

j This is an example of woolly thinking resulting in ambiguity of expression, and is made worse by trying to compress too many points into too few words:

... dependent upon either lowering or raising the price or the quality ...

What the writer probably means is 'either lowering the price or raising the quality'.

By the same token whatever the 'latter' option may be, it in turn will either result in 'increased competition or' a 'reduction in gross profits'. Or both?

To rectify this extract it would be necessary to start from square one and first to list the main points to be made and then to make them probably one sentence at a time.

k In this extract, although the words themselves are simple and straight-forward enough, the writer loses control and the result is that the firmness he or she intended fades away. A more direct approach is more likely to prove effective:

Although I am very sympathetic towards your problems in nursing your elderly mother, I am unable to authorize any further leave of absence without jeopardizing the efficient running of the department.

This being so, I would suggest you approach the personnel manager directly to ask that he considers your situation as a special case, and I would support you provided that suitable temporary staff were made available to me.

7 Here is a model advertisement of one of the assignments for you to con-sider and to compare with the approach of the one you chose to compose:

GO WEST YOUNG MAN, OR WOMAN!
JOIN OUR ALL-ACTION   OUTDOOR ACTIVITY
WEEK-END IN SNOWDONIA!
Friday, Saturday, Sunday 23, 24, 25 June 19—
Fully Residential in Log Cabin Accommodation

If you have ever wanted to learn 'white water' canoeing, how to ride a horse or how to dangle expertly from a rock face, then this introductory residential week-end is tailor-made for you!

A wide range of outdoor activities is available, all expertly supervised with skills taught under safe conditions.

And the Cost?   Absolutely a Give Away!

You can enjoy full board, a comfortable bed, sports room, television room, bar for only:
£45.00
Inclusive of Minibus Travel Costs!
TO AVOID DISAPPOINTMENT AND DESPAIR!
Contact: David Jackson,
Social Affairs Representative,
Student Common Room,
1.00 p.m. to 2.00 p.m. Monday to Friday
AND BE SURE OF YOUR BOOKING!

As an extra assignment, write down the words and expressions in this advertisement which you think are particularly persuasive in their appeal to the reader.

Chapter 32 Style and the reader

1 The main points in your passage are likely to reflect the following:

- No piece of writing occurs in a vacuum – there is always a reason for it, a series of events it follows upon or body of knowledge it adds to.
- In almost everything we write – especially what we write in the context of work – we are communicating with people in a role – we as employees and perhaps they as customers. Thus there is always a context or situation in existence within which we write which usually has its own customs or conventions governing what constitutes a 'proper and acceptable' way of writing.
- The situation in which writer and reader communicate at the time of writing must be carefully considered since all people – writers and readers – will bring their emotions as well as their reasoning powers to the process of writing and reading. For example, the upset customer may need to be soothed, the government official reassured or the angry office clerk calmed.
- Remember that readers will not take in the content of a message if they have an emotional block or feeling of hostility towards the writer.
- The way a particular style of writing evolves in a piece will naturally depend on whether its context is disciplinary, selling, informing, warning, and so on.

2 In many ways, differences in status should make no difference at all. No one wants a return to the days when the farm labourer had to touch his forelock as a sign of respect every time he met his 'betters'.

Yet we all know and accept that in many contexts, differences in status *do* make a difference in how people communicate. We are far less self-conscious and informal among people we know well and who are our equals – fellow students or workmates – than we are with senior teaching staff or managers.

Briefly put, the whole business of status (excepting that which snobbish people like to think they have acquired) is part of our society because it helps it to work. We would write respectfully to a judge or a bishop or a senior member of a large industrial organization partly because in doing so we acknowledge the responsibilities they have taken on, or at another level, because we feel more comfortable in the formal register.

Even if this is the case, do keep in mind that there is a world of difference between a style which is formal or which gives due respect and that which is ingratiating and what in slang terms would be called 'crawling'.

3 Your advice is likely to reflect upon the guidelines given in 'Meeting the Reader's Needs' and will include points like:

- If you alienate your reader, don't expect to win him to your side!
- It pays to know as much as possible about a reader's background.
- As readers we all have views and opinions – even prejudices – which we cherish. The clever writer accepts this fact and makes his points without riding roughshod over the reader's own opinions and attitudes.

Keeping a piece of writing at the appropriate pitch so as to get and hold its reader's interest is by no means easy. It means keeping the choice of words, types of sentence structure and paragraph construction etc. under constant review.

4   The characteristics we have concentrated upon are:

Age   Background   Education   Interests and Outlooks   Specialisms and Responsibilities   Relationship of Reader to Writer

5   The sort of unwished-for outcomes which are likely to occur will most probably include the following:

Shortcoming	Outcome
The language is inappropriately technical and specialized for its layman readership	Reader feels 'put down' and goes out to find an alternative source of information.
The register is set at the wrong level	Reader takes offence and the irritation obstructs the transmission of the message.
The way the points are made is provocative in terms of the readership's set of views	Reader tends to disregard the value or truth of the points in taking exception to the way they are made.
Writer's language is tired, stale and boring	Reader falls asleep and document falls unread on to the floor.
Writing is woolly, vague and longwinded	Reader gives up the attempt to follow the argument and finds some other urgent task to perform.

Though the list is by no means a complete one, the above examples do illustrate how readily the writer may fail in getting his message across if he fails to meet the needs of his reader!

6   Your own straw-poll may include some of the following:

- 'Never gets to the point.'
- 'Repeats the same thing umpteen times!'
- 'Specializes in making the interesting seem tedious!'
- 'Uses too many complex words – likes to show off his knowledge, I suppose.'
- 'Always trying to be funny or witty when most of the time his jokes fall flat.'
- 'Takes himself far too seriously and his writing always seems pompous.'
- 'Can't seem to write in short, clear sentences – one of hers can cover an entire page!'
- 'Always talks down to you when she writes anything – you'd think she was the Big I Am!'

Such criticisms reflect the common need most people express of having a message written simply, clearly and briefly, and knowing where they stand with a writer who writes to them courteously and with due regard for their own feelings, status or views.